teaching about the dynamics of the Christian life. His combination of biblical word studies, generous scriptural cross-referencing, and humble, heart-searching questions for personal application (especially at the end of each chapter) all make for a fresh understanding of the so-called love chapter in our Bible. Take my advice and read 1 Corinthians 13, and alongside it, Wayne Mack's book. You'll be so grateful you did!

—**Lance Quinn,** Pastor-Teacher, The Bible Church of Little Rock

This book is one of those can't-put-it-down volumes, which quickly draws the reader in by the pastoral heart and practical insights of the author. From years of ministry and pastoral counseling experience, Dr. Mack brings out implications from Scripture rarely considered in today's superficial culture of cheap love and throwaway relationships. His challenging questions at the end of each chapter are a tremendous tool for churches and Bible study groups that desire a deeper, yet intensely practical guide to loving one another in a way that brings maximum impact to your life for the glory of Jesus Christ. I wholeheartedly recommend it!

—**Jerry Wragg,** Pastor, Grace Immanuel Bible Church

*Maximum Impact* is Dr. Mack's magnum opus! It encapsulates his lifelong teaching, counseling, and service to the people of God. With this tender exposition of one of the most familiar passages in the Bible, he has taught us in word what he and his precious wife live out in practice. Knowledge and application of these important principles are the basis to guide our every relationship and every endeavor. The Bible provides everything we need for life and godliness, and as you'll soon see, this life-changing passage (1 Corinthians 12:31–13:18) may be the most important teaching to affect our influence for Christ in our own world—in the situations and places that God has sovereignly assigned for us.

—**Deborah Howard,** Author of *Where Is God in All of This?*

Wayne and Carol Mack came into my life when they moved to South Africa in 2005. They both ooze a joyful, caring, and loving attitude. Their theology is spot-on and deeply ingrained. But most of all, they humbly, obediently, and visibly live out what they believe. And that has more impact than flowery words and impressive proclamations. They showed me love, and I felt it; they did not have to tell me that they loved me. And here in this book Wayne lifts the veil to how they manage to live out love in such a practical and tangible way. If you and I can manage to apply only 20 percent of what Wayne teaches us in *Maximum Impact*, your life and those around you will be greatly enriched and God will be glorified.

—**Ian Murray,** Elder, Grace Fellowship Church

Dr. Mack has been one of the biggest mentors in my life, and now he can be yours too through this book. If ever I have known a man committed to living a fruitful life and having maximum impact, it is Dr. Mack. What a great opportunity in this book for us to learn better how to imitate such fruitfulness in our own lives.

—**Timothy Cantrell,** Pastor, Antioch Bible Church

Dr. Mack's book *Maximum Impact* provides readers with a look into ways they can personally make an eternal mark on the lives of others for Christ's sake. He uses very practical examples to show one's own need for growth in God's truth and in the lives of others to the glory of God.

—**Douglas Nichols,** Founder and Director Emeritus,
Action International

Wayne skillfully uses God's Word as a broom to sweep out motives, attitudes, and actions that keep us from loving others and having a maximum impact for Christ. Practical applications pulsate through this book and leave you no room to escape. If you don't want to change, put it down now.

—**Sybrand de Swardt,** Pastor,
Lynnwood Baptist Church

Dr. Mack does the church the immense favor of calling attention, in a thoroughly biblical way, to Christian fruitfulness, thereby raising it to the lofty standard by which God would have us measure it. Pastors seeking authentic congregational love should not hesitate to commend *Maximum Impact* to their flock.

—**Choolwe Mwetwa,** Pastor, Central Baptist Church

Through *Maximum Impact*, God teaches Christians how to have a maximum love impact in a world of un-love. This thorough biblical exposition of 1 Corinthians 13 by Dr. Wayne Mack is matched with vivid practical application, challenging the reader to examine and change his heart and life. I candidly recommend it, especially for personal reflection and group discussion.

—**Vorster Combrink,** Executive, Association for Biblical Counseling and Education, Manager, Counseling Ministry of Radio Pulpit

Comprehensive, convicting, and packed with gems of priceless truth. Another book that is vintage Mack! Some write from an armchair. Others from a heart shaped by Christ and His Word. Wayne Mack is one of the latter. Handle with care—you will never love or attempt to love in quite the same way again!

—**Roland Eskinazi,** Pastor, Goodwood Baptist Church

For almost two decades of pastoral ministry I have prayed, "Lord, since You taught the Thessalonian believers to love (1 Thess. 4:9), I am confident You can teach me too. Please teach me to love." The book you hold in your hands is an answer to my prayers. Like a good friend and loving mentor, Wayne Mack comes alongside, as an instrument in the Spirit's hand, to give us a Bible-saturated challenge to love others as Christ loves us. Read this book, apply it, and you will never be the same.

—**Paul Tautges,** Pastor-Teacher, Immanuel Bible Church

Worldly philosophy and effort have failed us. In *Maximum Impact*, however, Wayne Mack placards something that will never fail us—Christlike love (*agapē*). All who care to read and practice the words of this book will have no less than an ennobling experience.

—**Ronald Kalifungwa,** Pastor, Lusaka Baptist Church

If every Christian lived according to what is exhorted in this book, the local church would be a wonderful place and nonbelievers would be drawn to the church like bees to honey.

—**Chee-Eng Tan,** Elder, The Fisherman of Christ Fellowship

# MAXIMUM
# IMPACT

# MAXIMUM IMPACT

## LIVING AND LOVING FOR
## GOD'S GLORY

WAYNE A. MACK

P&R PUBLISHING
P.O. BOX 817 • PHILLIPSBURG • NEW JERSEY 08865-0817

Printed in the United States of America

**Library of Congress Cataloging-in-Publication Data**

Mack, Wayne A.
  Maximum impact : living and loving for God's glory / Wayne A. Mack.
     p. cm.
  Includes bibliographical references and index.
  ISBN 978-1-59638-204-6 (pbk.)
  1. Christian life--Textbooks. 2. Spiritual life--Christianity--Textbooks. 3. Love--Religious aspects--Christianity--Textbooks. 4. Bible. N.T. Corinthians, 1st, XIII--Criticism, interpretation, etc. 5. Bible. N.T. Corinthians, 1st, XIII--Textbooks. I. Title.
  BV4501.3.M23425 2010
  248.4--dc22
                              2010027081

# CONTENTS

# ACKNOWLEDGMENTS

In the opening pages of this book, I want to do the biblical thing in giving honor to whom honor is due (Rom. 13:7).

First, I want to acknowledge my deep appreciation to Deborah Howard, who took my extensive notes and used her considerable writing skills to shape them into the form that you find in this book. At times, I was tempted to scrap the whole project in that I was already extremely busy, plus I did not want to produce a book just for the sake of producing a book. At those times, my words to her were something like this: "Our bookshelves and bookstores are already clogged with books that contain shallow and unbiblical material. If the whole project should be scrapped, now is the time to decide, before I sign the contract. Let's publish this book only if it can make a valuable contribution to the church and to Christians." Her words to me, which kept me at it, were, "It's a great book! Of course it should be published! It is going to be an important book, Dr. Mack." So with that encouragement from someone whose editorial skills and Christian commitment I respect, I joyfully pressed on, preparing this book for publication. Thank you, Deborah.

In terms of giving honor I also want to express my thanks to Marvin Padgett, vice president-editorial of P&R Publishing, who immediately warmed to the idea of producing this book. As we proceeded, his positive and enthusiastic remarks ("What good news about *Maximum Impact*. Looks great! We want to publish your book. A study of 1 Corinthians 13 will be super. I have always been challenged by the message of this passage.") reinforced the idea that the contents of this biblically based tome could be of significant value to God's people. I could not ask for a better editorial relationship than the one I have enjoyed with Marvin. So thanks, my brother, for your valuable assistance.

Again, I must express my gratitude to the dear woman whom God has given to me as a suitable "helper" in every area of my life and ministry. As usual, she has assisted me in writing this book by her prayers and careful proofreading and by making suggestions about grammar and words or expressions that might improve the way some statement was made. Carol has spent long periods of time skillfully reworking some sections of the book so that the truth is still there, but it is presented in a much more readable and interesting way. What a joy it has been for me to work together with my wife on this project. So many thanks to the one who has stood with me as we have ministered together for over fifty-two years.

I gratefully acknowledge my indebtedness to certain men, who aren't even aware that I have written this book, for the help they have been to me as I have recorded its contents on paper. During the more than twelve months in which this manuscript was being developed, I was blessed and challenged by the insights and stimulation I gained from books by Jonathan Edwards (*Charity and Its Fruits*), Alexander Strauch (*A Christian Leader's Guide to Leading with Love*), John MacArthur (*Commentary on 1 Corinthians*), and several commentaries by other Bible scholars. I also want to mention my deep appreciation to Ian Murray and Elsa Marais, who carefully read the book and made useful stylistic comments; to Steve Viars for writing a meaningful and excellent foreword; and to all the men and women who have read the material in manuscript form and written endorsements for the book. Any errors in this book are totally my fault, but some of the worthwhile thoughts are certainly due to the influence of the people whose names I have just cited. So I thank them for the part they have played in the completion of this work.

# FOREWORD

I still remember the first day I laid eyes on Wayne Mack. I was a squeaky-clean doctoral student at Westminster Seminary, and Dr. Mack was one of my first-year professors in biblical counseling. I am not sure if doctoral students are supposed to be nervous, but I certainly was. It wasn't exactly the "first day of kindergarten" kind of nervousness, but I definitely had a lot of questions rumbling around my mind. Would I be able to handle the work? Would the instruction be based on Scripture? Would this degree program enhance my desire to help others?

Then Wayne Mack began speaking. Within minutes, I found myself praising God for what He was allowing me to experience. Wayne spoke with compassion, conviction, and clarity. He could pack more Bible verses into a single sentence than I could put into a sermon. I felt that I was listening to a cross between the apostle Paul, my grandpa, a trusted friend, and someone who gave clear evidence of having long walked with Christ. My concerns about the degree program melted away, and I decided then and there that I wanted to hear from Wayne Mack as long and as often as possible.

That occurred over twenty-five years ago, and I have since had the unexpected privilege of becoming one of Wayne's colaborers and associates. It was one of the sweet surprises of Christian ministry, when my teacher and mentor became my confidant and friend. I know that I speak for many when I praise the Lord for using Wayne to have maximum impact on my life by modeling biblical love to me.

I believe it is highly appropriate that Dr. Mack has written a book that unpacks the great love chapter in God's Word, 1 Corinthians 13. There are three reasons why I especially encourage you to read and carefully study this wonderful book.

First, Wayne's discussion of how to have maximum impact comes directly from the words of Scripture. So often in our day, books about leadership and impact are long on secular logic and short on the Word of God. Thankfully, Dr. Mack has taken the opposite approach. Paragraph after paragraph is devoted to a careful exposition of God's view on the subject of how to make a difference in someone else's life. Wayne takes time to set these verses in their original context so that people like you and me can confidently apply what we are reading.

Anyone familiar with Wayne's prior works can attest that fidelity to the Scripture is a hallmark of his ministry. I can even remember times back in school when I was tempted to take out a pen and make notes while Dr. Mack prayed. I do not think I have ever walked away from a discussion with Wayne when I have not learned or been reminded of something else from the Bible. This new book is equally trustworthy.

Second, *Maximum Impact* is intensely practical. It is obvious that Dr. Mack has spent many hours talking to real people with significant questions, hurts, and struggles. This book is anything but a dry theological treatise by an ivory-tower academician. Wayne knows people, and he loves them.

The time you spend studying these pages will provide solid and specific answers to the questions you have about how to grow in biblical love. You will not be left scratching your head about how to apply the principles, because, like any wise counselor, Wayne knows that the task is not complete until the hearer knows how to be a doer of the Word. You will be challenged to take definite and understandable steps in your quest to have maximum impact in the lives of those the Lord has placed around you.

Third, this book will challenge you at the level of the heart. Love is not a set of behaviors that are arbitrarily pasted on the outer man. As Wayne will carefully explain, you cannot *be* loving until you *are* loving.

That might mean taking the time to evaluate various areas of your heart that need to change. Before you can have maximum impact on others, you might have to allow Wayne to use God's Word to have maximum impact on you. But speaking for a long line of men and women who have been helped by Dr. Mack's life and teaching, I guarantee that the process will be more than worth it if the end result is a heart that has been transformed into the likeness of Christ.

Thank you, Wayne, for allowing God to make you into a loving man. And thank You, Lord, for allowing such a loving man to have maximum impact on me.

Pastor Steve Viars, Faith Baptist Church, Lafayette, Indiana

# INTRODUCTION

Little did I know on that cold, damp November day in 2007, when Carol and I arrived in Germany to begin a time of ministry there, that the end result of that ministry trip would be a book—a book about how to live a life of fruitfulness that will impact others. The weather was cold and damp, but we had a very wonderful time filled with joy, beauty, warm fellowship, rewarding service—and hard work. It was during this time that we visited with a seventy-year-old man who had lived in Napa Valley, California.

Napa Valley is famous for its fruit farms and vineyards. This man had worked in its fertile fields for more than forty years. In fact, he had gone to college and majored in agriculture, specializing in growing fruit trees and vineyards. As we visited with this man, I learned more about growing fruit and grapevines than I had ever known. He was a veritable storehouse of information about this subject, and we found it fascinating. We asked him many questions, and he gave us numerous insights about what is necessary if someone is to be a successful, productive fruit grower.

In a sense the conversations we had with this man motivated me to do a rather thorough biblical study of the theme of being a successful *Christian fruit* grower. I had already known that the Bible is replete with admonitions and instructions indicating that God wants all Christians—not just pastors or church leaders—to be prolific bearers of certain kinds of fruit. For example, I knew that we find this emphasis on bearing fruit in:

1. the Sermon on the Mount in Matthew 7:17–20
2. the parable of the four soils in Matthew 13:18–23
3. Jesus' teaching to His disciples in John 15:8, 16
4. Paul's teaching in Romans 7:4
5. Paul's prayer for the Philippians in Philippians 1:11
6. His teaching to the Colossians in Colossians 1:6

I also knew that these passages are the tip of the iceberg of many other passages that teach the same idea.

My study of Christian fruit-bearing also led me to the conclusion not only that it is God's will that every Christian bear fruit, but that it is God's desire for us to bear *different kinds* of fruit:

1. the fruit of personal character (Gal. 5:22–23)
2. the fruit of righteousness (Phil. 1:11)
3. the fruit of holiness (Rom. 6:22)
4. the fruit of goodness (Eph. 5:9)
5. the fruit of repentance (Luke 3:8)
6. the fruit of bringing people to Christ or building them up in Christ (Rom. 1:13; 15:25–28)
7. the fruit of living lives that will bring praise and glory to God (Heb. 13:15; Phil. 1:11).

In other words, the Bible makes it clear that God not only wants us to bear fruit, but wants us to bear many kinds of fruit. Sometimes being fruitful means that we are to live our lives in such a way that will bring glory and praise to God (Phil. 1:11). Sometimes, as the book of Hebrews teaches, the fruit He wants from us is the fruit of our lips, which involves giving praise and thanks to His name. "Through him then let us continually offer up a sacrifice of praise to God, that is, the fruit of lips that acknowledge his name" (Heb. 13:15).

There are times when the Bible speaks of God's desire for us to be fruitful in terms of the spiritual impact we have on others—having an effective ministry with others in terms of their spiritual lives, in terms of building up the church, in terms of bringing them to Christ, in terms of helping them to grow in Christ and become more like Christ and more useful in the church and world. In Romans 1:13 Paul refers to this kind of fruitfulness when he says, "I want you to know, brothers, that I have often intended to come to you (but thus far have been prevented), *in order that I may reap some harvest among you as well as among the rest of the Gentiles*" (see also Rom. 15:25–28; Col. 1:3–6).

This biblical emphasis on fruit-bearing has motivated me to write this book in which I will dwell on the theme of how to make a maximum impact for Christ. In it I will be presenting some suggestions and instruction aimed at helping us grow these different kinds of fruit! In it I will primarily focus on what God says is a fundamental requirement for bearing fruit in terms of our spiritual impact on others in our families, in our churches, and in our world.

While the primary focus of the book will be on making a maximum impact on others for Christ, I also write with the conviction that the different kinds of fruit we offer up to Christ with our lives cannot be easily separated. In other words, I understand that we will never be fruitful in making a spiritual impact on others or in bringing glory to God if we are not growing in personal holiness, and if we are not bearing the various aspects of the fruit of the Spirit in our lives.

In effect, I am saying that you can't have one kind of biblical fruit without the others—they are inextricably related and intertwined. At times, you can't see where one ends and the other begins!

And while I recognize this to be true, I want you to know that I still intend to make the primary focus of this book about how to live a life of fruitfulness *in terms of our spiritual impact on others*. Though all kinds of fruitfulness are important, I believe this one is among the "cream of the crop," because it causes us to carry out the Lord's frequently repeated great command to love our brothers.

# 1

## The "Over the Top" Way to Make an Impact: Part 1

I was with a friend several years ago who was quite annoyed at being asked if he was a senior citizen. (I was glad to be asked—it meant we qualified for a discount!) Because I am a senior citizen (at 74 waitresses don't ask me if I am a pensioner anymore) and have been a Christian for 58 years and in what is called full-time ministry for 52 years, I have often been asked to answer questions such as: What is involved in making a maximum impact for Christ in the lives of others? What is the most important factor in being a prolific fruit-grower in terms of bringing people to Christ and building them up in Christ? How do I keep from wasting my life and ending up with nothing but leaves on the tree of my life?

As I have thought and prayed about these questions and sought to discern the primary biblical answer to them, I have come to the conclusion that the main answer is found in one very familiar passage of Scripture. It's found in many other passages as well, and throughout this book we will allude to some of the other passages, but I want to primarily focus on one passage of Scripture, because it pulls the answer together in such a way that it is hard to miss.

The passage I'm referring to is 1 Corinthians 12:31–13:8. In this well-known passage, Paul, writing by the inspiration of the Holy Spirit, does several things. First he clearly identifies what the most important factor is; then he exposes some erroneous ideas about how to have a fruitful life and ministry; and third he uses a number of specific descriptive phrases to illustrate what this most important maximum-impact factor will look like in real-life relationships.

When you read that the contents of this book will involve an exposition and application of 1 Corinthians 13, some of you may be inclined to stop reading and put the book aside because this passage is certainly one of the best-known portions of Scripture. If that is your inclination, I can identify with you because that is what I might have been inclined to do if I were in your place. In fact, I resisted preaching on this passage and writing this book because I thought that I had already mined the depths of this section of Scripture. I had memorized this passage. I had often meditated on it. I had studied it. I had read Jonathan Edwards's exposition of this magnificent chapter. I had preached numerous messages on it at different churches and retreats. What more could I discover in this section of Scripture than I had already uncovered?

Besides that, I resisted preaching or writing on this portion because I thought that most people would think there was nothing contained in 1 Corinthians 13 that they didn't already know. Yet in spite of these thoughts, I couldn't get this passage about love out of my mind. I thought about it. I prayed for direction concerning the subject of my next series of messages and the next book I should write. I knew that I needed to be personally challenged in this area. From observation in ministry and especially in counseling, I was convinced that real love is woefully lacking in many lives and churches. I was aware that churches and families were being shattered by a lack of love. I was concerned about the relative spiritual fruitlessness of many Christians. I understood that we as Christians should be bearing much fruit for God. I became increasingly convinced, as I reflected on this passage, that our lack of fruitfulness as Christians is often connected with our lovelessness. My reflections on this portion led me to the conclusion that understanding and applying truths of 1 Corinthians 13 was a key factor in becoming a prolific bearer of spiritual fruit, which would bring glory to God (John 15:8).

As I prayed and pondered, my initial resistance was overcome, and I decided that there were many valid godly reasons for expositing and writing on this important section of Scripture. As we go through the rest of chapter 1 and chapter 2 (and other chapters), I'll be explaining and emphasizing why this passage and its teaching on real love are so significant. For now, if you still are not fully persuaded that this passage and its subject are of utmost importance, please read on; and if you have a sensitivity to biblical truth, you will soon see why I am excited about the potential for good that the teaching found in this book may bring to fruition.

Over the years, it has been my privilege to write many other books, but I have not written any that I am more passionate about than this one. I say that because my newer, and deeper, examination of this passage in the last two years has rocked my world in a way that it has never been rocked before. My hope is that what God has done and is doing in my life through the deeper insights I have gleaned through my intense study, He will do in the lives of many others as they peruse and reflect on the truths found in this great passage of God's Word. So if your first thought was that a new study of 1 Corinthians 13 would not be worth your time, please hang on—don't jump to that conclusion too fast. Instead, I urge you to come to a study of this book expecting that you will be challenged, enlightened, convicted, and changed into an even more loving person.

As you read the chapters of this book, I encourage you to begin your consideration of every portion with prayer. In that prayer, ask God to give you a submissive heart, a heart that is eager and willing to be challenged, enlightened, instructed, convicted, and changed. Then, carefully and thoughtfully read the contents of the chapter, seeking to understand in a new and fresh way what each part of this magnificent passage says about how to have a fruitful, God-honoring, and impactful life. Conclude each reading session by completing the review, reflection, application, and discussion assignments at the end of each chapter.

And now, before we begin to explore the meaning of each phrase, let's begin our actual study of 1 Corinthians 13 by quoting the passage itself:

> But earnestly desire the greater gifts. And I will show you a still more excellent way. If I speak with the tongues of men and of angels, but do not have love, I have become a noisy gong or a clanging cymbal. And if I have the gift of prophecy, and know all mysteries and all knowledge; and if I have all faith, so as to remove mountains, but do not have love, I am nothing. And if I give all my possessions to feed the poor, and if I surrender my body to be burned, but do not have love, it profits me nothing. Love is patient, love is kind and is not jealous; love does not brag and is not arrogant, does not act unbecomingly; it does not seek its own, is not provoked, does not take into account a wrong suffered, does not rejoice in unrighteousness, but rejoices with the truth; bears all things, believes all things, hopes all things, endures all things. Love never fails. (1 Cor. 12:31–13:8 NASB)

## The Broader Context

First, as we look at this passage I want to mention the broader context for this wonderful passage of Scripture. This passage was originally written to the church at Corinth, located in Greece, while Paul was ministering in Ephesus, which is in present-day Turkey.

Regarding the Christians who were part of the church in this place, Paul tells us that they had been sanctified (1:2), that they were recipients of the grace of God (1:4), and that many of the people in the church at Corinth were gifted by God (1:5–7). In the first twelve chapters, Paul deals with a number of issues that were going on in the church and lives of the people there.

For example, he wrote that he had heard that some of the people in the church were manifesting pride and arrogance. Others were guilty of immorality, and the church wasn't handling the situation rightly. He covered other topics such as the matter of believers' taking other believers to court, marriage and divorce concerns, Christian liberty issues, and the idolatry question. He helped the Corinthian church, and us, understand why we feel and behave as badly as we sometimes do. He explained issues related to relationships between men and women as well as relationships in the church—including how we are to practice the Lord's Supper (communion).

In chapters 12–14, Paul explores the difficult issue related to misunderstandings and confusion about spiritual gifts. In this section, he deals with mistakes made in trying to live a fruitful life and have an affirmative ministry for Christ. It was evident that the Corinthians were confused about how to make an impact for Christ, which involved erroneous thinking about the extraordinary gifts of the Holy Spirit and the role they play in church growth and maturity.

Chapter 12 indicates their confusion about the gifts of the Spirit—among other things, they considered those in possession of some of the more spectacular gifts more important or personally holy than others in the church. They didn't seem to comprehend why everyone couldn't have *all* the gifts. Some apparently believed the extraordinary gifts were more important and useful than the ordinary gifts of preaching and teaching.

We also read in chapters 12–14 that the apostle Paul believed he needed to make it clear that the erroneous way the church was using these gifts was causing confusion and becoming a hindrance to the work of Christ. The people who believed they possessed these gifts were becoming proud and unsubmissive. In fact, several passages in this book to the Corinthians indicate that having extraordinary and unusual spiritual gifts doesn't necessarily equal being godly and spiritual (see 1:10–11; 3:1–3, 16–21; 4:1–5, 17–19; chaps. 5–6).

These people didn't understand the purpose for which the extraordinary gifts of the Spirit were given. They didn't realize that until the whole canon of Scripture was completed, these gifts of the Spirit served a very useful purpose, but after that were not needed. According to Hebrews 2:3–4, these gifts were given to validate the message of the apostles who had heard Jesus. They were limited to the apostolic age, and were to be operative as long as there were apostles around, and until the canon of Scripture was complete.

Read what Jonathan Edwards wrote about these gifts in his excellent book *Charity and Its Fruits*:

*Ordinary and extraordinary.*—The extraordinary gifts of the Spirit, such as the gift of tongues, of miracles, of prophecy, etc., are called extraordinary, because they are such as are not given in the ordinary course of God's providence. They are not bestowed in the way of God's ordinary providential dealing with his children, but only on extraordinary occasions, as they were bestowed on the prophets and apostles to enable them to reveal the mind and will of God before the canon of Scripture was complete, and so on the primitive Church, in order to the founding and establishing of it in the world. But since the canon of the Scripture has been completed, and the Christian Church fully founded and established, these extraordinary gifts have ceased. But the ordinary gifts of the Spirit are such as are continued to the Church of God throughout all ages; such gifts as are granted in conviction and conversion, and such as appertain to the building up of the saints in holiness and comfort.

It may be observed, then, that the distinction of the gifts of the Spirit into ordinary and extraordinary, is very different from the other distinction into common and special; for some of the ordinary gifts, such as faith, hope, charity, are not common gifts. They are such gifts as God ordinarily bestows on his Church in all ages, but they are not common to the godly and the ungodly; they are peculiar to the godly. The extraordinary gifts of the Spirit are common gifts. The gifts of tongues, of miracles, of prophecy, etc., although they are not ordinarily bestowed on the Christian Church, but only on extraordinary occasions, yet are not peculiar to the godly, for many ungodly men have had these gifts (Matt. vii, 22, 23)—"Many will say to me in that day, Lord, Lord, have we not prophesied in thy name? and in thy name cast out devils? And in thy name done many wonderful works? And then will I profess unto them, I never knew you: depart from me, ye that work iniquity."[1]

Further, the Corinthians were confused about the significance of these extraordinary gifts to the person possessing them—what did

---

1. Jonathan Edwards, *Charity and Its Fruits* (London: Banner of Truth Trust, 1969), 29–30.

it mean about that individual? If someone had the gift of speaking in tongues, of working miracles, did that mean this person was especially godly and spiritual? Absolutely not!

In fact, sometimes in the Bible we're told that extraordinary gifts were given not only to the godly servants of the Lord, but sometimes to ungodly men, as was the case with Balaam (2 Peter 2:15; Jude 11; Rev. 2:14), King Saul (1 Sam. 10:11), and Judas Iscariot (Matt. 7:21–23; 10:1–8).

The Corinthians needed to learn that the ultimate purpose for which God gives spiritual gifts to His people, whether ordinary or extraordinary, is not to exalt the person who has them or to impress or entertain others. The ultimate purpose (as in Eph. 4:11–16) is that the body of believers might be built up in love. This has a double meaning. The first is that the means by which the body is built up is through love, but also the goal of the building-up process itself is love. So these Corinthians had an improper understanding of:

- what is really important to God
- what is most useful in the cause of Christ
- how to resolve fighting and squabbling with one another
- why they were not to sit in judgment on one another
- what it means to properly relate to one another
- the most important ways to do the work of the church

It is in this context that Paul is led by the Spirit of God to write 1 Corinthians 13. It's in this context that Paul says what he does in 12:31 and then, in chapter 13, goes on to expound just what that more excellent way is.

## The Most Excellent Way to Make an Impact for Christ

And now, having considered the setting of chapter 13, let's move forward in understanding what Paul has to say about the more excellent way to make an impact for Christ, as he does in verses 1–3.

First, in verse 1, Paul wants the Corinthians (and us) to know that having a life that is permeated and motivated by real love is a far more excellent way to make an impact for Christ than being a person who has the spectacular gift of tongues.

The way Paul makes his point in these three verses is interesting. He does this by hypothetically using himself as an example of someone who possessed extraordinary abilities and did amazing things. In this section, he says that even if all these things were true but were not permeated and motivated by sincere love, they would be worthless. The point isn't that all these things are wrong and totally useless. The point is that unless they are permeated and motivated by love, they serve no God-honoring purpose.

Paul begins the discussion with the issue of speaking in the tongues of men and of angels. The word used here for the tongues of men is found in Acts 2:4. This word means to speak in another language without having learned that language. What it doesn't mean is that some senseless gibberish is some kind of magic spiritual language with which we must converse with our Lord.

To understand what this gift is about, we must go to Acts 2:5–11:

> Now there were dwelling in Jerusalem Jews, devout men from every nation under heaven. And at this sound the multitude came together, and they were bewildered, because each one was hearing them speak in his own language. And they were amazed and astonished, saying, "Are not all these who are speaking Galileans? And how is it that we hear, each of us in his own native language? Parthians and Medes and Elamites and residents of Mesopotamia, Judea and Cappadocia, Pontus and Asia, Phrygia and Pamphylia, Egypt and the parts of Libya belonging to Cyrene, and visitors from Rome, both Jews and proselytes, Cretans and Arabians—we hear them telling in our own tongues [languages] the mighty works of God."

This perspective on speaking in tongues is certainly in harmony with the teaching of 1 Corinthians 14:6–12, 19.

Paul mentions not only tongues of men, but tongues of angels as well. We don't know what language the angels speak. In the Bible, they are able to speak—and understand—the same language as the people to whom they are ministering. So we may infer that to speak in the tongues of angels means that we would have the incredible ability that the angels have to speak in and understand every language.

Here Paul supposes, for the sake of argument, that he has that miraculous ability to go anywhere in the world and speak the language of the people who live there. He says that if he has this incredible God-given ability to speak in any language and he is able to speak, preach, and exhort, all that ability is worthless and would accomplish nothing in God's church, unless it is permeated, motivated, and saturated with love.

In fact, Paul says that being the greatest linguist in the world and having the ability to clearly articulate truth will be not only worthless but harmful, a hindrance to the church, if he's doing it for any other reason than love for God and genuine love for others. So whether it's the apostle Paul, you, or I who make this claim, we will come across to people like a noisy gong and a clanging cymbal if we have not love.

I'm sure you have been around people whose sincerity is suspect. How much attention do you pay to their words—even loudly and enthusiastically uttered? Sometimes they might just as well be saying, "blah, blah, blah." They're all noise and hot air!

I read about a preacher who when expositing on this verse would take a steel pot and a hammer with him into the pulpit. Then he'd begin to beat and beat upon the steel pot. At first, people were a bit amused, but after he beat on it awhile, they weren't laughing or smiling anymore. When he continued to beat on the metal pot, the people became annoyed and irritated. Finally this pastor would ask, "Are you enjoying this? Does this please you? Do you find it helpful? Would you like me to continue to beat on this pot for the remainder of the message?" You see, it's just meaningless noise.[2]

By way of application, you and I may be able to speak in the language of the people with whom we associate and say words that they can understand. We may be able to talk to children in one way, talk to our mates in another, talk to neighbors, talk to other church members, saying things that are true, and things they need to hear, but if our words are not permeated, motivated, and saturated, if they don't *drip* with love,

2. Alexander Strauch, *Leading with Love* (Littleton, CO: Lewis and Roth, 2006), 10.

not only will the best of our words be useless, but many people will be turned off and annoyed.

Ah! How important is love to the cause of Christ? It is so important that though our message is concise and relevant, it is meaningless if we don't have that remarkable aspect of love within our hearts.

## Review, Reflection, Application, and Discussion Questions

1. What is the broader context of the 1 Corinthians 13:1–7 passage?

2. What does the broader context of this passage indicate about the people to whom Paul was writing?

3. What mistakes were some of the people in the church at Corinth making about the extraordinary gifts of the Spirit?

4. Summarize what Jonathan Edwards wrote about the ordinary and extraordinary gifts of the Spirit.

5. Explain the meaning of "tongues of men" and "tongues of angels" in verse 1. What is the biblical basis supporting your view?

6. Do you agree that having a life that is permeated with 1 Corinthians 13 is the excellent, "over the top," "beyond greatness" way of making an impact for Christ? If so, why do you agree? If not, why don't you agree?

7. In terms of the way this chapter defined what it means to speak in the languages of the people (i.e., not literal languages such as German or French, but in the sense of being gifted to communicate clearly to certain segments of people, be they children, young people, neighbors, fellow employees, personality types, men, women, well-educated, poorly educated, sports fanatics, artists, music devotees, people from different ethnic or cultural backgrounds, etc.), what languages or what abilities do you have to communicate God's message clearly to certain groups of people that need to be per-

meated with love if you are going to be a blessing to them? What implications does all this have for our ministries?

8. What application can you make of the teaching of verse 1 to your own life and to the ministry of the church? How should you and will you, by God's grace, change in the way you relate to your family and church and people outside the church?

9. And now an important reminder that you will find after every chapter in this book: please remember as you reflect on the love principle presented in this chapter that the purpose of evaluation and application is:

    a. not to discourage or destroy us;

    b. but to motivate us to see our constant need of the cross and how much we owe to Jesus—without Him we'd never make it, but praise God we are not without Him;

    c. and to motivate us to understand our constant daily need of grace—that our salvation never has been and never will be by the works we have done, but always by the work Christ has done and is doing for us; I want our studies in 1 Corinthians 13 to be a reminder that we need to live a cross-centered life; we need the application of the cross work of Jesus every day of our lives; remember there's not a day in our lives when we are so good that we don't need the cross, and there is never a day in our lives when we are so bad that what Christ did on the cross is not sufficient to provide forgiveness for us (Rom. 3:24; 5:20; Eph. 1:7; 1 John 1:7; 2:1–2);

    d. and to cause us to understand that we must and can, by His grace, on a daily basis put off from our lives the "unlove" that is displeasing to God and put on in our lives the love that is beautifully described in 1 Corinthians 13, so that we might become more and more like our Savior and more prolific in bearing fruit for Him as others see the grace of God at work in our lives, changing and transforming us (Eph. 4:22–24; 1 Tim. 4:7).

# 2

# The "Over the Top" Way to Make an Impact: Part 2

What passage of Scripture was read at your wedding—or at the last wedding you attended? 1 Corinthians 13 is one of the most familiar passages in all the Bible. It is a passage that is probably quoted in weddings and various settings by Christians and non-Christians more than almost any other section of Scripture. I can't think of a wedding that I have attended or one in which I have had an officiating role when this beautiful portion of the Bible was not read as part of the ceremony. Unfortunately, when it is read or quoted, I wonder how many people really pay attention to the context in which it is found or the main purpose for which Paul penned these words.

As we noted in the first chapter, 1 Corinthians 13 forms a part of a larger context where Paul discusses the role that spiritual gifts have in the life of the church and in the lives of individual Christians. In the context of 1 Corinthians 12–14, Paul corrects some wrong ideas about the role of spiritual gifts that were held not only by the Corinthians but by many people today. This topic is as important now as in Paul's day, because so many people today are confused about this. Because that is true and so important for a proper understanding of the full import of this passage, I want to briefly review some of the highlights of the previous chapter.

In this section Paul corrects the idea held by many of the Corinthians that some of the extraordinary gifts of the Spirit mentioned in 1 Corinthians 12 were the most important factors for making an impact for Christ. He refuted their erroneous beliefs that every Christian should have some or all of these extraordinary spiritual gifts. They apparently went even further, thinking that if a person didn't possess these gifts, there had to be something wrong with him.

Paul countered the idea that possessing certain of these spiritual gifts made a person more important, holy, or influential than others in the church who either didn't share the same gifts or didn't have them to the same degree. He corrected the thought that everyone should be as effective as everyone else in the church—and get the same results as well (vv. 4–11, 18). In fact, a Christian can certainly be fruitful without displaying any of these special gifts. Paul goes on to explain that the ones who possessed these gifts were not somehow superspiritual or more important to the body of believers than other members.

## Why the Big Fuss about These Issues?

Why am I devoting so much space to correcting these erroneous ideas? We'd do better to ask why Paul took all that time to correct them. Why should he concern himself so much with these errors in thinking?

- He knew that they were wrong ideas.
- He knew that they were harmful attitudes that were causing confusion, contention, pride, and arrogance among professing Christians.
- They were causing some Christians to question Christianity and become discouraged.
- He knew that the purpose of all spiritual gifts, whether ordinary or extraordinary, was to edify, console, and exhort to godliness

(Eph. 4:12, 15–16). The Corinthians did not understand this and needed his correction.

- He knew that the purpose of the extraordinary spiritual gifts was to validate the message and ministry of the apostles until the whole canon of Scripture was completed. They were designed to provide the church with new revelation about Christ and the Christian life that was not found in the Old Testament. (Remember that at this time Christ had died and risen again only about twenty years previously and that even though a few of the New Testament books may have been written—most of them weren't—they were not widely available. There were no printing presses, you know, so all the New Testament Christians had was the Old Testament—and verbal communication [see 2 Cor. 12:11–12; Heb. 2:3–4].)
- One other reason why Paul made these corrections was that he knew, as he wrote in 1 Corinthians 12:31, that there was a more excellent way for Christians and the church to be fruitful for Christ.

Please note that in 12:31 and 14:1–3, Paul doesn't say that it is *wrong* for the Corinthians to desire spiritual gifts. He just wanted them to desire gifts for the *right reason*. Possession of these gifts was not designed to exalt self, to impress others, to make themselves look good, but to cheer up, edify, console (*paramytheomai*), exhort (*parakaleō*), come alongside to urge, entreat, motivate, and persuade.

Paul wrote in 1 Corinthians 12:31, "And I will show you a still more excellent way." Previously, he'd dealt with desiring those higher gifts. Now he is going to move on to a more excellent way to build the church. The Greek word for *excellent* is *hyperbolē*, which means "over the top." Literally, it means "exceedingly great; goes beyond great." It is taken from the verb *hyberballō*—"to throw beyond, overthrow."

## A More Excellent Way

So what is this more excellent way to build a church? The way of real love. In verses 1–3 of our passage, Paul begins detailing the better way by demonstrating the supremacy of love over the erroneous views the Corinthians had previously held. The most important aspect of the building up of the church is not extraordinary gifts—it is love. Love is the way to impact others for Christ.

Paul wants the Corinthians (and us) to know that the way of love is more excellent, more powerful, and more important than having a whole church full of people with the supernatural gift of tongues. That brings us to the second point Paul wants to convey—that when it comes to this matter of bearing fruit, it is far more important for us to have lives permeated and motivated by real love than it is to have the gift of prophecy and understand all mysteries and possess all knowledge.

In these opening verses, Paul portrays himself as a person who has an unusual gift of prophecy, the ability to understand mysteries, and the possession of special knowledge. In so many words, he is saying, "Let's suppose I have been gifted by God to be a prophet," which, of course, he was. He continues by saying, "I want you to know that even if I have been called and equipped by God to be a prophet and I exercise that gift, but my ministry is not permeated, saturated, and engulfed in love, I am an absolute zero. Not only am I not very significant, I am totally *in*significant. I'm a nobody. I am personally irrelevant and will accomplish nothing for the cause of Christ." He explains that having that gift in and of itself doesn't make an individual important or useful. In other words, having a life permeated and motivated by real love is far more important than any extraordinary spiritual gift we could possess. This concept was completely foreign to the Corinthians.

Ephesians 2:19–21 says:

> So then you are no longer strangers and aliens, but you are fellow citizens with the saints and members of the household of God, built on the foundation of the apostles and prophets, Christ Jesus himself being the cornerstone, in whom the whole structure, being joined together, grows into a holy temple in the Lord. (See also 1 Cor. 12:28; Eph. 4:11)

God has appointed first apostles, then prophets. The term *prophet* is a familiar one. But what does it really mean to be a prophet? Prophets, according to 1 Corinthians 13:2, are those who have unusual insights into the truths of God, into His mysteries, which can be known only by direct revelation; they are stewards of the mysteries of God. A prophet was divinely equipped to understand things the average person didn't. He possessed knowledge not available to everyone.

With that in mind, look forward to 1 Corinthians 14:1, 4–5, 29–31, 37–38, where Paul continues to discuss the ministry of a prophet. The ministry of prophets was especially important in the early church, which didn't have the New Testament. God delivered His new revelation through apostles and prophets.

So Paul says, "Let's suppose I have the gift of prophecy. Let's suppose I understand all mysteries—that I have all the knowledge it is possible to have. Let's assume that there is absolutely nothing I don't comprehend about God, about the Trinity, about the incarnation, about the Holy Spirit, about God's plans and purposes. Let's suppose that I understand everything about theology, everything there is to know about everything, including eschatology. Let's assume you could ask me any question you wanted and I could answer it, that I am the smartest, most intelligent, most perceptive person in the world. Do you know how meaningless that would all be if my life and ministry were not permeated and motivated and saturated with real love? I would be a nothing. I would not be the greatest person in the world, deserving all kinds of respect and adoration, having people bow down before me. Instead of being a person who deserved to have people hang on my every word, I would be . . . nothing—a noisy gong or a clanging cymbal."

What a powerful concept! What a surprising statement!

How does that apply to us? What does that mean in terms of our lives and ministries? Now, I know that none of us would claim to be a prophet in the sense in which Paul used the word. Surely none of us would think we know it all, that we have all the answers. None of us would be so arrogant as to think he has nothing more to learn—about *anything*.

Yet some of us do know quite a bit about theology, about the Word of God; some of us do have an above-average understanding of God and His Word. And all of us believe we understand some things that others don't. That might be about life, marriage, raising children, or many things, and we want to communicate those things to others.

Paul would say, if it's true that you have insights that others do not have—whether as a parent, friend, neighbor, fellow church attendee, fellow employee—having that certain knowledge doesn't make you a somebody. In fact, it is absolutely useless unless you communicate that knowledge to others in an attitude of real love. God does not give anyone a spiritual gift (ability) to put other people down, or to show off or impress others. Whatever unusual insight (knowledge) He may give to anyone is worthless unless the person possessing that knowledge dispenses it to others out of a real love for the people to whom he is ministering and, even more important, unless he does it because he is passionately in love with his God.

## Is Love More Important than Having Great Faith?

The next factor about effective ministry that Paul wants the Corinthians and us to understand about having a fruitful life and ministry is that it is far more important for us to have lives that are permeated and motivated by real love than it is for us to be people who have great faith.

Again, Paul supposes. He says, in essence, "Let's suppose I am a person who possesses *all* faith—as much faith as is humanly possible. Let's suppose I have mountain-moving faith that never wavers, that is always at maximum strength. I never doubt. I never fall to the influence of the world. In fact, let's suppose I have the faith Abraham had when he was told that at a hundred years of age, he was going to have a child—and that faith never wavered. Sarah wavered, but not Abraham. Let's suppose I have the faith that Shadrach, Meshach, and Abednego had when they were told they were going to be thrown into the fiery furnace; or the faith that Daniel had; or that David had when he faced Goliath. Well," Paul says, "let's suppose that all of that is true, but let's also suppose that my life and ministry is not permeated and saturated with and motivated by real love; do you know what that would make me? Do you know what I would be? I would be a zero—a nothing."

Of course, no one who reads the Bible, much less the writings of Paul, can come away thinking Paul didn't believe faith was a crucial factor in the Christian life and ministry. Among his statements on faith:

- We are justified by faith (Rom. 5:1).
- We have access to God through faith (Rom. 5:2).
- Faith produces joy and peace (Rom. 15:13).
- We are saved by faith (Eph. 2:8).
- We are to stand by faith (1 Cor. 16:13).
- We live by faith (Gal. 2:20).
- Faith produces joy (Phil. 1:25).
- Faith causes people to serve and to sacrifice (Phil. 2:17).
- Faith produces steadfastness (Col. 2:5).
- Faith produces works (1 Thess. 1:3).
- Faith makes us bold (1 Tim. 3:13).

And these are just the passages Paul wrote! So he isn't minimizing the importance of faith. Yet he explains in our passage that faith without love is powerless. In Galatians 5:6, he says that faith works by love. The way faith expresses itself is in love toward others.

In the Bible, we often find faith and love linked together. In fact, Paul summarizes 1 Corinthians 13 with verse 13, "So now faith, hope, and love abide, these three; but the greatest of these is love."

What does all of this mean in terms of our fruitfulness with others? It means that we may have strong convictions, may believe that God is sovereign, that God is all-wise, that God is just, that God will work all things together, that Christ is the only Savior, that people need to repent and believe, that people are lost, and that sin is awful. We may try to communicate all of that to others, but unless we do it with love, people will often reject, ignore, or even resent what we have to say.

Most of us have heard of the man who became known as Saint Augustine. He was a wicked man prior to conversion, yet he had a gigantic intellect. He also had a godly mother who prayed for him. What you may not know is that one of the reasons he was eventually willing to consider Christ was the loving life of a Christian by the name of Ambrose. Augustine often heard him preach. Of course, he rejected what Ambrose had to say. Though he was turned off by what Ambrose said, one thing he couldn't turn off was the love Ambrose showed.[1]

Many share this testimony. They disclose that they heard the gospel, but that it was the love shown them by a humble believer that impacted them the most—that made their hearts tender ground for planting godly seed. Speaking the truth is important. People *must* hear the message of the gospel. But our speaking the truth must be accompanied by a faith that works through love. Without love our faith will not make an impact.

An interview with Greg Livingstone, the general director of Frontiers International (an organization that works with Muslims), illustrates the importance and power of "faith working through love" (Gal. 5:6). In 1982 Greg and his wife started the Frontiers organization dedicated to planting churches that would be led by men converted from a Muslim background. Over the last thirty years, Livingstone says, "more Muslims have come to Christ than ever before in history. Thousands are coming to Christ." In Algeria, for example, where for 120 years the church had disappeared, it has exploded to more than fifty thousand converts from Islam in the last fifteen years. In Mauritania, a country that had not had a church for a thousand years, a church has been planted that has 550 members. In addition to personal verbal witnessing, what paved the way for impacting people in this country was a mercy ministry through which they fed and ministered to fourteen thousand mothers and babies. Livingstone indicates that throughout countries with a large Muslim population, 188 churches have been established during the last thirty years. While recognizing that ultimately it is the power of God that brings people to Christ and builds them up in Christ, Greg states that Frontiers International sends teams to demonstrate and proclaim the love of God, while also adapting to the local culture and learning the best ways to explain Christ's cross to Muslims. "Very few people," he says, "come to the Lord because they read a book or hear a sermon—there is no substitute for living among people and becoming a trusted person."[2]

1. Alexander Strauch, *Leading with Love* (Littleton, CO: Lewis and Roth, 2006), 45.
2. Katherine Anderson in *Wheaton Alumni Journal*, 12.4 (Autumn 2009): 27.

In other words, showing real love to people in the context of relationships is the most important factor in reaching Muslims for Christ. And, according to Paul's inspired words in 1 Corinthians 13:1–8, what Livingstone says about making an impact on Muslims for Christ is true in terms of reaching anyone for Christ.

Someone has rightly said that it's possible to be an effective doctor, lawyer, contractor, auto mechanic, or computer expert without love, but we *cannot* be a fruitful servant of Christ without it.

## Love-Saturated Lives Are More Important than Being Super Generous

Another point Paul makes to us, as to the Corinthians, is that when it comes to the matter of bearing spiritual fruit in our lives and ministry, it is far more important to have lives permeated and motivated by real love than it is for us to willingly give all our money to the poor! When Paul wrote, "If I give away all I have, and if I deliver up my body to be burned, but have not love, I gain nothing" (1 Cor. 13:3), he was saying, "Let's suppose that I am willing to be generous with the poor. In fact, let's assume that I am willing to give not just a portion, but all I have to the poor." In other words, if you have a home, sell it. If you have cars, sell them. Jewels? Computers? Furniture? Get rid of them and use the money to help the poor. Let's assume we actually do what the rich young ruler in Mark 10 was not willing to do. Wouldn't that be admirable?

The Greek word for *give* means "to dole out over a period of time, to continue to give"—and not just on a whim. In reality, this is what Paul really did. In Philippians 3:7–8 he says:

> But whatever gain I had, I counted as loss for the sake of Christ. Indeed, I count everything as loss because of the surpassing worth of knowing Christ Jesus my Lord. For his sake I have suffered the loss of all things and count them as rubbish, in order that I may gain Christ.

In 2 Corinthians 6 he tells the Corinthians that he was poor, that he often went hungry, and that he had nothing. It also shows his perspective on his poverty in verse 10 where he says, "as having nothing, yet possessing everything."

In Acts 20:33–35 he wrote:

> I coveted no one's silver or gold or apparel. You yourselves know that these hands ministered to my necessities and to those who were with me. In all things I have shown you that by working hard in this way we must help the weak and remember the words of the Lord Jesus, how he himself said, "It is more blessed to give than to receive."

As noted in these passages, Paul gave and continued to give. Obviously, his goal was not to amass a fortune or live a life of comfort. It is evident that he believed we ought to be generous with poor people. He believed what he wrote in Ephesians 4:28, "Let the thief no longer steal, but rather let him labor, doing honest work with his own hands, so that he may have something to share with anyone in need."

He held that believers should be willing to do what Barnabas did in Acts 4:36: "Thus Joseph, who was also called by the apostles Barnabas (which means son of encouragement), a Levite, a native of Cyprus, sold a field that belonged to him and brought the money and laid it at the apostles' feet." In the early days of the church, what one had, they all had.

Paul believed so strongly in helping the poor people of Jerusalem that he took it upon himself to raise funds for them. We see this in 1 Corinthians 16:1–3 and 2 Corinthians 8 and 9.

Back in our passage, we see that Paul says one could do all this and still do it without love. Good deeds may be motivated by many things other than genuine love.

- Like the deeds of Ananias and Sapphira, a person's good deeds may be motivated by a desire to win the approval of people. They weren't genuinely concerned about the needs of the poor, but in elevating themselves (Acts 5).
- Like the Pharisees, of whom Jesus spoke in Matthew 6:1–4, a person may perform good deeds to impress people with his

generosity. The Pharisees engaged in good works so "that they may be praised by others."

- The Pharisee described in Luke 18:12 gave, but for the wrong reason. He was trying to impress God with his giving and in doing so became selfish and legalistic.
- Some people give to relieve a guilty conscience. It makes them feel good about themselves and gives them something to brag about.
- Others may give out of a feeling of obligation and duty, which often translates into a grudging giver, as in 2 Corinthians 9:7, "Each one must give as he has made up his mind, not reluctantly or under compulsion, for God loves a cheerful giver."

Paul says that even if a person is extremely generous, if his giving is not motivated by love, it profits him nothing. He might think it does, but he'd be wrong about that. The only kind of giving that pleases God is sacrificial and cheerful, motivated by genuine love and compassion.

## What Does All This Mean to Us?

You might be asking yourself that question about now, wanting to find out how this relates or applies to you! How does this relate to the matter of being fruitful—especially in terms of making an impact for Christ in the lives of others?

It applies in the sense that God knows whether we give or not; and God not only knows whether we give, but also knows what's going on in our hearts as we give! God will withhold His blessing from those who don't give. This is the principle found in 2 Corinthians 9:6, which says, "The point is this: whoever sows sparingly will also reap sparingly, and whoever sows bountifully will also reap bountifully."

But more than that, God will withhold His blessing from those who give but whose giving is not motivated by compassion and genuine love. The principle is found here in the passage we're considering. God uses churches and people who are unselfish—who are genuinely concerned about the poor and needy around them.

Still further, Paul says that it is far more important for us to have lives that are permeated and motivated by real love than it is for us to be willing to suffer and even die and be martyrs for the cause of Christ. Again Paul uses himself as an illustration. He is saying, "Let's assume that I am willing to deliver up my body—sacrifice myself. Let's assume that I don't just talk about being willing to sacrifice. Romans 12:1 says, 'I appeal to you therefore, brothers, by the mercies of God, to present your bodies as a living sacrifice, holy and acceptable to God, which is your spiritual worship.' Let's assume that I go beyond doing what that verse says—that I'm willing to do more than offer up my body as a living sacrifice. Let's assume that I am in a position where my life is in danger. Something horrible and painful may actually happen to me, and I am faced with the possibility of not simply dying, but dying a horrible, painful death—for example, being burned to death, or being drawn and quartered. Wouldn't that please God? Wouldn't that make an impact on others? Wouldn't that be profitable for Christ and for me?"

The Bible makes it clear that we as Christians will be persecuted. Things will not always be easy for us (Matt. 5:10–12; James 1:2; 1 Peter 4:12–14). The Bible makes it clear that we ought to be willing to suffer for Christ's sake (Phil. 1:29; 2 Tim. 3:12).

What Paul describes here is not a mere hypothetical situation. This kind of suffering and persecution was something that he actually experienced! In Acts 14, we read that he was stoned; in Acts 16, he was flogged and beaten; in 2 Corinthians 11, he says that he was beaten with rods three times, that he was stoned, that he suffered dangers from countrymen, robbers, heathen, in the cities, in the wilderness, that he was attacked by false brethren; in 2 Corinthians 4:11 that he was constantly being delivered over to death . . .

Throughout the centuries, there have been thousands of Christians who have been martyred for the cause of Christ—hanged, burned at the stake, put in prison—and it's still happening today in China, India, North Korea, and Islamic countries.

Paul says that it is possible that all that he suffered and all that others may suffer may be of no value, and may be unprofitable—that is, of no profit to himself, to others, or to the cause of Christ. A person may do this for selfish reasons, for instance. People of other religions often suffer and die because they are promised immediate acceptance into paradise, or promised a harem of young virgins, or may do it because they want to be remembered as a brave person—a hero of the faith—or they don't want to be known as a coward. They may do it because they want to escape hardship or embarrassment.

In keeping with what Paul said in verse 3, Jonathan Edwards wrote this:

> Many have undertaken wearisome pilgrimages, and have shut them-selves out from the benefits and pleasures of the society of mankind, or have spent their lives in deserts and solitudes; and some have suffered death, of whom we have no reason to think they had any sincere love to God in their hearts. Multitudes among the Papists have voluntarily gone and ventured their lives in bloody wars, in hopes of meriting heaven by it. In the wars carried on with the Turks and Saracens, called the Holy Wars, or Crusades, thousands went voluntarily to all the dangers of the conflict, in the hope of thus securing the pardon of their sins and the rewards of glory hereaf-ter; and many thousands, yea, some millions, in this way lost their lives, even to the depopulation, in a considerable measure, of many parts of Europe. And the Turks were many of them enraged by this exceedingly, so as to venture their lives, and rush, as it were, upon the very points of the swords of their enemies, because Mahomet has promised that all that die in war, in defense of the Mahometan faith, shall go at once to Paradise. And history tells us of some that have yielded themselves to voluntary death, out of mere obstinacy and sturdiness of spirit, rather than yield to the demand of others, when they might, without dishonour, have died for their country, and many as martyrs for a false faith, though not in anywise in such numbers, nor in such a manner, as those that have died as martyrs for the true religion. And in all these cases, many doubtless have endured their sufferings, or met death, without having any sincere divine love in their hearts.[3]

3. Jonathan Edwards, *Charity and Its Fruits* (London: Banner of Truth Trust, 1969), 54.

What Paul—with Edwards—is suggesting is that our hearts are so deceitful that we may be willing to do the right thing, but do it for the wrong reason. In other words, we don't do it for the good of others.

What does all this have to do with making an impact for Christ on others? It's the same as mentioned when discussing giving all to feed the poor. God not only wants us to be willing to suffer—He wants us to be willing to suffer for the right reasons, not to avoid embarrassment or because we have no other alternative, but for the good of others and for the glory of God. Unless we do it for the right reason, even suffering for Christ will not be used of God to make an impact on others. Without genuine love, it will profit nothing in terms of our spiritual impact on others.

What does all this mean? Let me sum it up with an illustration from Jerry Bridges:

> Write down, either in your imagination or on a sheet of paper, a row of zeros. Keep adding zeros until you have filled a whole line on the page. What do they add up to? Exactly nothing! Even if you were to write a thousand of them, they would still be nothing. But put a positive number in front of them and immediately they have value. This is the way it is with our gifts and faith and zeal. They are zeros on the page. Without real love they count for nothing. But put this quality in front of them and they have value. And just as the number two gives more value to a row of zeros than the number one does, so more and more of real love in our lives can add exponentially greater value to our gifts.[4]

God wants each of us to bear fruit in the lives of others. What will it take for that to occur? What is the best way to get that done as individuals and as a church? What will make us a more powerful instrument in our world? Some of the Corinthians believed the best way was by way of extraordinary gifts, prophecy, or huge amounts of faith. Today, people are telling us the same things. Don't listen to

4. Jerry Bridges, *Growing Your Faith* (Colorado Springs: NavPress, 2004), 164–65.

them. Rather, let's listen to Paul. Examine what he tells us. Paul tells us that the more excellent way is the way of love. It is not simply a *good* way. It's the *best* way—the *hyperbolē* way, the "over the top" way, the "goes beyond excellent" way.

Brothers and sisters in Christ, as I close this chapter I want to ask you, do you want to be a person who makes a powerful impact for Christ? I do, and I'm sure that if you're a believer you do, too. So allow me to invite you to join with me, through the remainder of this book, to learn more fully about the specifics of what is involved in living a life of love.

## Review, Reflection, Application, and Discussion Questions

1. Why did Paul take the time to correct some of the wrong ideas that the Corinthians had about the extraordinary gifts of the Spirit?

2. Biblically speaking, what does it mean to be a prophet?

3. Why was the ministry of a prophet so important to the church during the middle part of the first century? What relevance does this fact have to the church today?

4. Though none of us have the unique gift of a prophet in our time, how does what Paul writes about the ministry of a prophet apply to us today?

5. What possible application can Paul's statement about having mountain-moving faith have for us today in terms of what is important in ministry?

6. What possible application can Paul's statement about giving away all that we have to feed the poor have for us today in terms of what is important in ministry?

7. What are some reasons for saying that good deeds such as giving away all we have to feed the poor are not always motivated by genuine love?

8. What are the reasons for saying that suffering martyrdom for the cause of Christ is not always motivated by genuine love? What other motives might cause someone to do this kind of thing?

9. What does all this have to do with making an impact for Christ?

10. Summarize what Jerry Bridges says about the importance of love if we are to have a fruitful ministry for Christ.

11. In terms of what this chapter has to say about the meaning of verses 2 and 3, what implications does all this have for the way we view and conduct the ministries of the church?

12. What application can you make of the teaching of verses 2 and 3 to your own life in your family and with other people and to the ministry of your church? How could you, should you, and will you, by God's grace, change in the way you relate and minister to people?

13. And now an important reminder that you will find after every chapter in this book: please remember as you reflect on the love principle presented in this chapter that the purpose of evaluation and application is:

   a. not to discourage or destroy us;

   b. but to motivate us to see our constant need of the cross and how much we owe to Jesus—without Him we'd never make it, but praise God we are not without Him;

   c. and to motivate us to understand our constant daily need of grace—that our salvation never has been and never will be by the works we have done, but always by the work Christ has done and is doing for us; I want our studies in 1 Corinthians 13 to be a reminder that we need to live a cross-centered life; we need the application of the cross work of Jesus every day of our lives; remember there's not a day in our lives when we are so good that we don't need the cross, and there is never a day in our lives when we are so bad that what Christ did on the cross is not sufficient to provide forgiveness for us (Rom. 3:24; 5:20; Eph. 1:7; 1 John 1:7; 2:1–2);

d. and to cause us to understand that we must and can, by His grace, on a daily basis put off from our lives the "unlove" that is displeasing to God and put on in our lives the love that is beautifully described in 1 Corinthians 13, so that we might become more and more like our Savior and more prolific in bearing fruit for Him as others see the grace of God at work in our lives, changing and transforming us (Eph. 4:22–24; 1 Tim. 4:7).

# 3

## LOVE'S FIRST CHARACTERISTIC

### Our Passion and Our Focus in This Life

Do you want your life to count for Christ? Do you want your life to bear every kind of fruit for Christ? I don't know how you would answer that question, but I do know I want my life to count for Christ. I want my life to bear every kind of fruit the Bible describes. When God calls me home and I stand in His immediate presence, I want Him to be able to say, "Well done, good and faithful servant. You have borne the fruit of holiness, bringing praise and glory to God, and impacting others for Christ through evangelizing unbelievers and building up believers."

On the day we stand in His immediate presence, most of the things we now consider to be important won't matter anymore. On that day it won't matter whether we had a big house or a small one, whether we had a big bank account or no bank account, whether we had an extensive education or very little, or whether we were beautiful or ugly.

On that day the only thing that will really matter will be whether we lived the way God wanted us to live. You have to ask yourself, "Have I done what He wanted me to do? Have I loved and served Him the way He deserves to be served?"

29

On that day, will we be able to say with Paul, "By His grace and power to equip and enable me to serve Him, I have fought the good fight"? "I have kept the faith"? "I've done my Master's will"? "I've obeyed Him in seeking to make disciples"? "I've obeyed Him in encouraging and building up the brethren"? "I've borne the fruit of holiness in my own personal life"? "I've lived in such a way that praise and glory were brought to God"? "I have made an impact for Him in the lives of other people"? "I've strengthened the church"? "I've borne the fruit of holiness"? "I've been an instrument through whom others were saved and strengthened"?

I believe these things should be the passion and focus of our lives as long as we are in this world! We are to work for Christ while it is still day, for the night is coming. As we work to our maximum effort, we are to be ever mindful that it is only by His grace, His power, and His will that we can do so.

## The Most Important Factor in Achieving This Spiritual Goal

The question is this: what is the most important factor in being able to bear the fruit that God wants from our lives? If I were to ask you to answer that question, how would you answer it?

Would you say that the most important factor is having the gift of evangelism or teaching? Maybe you would say that the most important factor is having the gift of speaking clearly and articulately. Or perhaps you would say that the most important thing is having a thorough understanding of theology, possessing a wealth of Bible knowledge, or being able to do block diagrams of Scripture.

Would you say that having a great faith is the primary factor? How about earning more than enough money so that we can give large amounts of money to the church and to the poor? Would you say that not enough of us have sufficient courage, enough boldness? Being willing to suffer or to run risks for Christ? Is the biggest need to not be afraid of people? Is it of monumental importance to get the right kind of training in evangelism, in counseling, in teaching methodology and techniques?

Well, many of the things I've just suggested are good things. In fact, none of them are unimportant. I certainly don't want to minimize the importance of any of these things. But as good as all these things are, I am convinced that if you were to ask the apostle Paul, "What do you think is the most important factor for making an impact for Christ?", his answer would be different from any of the ones I've just mentioned.

In fact, I don't just think his answer would be different. I know his answer would be different; and I know that because he answered this question in our passage—1 Corinthians 12:31–13:13.

In 12:31 Paul tells us that having spiritual gifts is good, but there's something that is even better. There is something that is much more excellent, much more important.

In 13:1–3 he tells us what that more excellent way is. It is the way of love. In these verses, Paul tells us that love is more important or excellent than the ability to speak well. It is more important than having the gift of prophecy or being able to understand all the mysteries of God. It is superior to having an incredible amount of knowledge or having the gift of mountain-moving faith. Love is more important than being extremely generous with your money. It is even more valuable than being willing to suffer and die for the cause of Christ. So Paul is saying that when it comes to making an impact for Christ, being a really loving person is at the top of the list.

In 13:4–8 Paul goes on to describe for us the kind of love that he is talking about. In this passage he goes into great detail to explain what real love is, and he does this because he knows that many people talk about love and think they are loving people.

## The Real Thing versus the Imagined Thing

If you were to ask most people, "Are you a loving person?" they would tell you, "What a foolish question! Why do you even ask that question? Of course, I am an absolutely loving person." I have yet to hear anyone describe himself in the way Paul describes us in Titus 3:3. I have yet to hear anyone say, "I am a hateful person and I hate other people."

In his book *Testaments of Love,* Leon Morris describes the way most people think about love; he suggests that the way most people think about love is erroneous and deficient. He goes on to describe what needs to be done to correct the situation:

> There is no need to tell our generation that love "is the greatest thing in the world." Christian and non-Christian alike, we take that for granted. We write about it, talk about it, and preach about it; we praise it and appraise it; we emblazon the word on T-shirts and on protest banners. We see ourselves as loving people, and it distresses us when others don't love as they should.
>
> There is a great deal written and said about love these days. It can scarcely be denied that many people think love is very important. It is also widely realized that Christianity emphasizes the practice of this virtue. Accordingly, it is curious that there are so few studies of what the Bible means when it uses this word. We usually assume that everybody knows what the word means, and that it is a generally agreed upon meaning.
>
> But I am not sure that this idea is justified, because the word love can be understood in one of a multitude of ways. It seems to me that we should be better off if we did not assume quite so much and gave more thought to exactly what we understand love to be. For Christians the starting point for such an exercise is the Bible.[1]

In my judgment, Leon Morris is "right on" in everything he said about the way most people think about love. He is also "right on" when he intimates that most people assume that everyone knows what real love is, and he is also absolutely correct when he says that our starting point for understanding love must be the Bible. That's why he wrote the excellent book that he did and why I've written the book that you are now reading.

The reason most people think of themselves as loving is either that they don't really know themselves or that they haven't rightly defined what real love is. Paul understood that most people do not really understand what God's style of real love is, so writing by inspiration of the

---

1. Leon Morris, *Testaments of Love* (Grand Rapids: Eerdmans, 1981), 1–2.

Holy Spirit, he takes the time to carefully explain God's concept of real love. In his explanation he gives us fifteen characteristics of God's kind of love, the kind of love that is more important than anything else in terms of our life and ministry for Christ.

And now, before I actually begin to exposit what Paul says about God's kind of powerful love, I want to give you a warning. If you don't want to be convicted and challenged by God's Word, you will not enjoy this topic of study. Better to just put this book down right now, because the very spirit of this passage rebukes, convicts, and challenges all of us!

I say this because of what has happened to me as I've done an in-depth study of this passage. From my own study of this passage, I'm convinced that when rightly understood there isn't a more challenging or convicting passage in all of God's Word. That's a strong statement, for sure.

So if you're really serious about spiritual things, I want to encourage you to be prepared for some heart surgery as we work our way through what God has to say about love in 1 Corinthians 13. I need to sound out a warning that this passage may be dangerous to the good opinion you have of yourself. If you're wallowing in positive self-esteem or working on building up a good self-image, you'll want to stay away from this passage. *On the other hand, if you want to grow as a Christian and as a witness for Christ, then this is the passage for you.*

Now, with this warning, let's turn to the passage itself and reflect on the first characteristic of real love in 1 Corinthians 13:4.

## Love Is like a Diamond

Real love is like a diamond that has many facets—all of them beautiful. And these beautiful facets are all essential. All complement one another, but all of them stand alone in their uniqueness, and Paul describes them all in this marvelous passage. For the remainder of this book I want to carefully study and apply and be challenged by each of the fifteen facets (or characteristics) of God's kind of love that form the main part of this well-known piece of Scripture. This has been a fascinating and useful study for me, and I pray it will be for you as well.

At the beginning of 1 Corinthians 13:4, Paul tells us that the kind of love that will make you a powerful influence for Christ is long-suffering. The Greek word *makrothymeō* found here is made up of two parts: *macro* = long; *thymeō* = to suffer. This was a word that was used to describe a calm and gentle response to the kind of suffering, pressures, difficulties, or injuries that are caused by people, not circumstances. This word meant to suffer long without losing your temper, without becoming upset or angry, without retaliation or seeking vengeance.

Jonathan Edwards said that the word means that we should be willing to suffer injuries without doing anything to get revenge either with injurious deeds or with bitter words. It means that we will bear injuries from others without losing the quietness and repose of our own hearts and minds—that when we are injured we will be willing to suffer much for the sake of peace, rather than do what we have the opportunity and perhaps right to do in defending ourselves.[2]

This word means we will bear not only a small injury, but also a great deal of injurious treatment from others without retaliation. We are to meekly bear these injuries without retaliation though they go on for a long time. We should be willing to suffer a great while in reference to our own interests before we defend ourselves. If we must eventually defend ourselves, we are to do it because we have been driven to it. Even then we do it in such a way that we do not do unnecessary injury to the person who has injured us.

We are told to be long-suffering. But what does that mean exactly? It means that we will do what Paul advised the Corinthians to do in 1 Corinthians 6:7 when they were being treated unfairly. "To have lawsuits at all with one another is already a defeat for you. Why not rather suffer wrong? Why not rather be defrauded?"

Jonathan Edwards explains that having a love that is long-suffering in actual practice means that a person will receive injuries with a soul filled with meekness, quietness, and goodness. Being long-suffering means that we will be meek and gentle and will literally suffer long:[3]

2. Jonathan Edwards, *Charity and Its Fruits* (London: Banner of Truth Trust, 1969), 71.
3. Ibid, 72.

1. When others are unfair or dishonest in their dealing with us;
2. When others make promises they don't keep;
3. When others injure us by reproaching us, slandering us, gossiping about us, spreading evil reports, or saying things about us that are not true;
4. When others misrepresent us or exaggerate our faults and mistakes;
5. When others injure us in their minds and entertain belittling thoughts about us;
6. When others express those evil, demeaning thoughts in words to us or by the expressions on their faces;
7. When others over whom we have God-given authority deny us the respect and honor and cooperation that our position rightly deserves;
8. When others who have God-given authority over us misuse that authority by behaving in a proud, selfish, arrogant, and uncaring way;
9. When others seem to be concerned about only their own interests in any given situation;
10. When others are stubborn and determined to have their own way and will not listen to the ideas of others even if their way is unreasonable and others will be hurt by it;
11. When others seem pleased when we are cast down because they wickedly think that our fall will elevate or benefit them;
12. When others keep up a grudge toward us and carry about with them a spirit of revenge and malice;
13. When others blame us for something we didn't say or do;
14. When others don't cooperate with us;
15. When others take longer to do something than it ought to take;
16. When others don't close doors, turn off lights, hang up clothes, or put tools away, or when they borrow books and then don't put them back where they got them;
17. When others don't listen well and we have to repeat ourselves;
18. When others constantly repeat themselves;
19. When others are late for appointments.

These are some "rubber meets the road" examples of occasions when a long-suffering love is needed. Now let me give you some specific real-life pictures of what this long-suffering love looks like in practice.

In 2 Corinthians 6, Paul gives us a great example of what long-suffering love looks like in practice from his own life. In verses 4–5, he mentions that he suffered afflictions, hardships, and distresses, was beaten and imprisoned, experienced tumults or disturbances, was slandered as a deceiver, was unrecognized, was shown disrespect, and was the subject of evil reports. How did he respond to this kind of treatment?

In verses 3, 4 and 6, he tells us that though he was being treated unfairly—in ways he didn't deserve—he was careful to give no offense in order that the ministry would not be discredited, commending himself as a servant of God by his long-suffering. He bore all of that without seeking to get revenge—without retaliation.

In 1 Corinthians 4:11–13, we read more of the same:

> To the present hour we hunger and thirst, we are poorly dressed and buffeted and homeless, and we labor, working with our own hands. When reviled, we bless; when persecuted, we endure; when slandered, we entreat. We have become, and are still, like the scum of the world, the refuse [rubbish, garbage] of all things.

So what does it mean to be long-suffering? It means that we are to respond to mistreatment in the way that Paul did in these passages.

And when we turn to Acts 7 we find another example of a love that was long-suffering. Stephen provides us with a great example. In verses 1–53 he preached to a group of people about Jesus. Verses 54–59 describe the horrible way they responded to his message of Christ. They violently stoned him in anger and disgust. But in verses 59 and 60 we read of the remarkable way he received this undeserved sentence:

> And as they were stoning Stephen, he called out, "Lord Jesus, receive my spirit." And falling to his knees he cried out with a loud voice, "Lord, do not hold this sin against them." And when he had said this, he fell asleep.

What does it mean to be long-suffering? Turn to Genesis 13 and read about a man called Abram (Abraham). See how he demonstrated a love that was long-suffering. Verses 1–7 tell of the strife that existed between the herdsmen of Lot and Abraham. Let's read Abraham's response in verses 8–12:

> Then Abram said to Lot, "Let there be no strife between you and me, and between your herdsmen and my herdsmen, for we are kinsmen. Is not the whole land before you? Separate yourself from me. If you take the left hand, then I will go to the right, or if you take the right hand, then I will go to the left." And Lot lifted up his eyes and saw that the Jordan Valley was well watered everywhere like the garden of the LORD, like the land of Egypt, in the direction of Zoar. (This was before the LORD destroyed Sodom and Gomorrah.) So Lot chose for himself all the Jordan Valley, and Lot journeyed east. Thus they separated from each other. Abram settled in the land of Canaan, while Lot settled among the cities of the valley and moved his tent as far as Sodom.

## The Greatest Example of Long-Suffering

I could go on giving other examples of the long-suffering aspect of love in the lives of biblical people, but I want to move on to mention the greatest example of what it means to be long-suffering.

Exodus 34:6 tells us that God is merciful and long-suffering. Romans 2:4 tells us that God is rich in goodness, forbearance, and long-suffering. Our God is a supreme example of long-suffering love.

The long-suffering love of God is manifested in the way He bears with the innumerable and continuous wrongs He experiences from men. They ignore Him, deny His existence, curse Him, rebel against Him. Yet God does not destroy them.

Think how His long-suffering love is manifested in the way He puts up with the filth and immorality that run rampant in the great cities, towns, and villages in every part of the world. Or consider how His long-suffering love is manifested in the way He spares and offers mercy to particular persons in all ages and all places. Consider how long-suffering and patient He has been with you over the years that you've been a Christian.

Think of the long-suffering nature of the love of Jesus as an example of this kind of love. In 2 Corinthians 10:1 we read about the meekness and gentleness of Christ. Matthew 11:29 tells us that Jesus was gentle and humble in heart. In fact, the long-suffering nature of the love of Christ is manifested throughout the Gospel accounts. Here are just a few instances:

- Matthew 11:16–24—People in Capernaum rejected Jesus and called Him names. Yet we read in 11:28–30, "Come to me, all who labor and are heavy laden, and I will give you rest. Take my yoke upon you, and learn from me, for I am gentle and lowly in heart, and you will find rest for your souls. For my yoke is easy, and my burden is light."
- John 10:20—Jesus is accused of insanity and being demon-possessed.
- John 10:33—He's accused of blaspheming God.
- Matthew 10:25—He is accused of being the devil himself.
- John 5:16 (and other places)—Enemies gathered together to make plans to kill Jesus.
- The long-suffering love of Christ was most marvelously illustrated in the events leading up to His crucifixion. It was manifested with Judas, with those who came to arrest Him, with those who lied about Him, with those who judged Him, with those who mocked Him, with those who spat upon Him. First Peter 2:21–23 says, "For to this you have been called, because Christ also suffered for you, leaving you an example, so that you might follow in his steps. He committed no sin, neither was deceit found in his mouth. When he was reviled, he did not revile in return; when he suffered, he did not threaten, but continued entrusting himself to him who judges justly." Isaiah 53:7 says, "He was oppressed, and he was afflicted, yet he opened not his mouth; like a lamb that is led to the slaughter, and like a sheep that before its shearers is silent, so he opened not his mouth."

Yet when He was on the cross, He prayed, "Father, forgive them, for they know not what they do" (Luke 23:34).

- Jesus was also long-suffering with His beloved disciples when they were slow to learn, when they were told about the cross and didn't understand—instead they were still looking out only for themselves when they fell asleep in the garden after He had asked that they pray.

- In John 13:34 (and many other places) Jesus commanded us to love one another as He has loved us. He told us that our love for others is to be modeled after His love for us. In fact, in John 15:12 He told His disciples (and us), "This is my commandment, that you love one another as I have loved you." And how did He love us? Just a few verses before, He had described this love: "As the Father has loved me, so have I loved you." Incredible! We are to love others as He loves us. And He loves us the way the Father loves Him.

Just what does that mean in practice? In part, it means that our love for others must be long-suffering, that we must be willing to meekly bear the injuries inflicted by others without internal or external retaliation or revenge—without harboring bitterness in our minds and without expressing it in our voices and behavior.

I have to wonder, at this point, what's going on in your minds as you read these words. I wonder if any of you reading this book would say, "I've been a perfect example of that kind of love. In fact, I'm always very patient and truly long-suffering."

I suspect that some have been thinking that what I'm writing about is correct, that it's indeed what the Scripture teaches. You've been reminded how often you've failed to respond in the right way. You may need to stop right here to seek forgiveness for the times you haven't shown this kind of love. You may need to seek God's help to become a more long-suffering person. I know I do.

But perhaps you're a person who responds, "That may be what the Scripture teaches, but it's completely impossible and unrealistic. Loving someone like that just cannot be done." Maybe you've been so hurt in the past that you dare not show others this kind of long-suffering love.

Why, they'd take advantage of you all the more, wouldn't they? That would just encourage them to continue and even increase the bad treatment toward you. Right?

I don't know what your response to this teaching may be, but I do know that what I am teaching in this book is God's perspective, and that if we reject this teaching, we are rejecting God's will and His design. I also know, as I prepared this book, that I was personally convicted and challenged. I know that I want to, with God's help, grow in this aspect of love. And I hope that's true of you also.

## Just a Little Reminder

Before we finish this chapter, I'd like to remind you of a few things:

- This passage was written to Christians. Paul is not telling us how to become Christians. He is telling us how we as Christians should live.
- Since this was written to Christians, he is writing to people who have become new creatures in Christ, who are indwelt by the Holy Spirit. If you're not a Christian, you can't possibly live or love this way because you don't have the nature or power to live this way apart from Him.
- Your great need is to see that loving this way is God's will. Acknowledge that you haven't been living this way, and then seek Christ for forgiveness. God will help you begin to develop more of this long-suffering aspect of real love. That's what you and I both need to do: confess that we've failed, ask Him for help, make a commitment for change, and promote this kind of long-suffering by remembering how long-suffering God the Father and Jesus Christ the Son have been with you.
- One more thing I'd like you to remember is the context in which this great truth is found. Remember the main point Paul is making: he wants us to know that developing and demonstrating this kind of love is the most important requirement for being a powerful witness for Christ in the midst of our families, church, and world.

We live in a dark world—a world filled with people like the ones described in Romans 1. This is a world filled with people who "suppress the truth" (v. 18), a world filled with people who "do not honor God" (v. 21), a world filled with people who have "exchanged the glory of the immortal God for images" (v. 23), a world filled with people who have "hearts given over to impurity" (v. 24), a world filled with people who have "exchanged the truth about God for a lie" (v. 25), a world filled with people who worship created things rather than the Creator, a world filled with people who are "ruled by their own passions" (v. 26), a world filled with people who do not want to acknowledge or submit to God (v. 28), a world filled with people who are unrighteous, wicked, greedy, malicious, arrogant, insolent, unloving, and unmerciful (vv. 29–30), a world filled with people who not only practice these things, but also give hearty approval to others who do (v. 32).

That was God's description of the situation in the time of Paul, and that's His description of the situation today. It's not a pretty picture, but it's into that world that God sends us to bear fruit for Him. It's into that dark world that God sends us to be a light.

And it's to Christians living in such a world to whom Paul writes 1 Corinthians 13. His goal is to tell them and us that if we're going to make an impact on this world around us, we must be people who love God with all our hearts and souls, people who love others in the way described here. John 15:16 tells us how we are to do it when Jesus says, "You did not choose me, but I chose you and appointed you that you should go and bear fruit and that your fruit should abide, so that whatever you ask the Father in my name he may give it to you." What's our most powerful weapon for getting the job done? It's developing a life that manifests the kind of love described in this passage.

## Review, Reflection, Application, and Discussion Questions

1. How would you answer the question: "What is the most important factor in being able to bear the fruit that God wants in our lives?"

2. What is the answer that the apostle Paul would give to this question?

3. What are the reasons for saying that Paul would give this answer?

4. What does Jonathan Edwards say Paul means when he states that "love is long-suffering"?

5. What are some of the times or occasions to which being long-suffering may apply? Go over the list of occasions mentioned in this chapter and evaluate yourself on each of these items in terms of always (4), usually (3), sometimes (2), seldom (1), never (0).

6. On the basis of this inventory, how would you rate yourself in terms of your love being long-suffering?

7. Give some biblical examples of what it means to be long-suffering. Describe what long-suffering meant to these people in terms of their experience.

8. Identify and explain occasions when Jesus demonstrated the long-suffering nature of love.

9. In what specific ways have you seen others manifest a love that is long-suffering as described in this chapter? Give specific examples.

10. In what specific ways have you personally manifested a love that is long-suffering?

11. In what specific ways or instances have you personally failed to manifest a love that is long-suffering?

12. What is your response to the teaching of this chapter? In what ways do you need to change to be more long-suffering in your love for others?

13. And now an important reminder that you will find after every chapter in this book: please remember as you reflect on the love principle presented in this chapter that the purpose of evaluation and application is:

a.  not to discourage or destroy us;

b.  but to motivate us to see our constant need of the cross and how much we owe to Jesus—without Him we'd never make it, but praise God we are not without Him;

c.  and to motivate us to understand our constant daily need of grace—that our salvation never has been and never will be by the works we have done, but always by the work Christ has done and is doing for us. I want our studies in 1 Corinthians 13 to be a reminder that we need to live a cross-centered life; we need the application of the cross work of Jesus every day of our lives; remember there's not a day in our lives when we are so good that we don't need the cross, and there is never a day in our lives when we are so bad that what Christ did on the cross is not sufficient to provide forgiveness for us (Rom. 3:24; 5:20; Eph. 1:7; 1 John 1:7; 2:1–2);

d.  and to cause us to understand that we must and can, by His grace, on a daily basis put off from our lives the "unlove" that is displeasing to God and put on in our lives the love that is beautifully described in 1 Corinthians 13 so that we might become more and more like our Savior and more prolific in bearing fruit for Him as others see the grace of God at work in our lives, changing and transforming us (Eph. 4:22–24; 1 Tim. 4:7).

# 4

## REAL LOVE AND KINDNESS ARE INSEPARABLE

### A Heavenly Meditation

If I were to ask you to give me a one-sentence description of heaven, what would you say? Someone might say, "Whenever I think of heaven, I think of seeing Christ face-to-face." Another might offer, "Whenever I think of heaven, I think of seeing my friends and loved ones who have gone on before." Still others might say, "Whenever I think of heaven, I think of being in a place where there is no more pain or hardships, no more wars, no more crying."

Those are all good answers. However, if you were to ask Jonathan Edwards that same question, do you know how he would answer? He would have answered, "When I think of heaven, I think of it as a world of love." We know that's the answer he would have given because he frequently referred to it that way.

In the annals of church history, Jonathan Edwards is one of the best-known and most respected figures. Many believe he was the greatest theologian and one of the most brilliant men that America has ever produced. But he was more than a theologian—he was first of all a pastor who preached hundreds of messages that have been reprinted and distributed widely even to this day.

Out of all those sermons, the one that is best known is a sermon entitled "Sinners in the Hands of an Angry God." It was first preached in 1741, and God used it to begin what has been called the Great Awakening, which was a period when hundreds of people—probably thousands—were brought to Christ and added to the church.

If "Sinners in the Hands of an Angry God" was his most famous, then the second most famous sermon that Edwards ever preached was probably "Heaven Is a World of Love." In that sermon, Edwards indicates that heaven is a place where love doesn't just trickle along in streams but gushes forth in mighty rivers. Then he goes on to say that these rivers of love swell as it were into an ocean of love, in which the souls of the ransomed may bathe in the sweetest enjoyment and have their hearts deluged with love.

After commenting on the kind of love we'll experience in heaven, he goes on to say, "If you would be in the way to the world of love [by which he means heaven], see that you live a life of love—of love to God, and love to men. All of us hope to have part in the world of love hereafter, and therefore we should cherish the spirit of love, and live a life of holy love here on earth."[1]

In that sermon, and many others, Edwards admonished his hearers that if they are citizens of heaven, they must bring heaven to earth. Doing this means, according to Edwards, shelving our personal agendas for the sake of our neighbors. It means that we will speak and demonstrate our love even, or perhaps especially, when it is costly and uncomfortable. Edwards says that in this world we must be real Christians and not just pretend Christians. We must live as real Christians and be much involved in deeds of love to our fellow men.

Moreover, Edwards calls upon us to imagine the impact we could have in the world if all of us, in the name of Christ, were much involved in deeds of love. In other words, Edwards is saying exactly what Paul said in

1. Jonathan Edwards, *Charity and Its Fruits* (London: Banner of Truth Trust, 1969), 367.

1 Corinthians 13—namely, that if we want to have fruitful lives and ministries, we must be people whose lives are characterized by real love.[2]

But the question is, what does the kind of love that will make us
fruitful in this world look like? That's the question Paul answers in
1 Corinthians 13:4–8.

In the previous chapter we focused on the first part of verse 4—where
Paul tells us that the kind of love that is powerful and impactful is patient
or long-suffering. In this chapter, we'll discuss the second element of
love in verse 4 where Paul says, "Love is kind."

## What Does It Mean to Have a Love That Is Kind?

The same Greek word used here is also used in Luke 6:35, "But love
your enemies, and do good, and lend, expecting nothing in return, and
your reward will be great, and you will be sons of the Most High, for he
is *kind* to the ungrateful and the evil." God is kind or good to ungrateful
men and evil men. In this context God does good to people who aren't
good to Him. He provides for people who ignore Him and do evil. He
lends to them even though He gets nothing back in return.

This word is also used in Matthew 11:30, "For my yoke is easy, and
my burden is light." Jesus says that His yoke is easy (or pleasant; kind)
and His burden is light. In Galatians 5:22–23, it is translated "gentleness":

> But the fruit of the Spirit is love, joy, peace, patience, kindness, good-
> ness, faithfulness, gentleness, self-control; against such things there
> is no law.

And in 1 Peter 2:3, "if indeed you have tasted that the Lord is good
[kind]." In Romans 11:22 the word for *kindness* is contrasted with
the word *severity*: "Note then the kindness and the severity of God."
So whatever kindness is, it is the opposite of severity. Severity would
involve being stern, lacking in compassion, lacking gentleness, being
harsh, not caring.

2. Summary of Edwards, *Charity and Its Fruits*, 321–68.

Ephesians 4:32 contrasts kindness with being bitter, wrathful, angry, and malicious (cf. v. 31). The Greek dictionary says that the word used here is describing not merely kindness or goodness as a quality, but goodness or kindness in terms of action. In other words, *kindness* may be defined as "love in working clothes." Kindness means being ready to help, to do good, to relieve burdens, to be useful, to be tender, to be genuinely sympathetic, and then actually doing something that helps someone in need.

Kindness involves doing good to the souls of men because you love them and love God. It involves:

- seeking to make disciples (Matt. 28:19)
- evangelizing and witnessing to those who are lost (1 Cor. 9:19–23; 10:32–33)
- teaching and admonishing one another in all wisdom (Col. 3:16)
- gently restoring our brothers who are in sin (Gal. 6:1–2)
- being filled with hope (Rom. 15:13)
- encouraging and building one another up (1 Thess. 5:11)
- admonishing the idle, encouraging the fainthearted, and helping the weak (1 Thess. 5:14)
- showing hospitality to one another and serving others to the glory of God (1 Peter 4:9–10)

Recently, a friend of mine, Deborah Howard, sent me an e-mail about a woman by the name of Edith Burns, who beautifully illustrated a very important aspect of what it means to be kind.

Happy Easter!

Edith Burns was a wonderful Christian. She was the patient of a doctor by the name of Will Phillips. Dr. Phillips was a gentle doctor who saw patients as people. His favorite patient was Edith Burns.

One morning he went to his office with a heavy heart because of Edith Burns. When he walked into that waiting room, there sat Edith with her big black Bible in her lap earnestly talking to a young mother sitting beside her.

Edith Burns had a habit of introducing herself in this way: "Hello, my name is Edith Burns. Do you believe in Easter?" Then she would explain the meaning of Easter. . . .

Beverly, the head nurse, called Edith into the room where certain procedures were performed. While her blood pressure was being taken, Edith began by saying, "My name is Edith Burns. Do you believe in Easter?"

Beverly said, "Why yes, I do."

Edith said, "Well, what do you believe about Easter?"

Beverly said, "Well, it's all about egg hunts, going to church, and dressing up." Edith kept pressing her about the real meaning of Easter.

After being called back to the doctor's office, Edith sat down, and when she took a look at the doctor she said, "Dr. Will, why are you so sad? Are you reading your Bible? Are you praying?"

With a heavy heart he said, "Your lab report came back and it says you have cancer, and Edith, you're not going to live very long."

Edith said, "Why, Will Phillips, shame on you. Why are you so sad? Do you think God makes mistakes? You have just told me I'm going to see my precious Lord Jesus, my husband, and my friends. You have just told me that I am going to celebrate Easter forever, and here you are having difficulty giving me my ticket!"

Dr. Phillips thought to himself, "What a magnificent woman this Edith Burns is!"

Edith continued coming to Dr. Phillips. Christmas came and the office was closed through January 3. On the day the office opened, Edith did not show up. Later that afternoon, Edith called and said she thought she would have to be admitted to the hospital soon.

"Will," she said, "I'm very near home, so would you make sure that they put women in here next to me in my room who need to know about Easter?"

Well, they did just that and women began to come in and share that room with Edith. Everybody on that floor from staff to patients was so excited about Edith that they started calling her Edith Easter—that is, everyone except Phyllis Cross, the head nurse.

Phyllis made it plain that she wanted nothing to do with Edith because she was a "religious nut." She had been a nurse in an army hospital. She had seen it all and heard it all. She was the original G. I. Jane. She had been married three times. She was hard and cold, and did everything by the book.

One morning the two nurses who were to attend to Edith were sick.

Edith had the flu and Phyllis Cross had to go in and give her a shot. When she walked in, Edith had a big smile on her face and said, "Phyllis, I love you, and I have been praying for you."

Phyllis said, "Well, you can quit praying for me. It won't work. I'm not interested."

Edith said, "Well, I will pray and I have asked God not to let me go home until you come into the family."

Phyllis Cross said, "Then you will never die because that will never happen," and curtly walked out of the room.

Every day Phyllis would walk into the room and Edith would say, "I love you, and I'm praying for you."

One day Phyllis said she was literally drawn to Edith's room as a magnet would draw iron. She sat down on the bed and Edith said, "I'm so glad you have come, because today is your special day."

Phyllis said, "Edith, you have asked everybody here the question, 'Do you believe in Easter?' but you have never asked me."

Edith said, "Phyllis, I wanted to many times, but I decided to wait until you asked, and now you have." Edith Burns took her Bible and shared with Phyllis Cross the Easter story of the death, burial, and resurrection of Jesus Christ. Edith said, "Phyllis, do you believe in Easter? Do you believe that Jesus Christ is alive and that He wants to live in your heart?"

Phyllis Cross said, "Oh, I want to believe that with all my heart, and I do want Jesus in my life." Right there, Phyllis Cross prayed and professed faith in Christ.

Two days later, Phyllis came in and Edith said, "Do you know what day it is?" Phyllis said, "Why Edith, it's Good Friday."

Edith said, "Oh, no, for you every day is Easter. Happy Easter, Phyllis!"

Two days later, on Easter Sunday, Phyllis Cross came in to work, did some of her duties, and then went down to the flower shop and got some Easter lilies because she wanted to go up to see Edith and give her some Easter lilies and wish her a Happy Easter.

When she walked into Edith's room, Edith was in bed. That big black Bible was on her lap. Her hands were in that Bible. There was a sweet smile on her face. When Phyllis Cross went to pick up Edith's hand, she realized Edith was dead. Her left hand was on John 14: "In my Father's house are many mansions. I go to prepare a place for you. I will come again and receive you to Myself, that where I am, there you may be also." Her right hand was on Revelation 21:4, "And God will wipe away every tear from their eyes; there shall be no more death nor sorrow, nor crying: and there shall be no more pain, for the former things have passed away."

Phyllis Cross took one look at that dead body, and then lifted her face toward heaven, and with tears streaming down her cheeks, said, "Happy Easter, Edith—Happy Easter!"

Phyllis Cross left Edith's body, walked out of the room, and went over to a table where two student nurses were sitting. She said, "My name is Phyllis Cross. Do you believe in Easter?"

Now, that's a challenging illustration of what it means to be kind—of what it means to be good to others because you have been loved by Jesus and because you love Jesus. Having a love that is kind involves doing good to others in terms of physical and temporal things, because you love them and love God; it involves doing what the good Samaritan did in Luke 10; doing what Phoebe did in Romans 16:1–2; what Aquila and Priscilla did, according to Romans 16:3–4; what Barnabas did in Acts 4; what Jesus did in John 8; what Jesus did in Mark 8—feeding four thousand; what Galatians 6:10 tells us to do; what 1 John 3:16–17 says; what Matthew 25:35–36 tells us God's people do; what Romans 12:17 says; what 1 Corinthians 12:26 talks about; what Paul did in Acts 20:34 and 1 Thessalonians 2:9; what James 1:27 tells us to do because we love God and His people; treating other people in keeping with the admonition of Matthew 7:12; it involves doing what Edith Burns did to Phyllis Cross and others.

And now as I bring this chapter to a close, I'd like to emphasize and highlight the fact that kindness will manifest itself in a comprehensive way. It will manifest itself in our words as well as in our actions. It will display itself in what we do say and what we don't say (Prov. 15:2 ; Eph. 4:29). Please reflect on the fact that it will manifest itself in:

- how we say things (Prov. 16:21, 24; Eph. 4:15; Col. 4:6; 1 Tim. 5:1–2)
- when we say things (Eph. 4:29)
- where we say things (Matt. 18:15; John 21:15–17)
- what we do and don't do—we will keep commitments and promises; will be a good example
- rejoicing with our brothers and weeping with them
- being willing to share with them and not be overbearing
- not being domineering or imposing our will
- not spreading evil reports about others or ignoring them
- listening to them and not lying to or about them
- not borrowing things from them without asking and, if we do borrow something, returning it in good condition

That's all part of having a love that is kind. And since God in His Word challenges us with this teaching, each of us should evaluate whether we can honestly say that we possess and manifest a love that is kind. Manifesting this kind of love is important for many reasons, with one of them being that it is an important aspect of the "excellent, over the top, beyond greatness" way of making an impact for Christ.

## Review, Reflection, Application, and Discussion Questions

1. What is the second-best-known sermon that Jonathan Edwards ever preached?

2. What do you think Jonathan Edwards meant when he said that we must bring heaven to earth?

3. How are you and others bringing heaven to earth?

4. What does Paul mean when he says that "love is kind"?

5. In what specific ways does this chapter indicate that a love that is kind will manifest itself?

6. What does the Edith Burns story illustrate about the way a love that is kind will manifest itself?

7. In what specific ways have you seen a love that is kind manifested by people in your church and in your family and by other Christians outside your church?

8. In what specific ways have you personally manifested a love that is kind to people in your church and in your family and to people outside your church?

9. In what specific ways have you failed to manifest a love that is kind to people in your church and in your family and to other Christians outside your church?

10. As a result of studying this chapter, are there ways in which you should and will, by God's grace, seek to develop more of the love that is kind? Please be specific.

11. And now an important reminder that you will find after every chapter in this book: please remember as you reflect on the love principle presented in this chapter, as I want you to do with our study of all the love principles, that the purpose of evaluation and application is:

   a. not to discourage or destroy us;

   b. but to motivate us to see our constant need of the cross and how much we owe to Jesus—without Him we'd never make it, but praise God we are not without Him;

   c. and to motivate us to understand our constant daily need of grace—that our salvation never has been and never will be by the works we have done, but always by the work Christ has done and is doing for us; I want our studies in 1 Corinthians 13 to be a reminder that we need to live a cross-centered life; we need the application of the cross work of Jesus every day of our lives; remember there's not a day in our lives when we are so good that we don't need the cross, and there is never a day in our lives when we are so bad that what Christ did on the

cross is not sufficient to provide forgiveness for us (Rom. 3:24; 5:20; Eph. 1:7; 1 John 1:7; 2:1–2);

d. and to cause us to understand that we must and can, by His grace, on a daily basis, put off from our lives the "unlove" that is displeasing to God and put on in our lives the love that is beautifully described in 1 Corinthians 13 so that we might become more and more like our Savior and more prolific in bearing fruit for Him as others see the grace of God at work in our lives, changing and transforming us (Eph. 4:22–24; 1 Tim. 4:7).

# 5

## KINDNESS VISUALIZED

At one point in his ministry at the Bethlehem Baptist Church in Minneapolis, John Piper did an extended series on the subject of love. In one of those sermons Piper made this statement to his congregation: "We are praying for revival. When it comes it will have to look like this or it will not be of the Holy Spirit—love is the fruit he bears." In context, what John Piper was saying was that when the Holy Spirit brings revival, it will always come in the form of a revival of love.

In that same sermon he emphasized the importance of love by saying, "I long personally to grow in love. I take heart from the apostle Paul that love is not an all-or-nothing affair. It is something you can grow in. So he prays in Philippians 1:9, 'I pray that your love may abound still more and more in real knowledge and all discernment.' That's what I want, as I get older."

Also in that sermon he emphasized the priority of love by reminding the people in his church that on one's deathbed no one ever looks up into the eyes of his family and says, "I wish I'd spent more time at the office." Piper's point is that when one is dying, the greatest grief is caused by the awareness that one should have been more loving to other family members.

In his conclusion to this sermon Piper again emphasized the priority of love when he quoted the words of Paul in 1 Corinthians 16:14: "May the Lord use these weeks in his loving Word to fulfill in us Paul's word in 1 Corinthians 16:14, 'Let all that you do be done in love.'"[1]

So it was John Piper's conviction that if and when the Holy Spirit brings revival, the fruit of that revival will be a revival of love; it was his conviction that growth in his own love quotient was a personal value; it was his conviction that at the time of our death what we will be most grieved about is a lack of love; and it was his conviction that everything we do should be motivated and conducted by love.

## The Biblical Basis for Making Love a Priority

Where did John Piper get his conviction about the importance of love in the Christian life and ministry? Well, he got it from many passages of Scripture, but in particular he got it from the passage we've been studying in 1 Corinthians 13. I know that from the fact that he quotes that passage and makes several references to it throughout the body of his sermon.

According to the apostle Paul, John Piper was absolutely right, for Paul said in verses 1–3, "If I speak in the tongues of men and of angels, but have not love, I am a noisy gong or a clanging cymbal. And if I have prophetic powers, and understand all mysteries and all knowledge, and if I have all faith, so as to remove mountains, but have not love, I am nothing. If I give away all I have, and if I deliver up my body to be burned, but have not love, I gain nothing."

So when it comes to being fruitful in ministry, Paul is saying that nothing is more important than love.

## Love That Is Kind in Actual Practice

But then the question comes: what does this love look like in actual practice—this love that will make us effective witnesses for Christ? That's

---

1. www.desiringgod.org/ResourceLibrary/TopicIndex/16/918_Dying_as_a_Means_of _Loving_Part_2/site.

the question Paul answers in 1 Corinthians 13:4–8 where he mentions that life-impacting love will possess fifteen characteristics. Previously we considered the first of these characteristics mentioned at the beginning of verse 4—love is long-suffering or patient. Then we began to consider the second of these characteristics that Paul mentions—also in verse 4—love is kind.

The Greek word for *kind* basically means to be good or gracious to people. It goes beyond being sorry for or pitying or being concerned about or compassionate toward people who have needs; kindness is more than an emotion or an attitude. It includes that, of course, but goes beyond that to do something positive as an expression of that attitude.

True loving-kindness manifests itself in doing something to help people who have spiritual needs. In this way, evangelism toward the unsaved and ministry or service to believers is an act of kindness. It will also manifest itself in doing something to help people who have physical needs.

## Let's Get Specific about the "Kindness" Aspect of Love

What I've covered so far in this chapter is the general answer to the question, "What does kindness look like?" However, if we're going to get our arms around what it means to have a love that is kind, it will be helpful for us to answer another question, "To whom does the Bible say we should show kindness or goodness?"

- Proverbs 31:26 says of the ideal wife and mother, "She opens her mouth with wisdom, and the teaching of kindness is on her tongue." Here kindness is demonstrated by the way this woman talks to her family.
- In Colossians 3:19 husbands are told that bitterness is the opposite of kindness: "Husbands, love your wives, and do not be harsh with them." Stated positively, "Love your wives and be kind to them."
- In 1 Timothy 3:4–5 Paul says that fathers are to treat children with dignity: "He must manage his own household well, with

all dignity keeping his children submissive, for if someone does not know how to manage his own household, how will he care for God's church?" Here is a man showing kindness by treating and managing his children with dignity and respect.

- Ephesians 6:4 says fathers are not to provoke their children to wrath.
- Colossians 3:21 says for fathers not to exasperate their children.
- Again in 1 Timothy, we read in 5:8 that piety ought to begin at home. Certainly kindness ought to begin at home by the way a man provides for the needs of his family.
- In Mark 7:10 we read that children are to honor their parents. That is, they are to do good and be kind to them.
- In Galatians 6:10 we are told that we should do good (be kind) to everyone—especially those who are of the household of faith (other believers).
- First Corinthians 12:25–26 says that it is God's design "that there may be no division in the body, but that the members may have the same care for one another. If one member suffers, all suffer together; if one member is honored, all rejoice together." Here kindness is suffering with others and rejoicing with them when they are blessed.
- Matthew 5:43–45 expands on the identity of those to whom we should be kind by saying that we are to do good (or be kind) to those who are our enemies, bless them that curse us, do good to those who hate us. In this matter of doing good (being kind) we are to follow the example of our heavenly Father, who makes His sun to rise on the evil and the good, the rain to fall on the just and the unjust.
- Jonathan Edwards wrote, "While we live in this world, we must expect to meet with some men of very evil properties, and hateful dispositions and practices. Some are proud, some immoral, some covetous, some very ungodly, some unjust or severe, and some despisers of God. But any or all of these bad qualities should not hinder our kindness, nor prevent our doing good as we have

opportunity. On this very account, we should be rather diligent to benefit them, that we may win them to Christ; and especially should we be diligent to benefit them in spiritual things."[2]

- Romans 12:17–18 presents the same challenge when it says, "Repay no one evil for evil, but give thought to do what is honorable in the sight of all. If possible, so far as it depends on you, live peaceably with all."
- First Thessalonians 5:15 joins with these passages when it commands us, "See that no one repays anyone evil for evil, but always seek to do good [to be kind] to one another and to everyone."
- In Luke 6:35 Jesus says, "But love your enemies, and do good [be kind], and lend, expecting nothing in return, and your reward will be great, and you will be sons of the Most High, for he is kind to the *ungrateful* and the *evil*."
- In reference to this matter of doing good and being kind, we need to remember the example of our Lord as described in Romans 5:8: "But God shows his love for us in that while we were still sinners, Christ died for us."
- Colossians 1:21–22: "And you, who once were alienated and hostile in mind, doing evil deeds, he has now reconciled in his body of flesh by his death."

## The Manifestations of Loving-Kindness

This brings us to another question we need to ask: "How should we manifest this loving-kindness to others?" The answer to that question is implied in the meaning of the word *kindness* and also in many of these same texts I've already mentioned.

As we have noted, the word *kindness* includes actually doing good, but behind the action, if it's to be real kindness, is a kindly attitude. This is an attitude that wants to do good to the other person, not because he deserves it, but because the kindly person is motivated by God's kind of love—a love that is not based on works.

2. Jonathan Edwards, *Charity and Its Fruits* (London: Banner of Truth Trust, 1969), 100.

Ephesians 2:4–9 says:

> But God, being rich in mercy, because of the great love with which he loved us, even when we were dead in our trespasses, made us alive together with Christ—by grace you have been saved—and raised us up with him and seated us with him in the heavenly places in Christ Jesus, so that in the coming ages he might show the immeasurable riches of his grace in kindness toward us in Christ Jesus. For by grace you have been saved through faith. And this is not your own doing; it is the gift of God, not a result of works, so that no one may boast.

Note that in the context of this passage God did this for us even though we were not walking in obedience to Him; rather, we were walking according to the course of this world. God did this for us even though we were living the way Satan wanted us to live rather than the way He wanted us to live.

That, my friends, is an example of how and when our kindness should manifest itself. This means, of course, that the kind of love we are to show to others must not be done in a mercenary spirit, in a "give to get" spirit.

- In Luke 6:35 Jesus teaches us about this aspect of kindness when He says that we are to give, expecting nothing in return.
- Luke 14:12–14 emphasizes the same truth when Jesus says, "When you give a dinner or a banquet, do not invite your friends or your brothers or your relatives or rich neighbors, lest they also invite you in return and you be repaid. But when you give a feast, invite the poor, the crippled, the lame, the blind, and you will be blessed, because they cannot repay you. You will be repaid at the resurrection of the just." You see, our doing good must be done freely. That also means that our kindness is to be manifested cheerfully and heartily.
- First Peter 4:8–9 says, "Above all, keep loving one another earnestly, since love covers a multitude of sins. Show hospitality to one another without grumbling."
- Second Corinthians 9:7 says, "Each one must give as he has made up his mind, not reluctantly or under compulsion, for God loves a cheerful giver."

- Deuteronomy 15:7–8 says, "If among you, one of your brothers should become poor, in any of your towns within your land that the LORD your God is giving you, you shall not harden your heart or shut your hand against your poor brother, but you shall open your hand to him and lend him sufficient for his need, whatever it may be."

Manifesting a love that is kind will mean that we will give liberally or bountifully. We will not give grudgingly, or because we were forced to do it. We should gladly contribute to the needs of the saints.

## The Motivation for Having a Love That Is Kind

This brings us to a final question about what a kind love really means: "Why should we be devoted to manifesting this aspect of real love?"

First, *we should be motivated to develop and sustain this aspect of love because this quality is part of the essence of what real love is.* You can't love without being kind. Kindness is to love what heat is to fire. Without heat, you don't have fire. There are imitative sources of heat, but those are just not the real thing. Try getting warm next to a fireplace that has a red light bulb as its heat source.

Kindness is to love what hydrogen and oxygen are to water. Without hydrogen and oxygen, you don't have water. So it is with love. Without kindness, you don't have love. First John 3:18–19 puts it this way:

Little children, let us not love in word or talk but in deed and in truth. By this we shall know that we are of the truth and reassure our heart before him.

Still further, *we should be motivated to want to manifest genuine love because of the way God has dealt with us.* Titus 3:5–6 says:

He saved us, not because of works done by us in righteousness, but according to his own mercy, by the washing of regeneration and renewal of the Holy Spirit.

God has been so kind to us. He saved us not by our own works of righteousness, but by Christ's unprecedented righteousness (see Rom. 5:8; 2 Cor. 8:9; Eph. 2:4–7; 1 John 4:10–11). We're told that we love because He first loved us. How can we not be kind to one another when God has been so kind to us?

Let me give you one more reason why we should want to develop and manifest a love that is kind. *This is the kind of love that will make us powerful and effective in our witness to unbelievers and in our attempt to build other Christians up in Christ.*

During the middle of the nineteenth century, at a time when black slaves in America were freed, Abraham Lincoln was president of the United States. Lincoln had many enemies, but one of the most outspoken was a man named Edwin Stanton. Prior to Lincoln's election as president, Stanton strongly opposed him and called him a "good for nothing clown" and "the original gorilla." Stanton said people were foolish to go all the way to Africa to see a gorilla when they could find one in Springfield, Illinois (Lincoln's hometown). When Stanton slandered him, Lincoln never responded, but when as president he needed a secretary of war, he chose Stanton. When his incredulous friends asked why, Lincoln replied, "Because he's the best man for the job." Instead of retaliating or defending himself, Lincoln gave evidence of being a Christian when he showed a love that was long-suffering and kind. The result? Stanton's resistance and animosity were broken down, and years later when Lincoln was shot and killed, Stanton came to his coffin and looked into it and said, "There lies the greatest ruler of men the world has ever seen."[3]

That story illustrates the truth Paul is teaching in 1 Corinthians 13—it illustrates the truth that real love can overcome opposition and can make a powerful impact on people with whom we associate.

Perhaps you have heard of Amy Carmichael, a woman who went to India to minister to poor, neglected, and abused children and young girls who were being forced by Hindu priests to become temple prostitutes. She began a work there that was called Dohnavur Fellowship, in which

3. John MacArthur, *1 Corinthians*, MacArthur New Testament Commentary (Chicago: Moody, 1984), 339.

hundreds of girls were housed and fed, brought to Christ, and trained up in Him. At the home she founded, she and others who came to work with her chose to wear Indian dress and gave the children they rescued Indian names. There she became known as a woman whose life was characterized by a love that was kind. She and her coworkers dedicated themselves to caring for the physical and spiritual needs of the girls they rescued. Amy said, "One cannot get people saved and then use a pitchfork to send them to heaven," meaning that you must care for the people you reach for Christ in a holistic way. Souls are more or less securely encased in bodies, and because you cannot get the souls out and deal with them separately, you have to take care of them both together.

One biographer said that Amy Carmichael lived a life of love. In fact, the love of God within her was so powerful a magnet that throughout her life people were irresistibly drawn to her. Even the Hindus began to call her "the child-catching Missie Ammal" (which was her Indian name meaning "Mother"). These Hindus believed that she was able to attract and influence Indian girls and women because she used some mysterious powder that drugged people and made them long to be near her and listen to her. The drug, of course, was the kind of love Paul describes in our passage in 1 Corinthians.

So for these three reasons and more, we should be concerned about developing and sustaining a love that is kind, because kindness is part of the essence of love. We should do it because of the kindness God has shown to us and others, and because without kindness we will never make a powerful positive impact on other people for Christ.[4]

## Concluding Evaluations and Applications for Personal Growth and for Discussion

As I close this chapter, I'm again wondering what your response is to what you've read about the importance, meaning, and power of

4. Adapted from www.traveltheroad.com/missions/missionaries/Carmichael.php Web site and Frank L. Houghton, *Amy Carmichael of Dohnavur: The Story of a Lover and Her Beloved* (Fort Washington, PA: Christian Literature Crusade, 1992), 219.

developing and sustaining a love that is kind. Again I ask you, brothers and sisters in Christ, do you want to have a fruitful life and ministry for Christ? I'm certain that if you're a Christian, you do.

Remember, according to the Bible, the most important factor in making an impact for Christ is not having great abilities or great knowledge, not giving up all your possessions, not being willing to be burned at the stake, but being a person whose life is characterized by real love. We've seen that the most powerful love is a love that is long-suffering and kind.

In the light of this fact, think now about your own response to this message of truth. What will you do with what you've read? If I were to ask you to give some examples of how you have manifested a love that is kind this week, what examples could you give? If I were to ask you to tell about how your love for people compelled you to tell someone about Christ or give someone a piece of evangelistic literature this week, could you give some examples? Or if I were to ask you to tell us of times you have manifested kindness to other Christians in the form of encouragement, comfort, or prayer, would you be able to think of such interactions? What about helping someone physically? What have you done? Whom have you impacted for Christ?

I have an idea that many of you who read this book can testify of times when you have done good to others. Some of you have probably sought to be a witness. Some have probably invited others to church services. Others may have given of their substance to those who don't have as much. Some may have prayed for or visited or sent a card to or called some hurting person this week. Many of you have shown kindness.

So to those of you to whom the previous paragraph applies, I would say the same thing that Paul said to the Thessalonians: "Now concerning brotherly love you have no need for anyone to write to you, for you yourselves have been taught by God to love one another. . . . But we urge you, brothers, to do this more and more" (1 Thess. 4:9–10). In essence he's saying, "You're doing well, but you can do better."

Many of you are doing good to your brothers and sisters in Christ. You are showing a love that is kind, that's true. But I doubt that there is any believer who could say, "My kindness quotient is 100 percent!

I couldn't do any better." So to those of you who are really devoted to showing a kind love, I call on you to commit yourself to turning up the intensity level of your kind love. Brethren, let's go out into the world with a new commitment to look for and pray for and welcome every opportunity to show this kind of love to unbelievers and believers. Will you make that kind of silent commitment to the Lord?

In conclusion, I would also like to write a few words to those of you who may not be very concerned about showing a kind love to others. Instead of reaching out to do good to others spiritually or physically, you've done very little or even nothing to make life better for anyone. If truth were told, some of you may have actually made life more difficult through your words or actions or lack thereof. In fact, it may be that you've shown a lot of what Amy Carmichael called "unlove."

If that's true of you and you claim to be a Christian, then you need to repent and ask God for forgiveness and for help because He saved you in order that you might bring forth fruit unto the Lord (Rom. 7:4).

However, if, as you look at your life, you discover that you don't have any concern about doing good spiritually or physically to people in your family or outside your family, if your "unlove" doesn't concern you, then it may be that you're not a Christian at all. God doesn't save you because you have a kind love for others, but if and when He does save you, He puts within you the desire and the power to have a kind love for others.

Peter puts it this way: "Having purified your souls by your obedience to the truth for a sincere brotherly love, love one another earnestly from a pure heart" (1 Peter 1:22). Peter is saying that no one becomes a Christian by having a kind love, but everyone who has repented of his sins and believed on Christ will have the desire and the ability to demonstrate that salvation by having a love that is long-suffering and kind.

Therefore, my word to you, if you have neither the desire nor the ability to love this way, is that you need to recognize that your lack of this kind of love is evidence that you are not a Christian and that you need to come to Christ to be saved and have your soul purified through what He did on the cross.

## Review, Reflection, Application, and Discussion Questions

1. What succinct definition of the word *kind* is given at the beginning of this chapter?

2. What erroneous or deficient idea about kindness does that definition eliminate?

3. What does the phrase "kindness is love in working clothes" mean?

4. Reflect on the answer that is given to the question: "To whom does the Bible say we should show kindness?" List the verses that fill in the details of the answer to that question.

5. Having identified the people to whom the Bible says we should show kindness, go on to specify ways in which kindness can be shown to these people.

6. What is meant by the statement that the kind of love we are to show to others must not be done in a mercenary spirit?

7. From your knowledge of Scripture and also historic or contemporary experience, have you observed what on the surface may appear to be kindness being done in a mercenary spirit? How might a husband or wife or parents or children or church members show what may appear to be kindness in a mercenary spirit?

8. How does this chapter answer the question: "Why should we be devoted to manifesting a love that is kind?"

9. Can you think of some reasons for manifesting a "love that is kind" that are not mentioned in this chapter?

10. What did Amy Carmichael mean by the statement "One cannot get people saved and then use a pitchfork to send them to heaven"? How does that statement relate to showing a love that is kind?

11. As a result of studying this chapter, are there ways in which you should and will, by God's grace, seek to develop more of the love that is kind? Be specific.

12. And now an important reminder that you will find after every chapter in this book: please remember as you reflect on the love principle presented in this chapter that the purpose of evaluation and application is:

a.  not to discourage or destroy us;

b.  but to motivate us to see our constant need of the cross and how much we owe to Jesus—without Him we'd never make it, but praise God we are not without Him;

c.  and to motivate us to understand our constant daily need of grace—that our salvation never has been and never will be by the works we have done, but always by the work Christ has done and is doing for us; I want our studies in 1 Corinthians 13 to be a reminder that we need to live a cross-centered life; we need the application of the cross work of Jesus every day of our lives; remember there's not a day in our lives when we are so good that we don't need the cross, and there is never a day in our lives when we are so bad that what Christ did on the cross is not sufficient to provide forgiveness for us (Rom. 3:24; 5:20; Eph. 1:7; 1 John 1:7; 2:1–2);

d.  and to cause us to understand that we must and can, by His grace, on a daily basis put off from our lives the "unlove" that is displeasing to God and put on in our lives the love that is beautifully described in 1 Corinthians 13, so that we might become more and more like our Savior and more prolific in bearing fruit for Him as others see the grace of God at work in our lives, changing and transforming us (Eph. 4:22–24; 1 Tim. 4:7).

# 6

## Envy and Jealousy Are Not Friends

In 1 Corinthians 13:13 Paul makes a statement about three of the most important qualities that should characterize the life of every Christian: "So now faith, hope, and love abide, these three." He's saying that when all is said and done, what God wants to see in our lives most of all is faith, hope, and love.

But Paul doesn't stop there. He goes on to say that if you're going to rank these three in terms of importance, love must be at the top of the list. He continues, "but the greatest of these is love."

Mind you, I'm not saying (nor is Paul) that faith and hope are not essential or important. Paul knew, and we know from the study of Scripture, that all of them are important and essential in Christian life. In fact, we really can't have one without the others. The person who has faith will have some degree of hope, and the person who has faith and hope will also have some love. That's why you'll find these three qualities frequently linked together in Scripture (Gal. 5:6; Col. 1:3–5; 1 Thess. 1:2–3). So Paul isn't saying that all three are not important, but still he does say that the greatest of the three is love.

## The Rationale for Saying That Love Is the Greatest

There certainly are a number of reasons why Paul says that love is the greatest. For my purpose in this chapter, I'm simply going to mention one reason that fits into the context of 1 Corinthians 13, namely, that when it comes to making an impact for Christ, you may have faith and you may have hope, but if you don't have love, your ministry will be ineffective.

In the first and last portions of 1 Corinthians 13, Paul tells us that when it comes to the matter of ministry, love is at the top of the list. He's saying that if you must rate these three qualities in terms of ministry importance, love must come first. In verses 4–8, he goes into great detail describing fifteen factors that characterize the kind of love that will inevitably make us powerful instruments for promoting biblical change in people. Thus far we've considered two of these characteristics. First we noted that Paul says the characteristic of love that will make us powerful influences for Christ is being long-suffering or patient. Then we noted that another characteristic of love that will make our ministries for Christ most effective is kindness.

## The Third Characteristic of a Powerful, Impactful Love

Moving on in this chapter to 1 Corinthians 13:4, we note that the third characteristic of the kind of love that will give us maximum impact in the lives of others is that our love must not be envious or jealous.

What does God mean when He says that love isn't jealous or envious? This is important for us to consider, because many misunderstand what envy or jealousy is. They're too quick to say, "That's one thing I don't have a problem with. You don't even have to bother talking about that one. We might as well move on to the next characteristic." I'd like to ask you to be a little patient with me until I give you several definitions I believe will help us to understand the real nature of envy, which is the opposite of love.

## Defining and Describing a Nonenvious Love

Envy consists of a disposition of dissatisfaction or dislike over the fact or thought that someone seems to be ahead of us or above us or superior to us in honor, position, respect, success, possessions, or effectiveness. The Bible is replete with examples of this kind of envy or jealousy:

- Satan was envious of the honor and position that God had in the life of Adam and Eve. He wanted that honor and resented the fact that God was claiming a right to an honor above the honor Satan received (Gen. 3).
- Cain became jealous of his brother Abel (Gen. 4).
- Sarai was jealous of her maidservant Hagar (Gen 16).
- Joseph's brothers became very jealous of him (Gen. 37).
- Korah, Dathan, and Abiram were jealous of Moses' authority and esteem (Num. 16).
- Saul became incredibly jealous of David (1 Sam. 18).
- The Pharisees were envious of the respect that Jesus received (Matt. 12).
- The elder brother became intensely jealous of his brother when he thought their father was treating his brother in a manner superior to the way their father had treated him (Luke 15).

Jonathan Edwards wrote, "It is very common that men . . . cannot bear a rival. . . . They love to be singular and alone in their eminence and advancement. Such a spirit is called envy in the Scriptures. . . . The desire to be distinguished in prosperity and honor is more gratified just in proportion that they are elevated, and others are below them (and I might add stay below them) so that their comparative eminence may be marked and visible to all."[1]

The man Haman as described in Esther 3:1–5:13 is an unmistakable example of the kind of envy to which Jonathan Edwards was referring.

---

1. Jonathan Edwards, *Charity and Its Fruits* (London: Banner of Truth Trust, 1969), 112.

Scripture indicates that Haman became indignant and that his indignation was due to several factors. One was the fact that he didn't think Mordecai gave him the respect he deserved. Another was that Mordecai was allowed to sit in the king's gate—a place of privilege. He was also aware of the close relationship Mordecai had with Queen Esther, and he also knew that Mordecai had foiled a plot to assassinate the king. He was mindful of the fact that Mordecai had risen in influence because of these factors, and this really bothered Haman. He wanted that favor and honor and position for himself! He was eaten up with envy and jealousy.

## Current-Day Examples

Let's take a couple of current-day examples. A preacher may not be envious of someone who is superior to him in the area of business or even in financial success, but he may be envious of other preachers who seem to be more honored and respected than he is. He might be jealous of preachers who have larger churches or may be envious of pastors who draw bigger crowds, or get more attention from the community.

A businessman may not be envious of an athlete who is far superior to him in terms of athletic ability and success, but he may struggle with envy toward another businessman who takes business away from him or whose business is growing faster than his.

A woman may not be envious of a television personality who is more beautiful or more popular than she is, but she may be envious of another woman whose children seem to be more respectful or obedient than her own. She could seethe with envy at a friend whose husband seems to be more gentle and considerate. She may be envious of another woman who came from a more affluent background, or whose parents were more loving and supportive than her own parents.

## Some Biblical Examples

Looking back to Genesis 26:12–14, we find that the Philistines became jealous of Isaac because he was richer—and continued to become more prosperous. I doubt that the Philistines would have been jealous of Isaac if the issue had been that Isaac was taller than they were or had a more beautiful singing voice. You see, the reason they were so intensely jealous was that Isaac had more of something that they intensely wanted—material wealth.

I doubt that Saul would have been jealous of David over the fact that David may have been a better harp player than Saul was or that David could lift more weight than he could. No, he was jealous because David was receiving more honor in an area that was especially important to Saul—military prowess (1 Sam. 18:1–31:13).

Let's take the case of Joshua in Numbers 11 when he thought Eldad and Medad were receiving honor and claiming the right to be prophets to the people of Israel, which Joshua thought should be the right of Moses alone. In verse 28, Joshua encouraged Moses to restrain them. Then, in verse 29, Moses rebuked him by saying, "Are you jealous for my sake? Would that all the LORD's people were prophets, that the LORD would put his Spirit on them!"

We can even see this aspect of envy illustrated in Galatians 1:13–14 where Paul says that before he became a Christian, he was extremely zealous for his ancestral traditions. He was afraid that the truths, convictions, and beliefs of Christianity would become equal to and even excel the traditions he had learned. As a result, he persecuted the church.

Gustav Mahler, a famous composer, married a woman who was also a very skilled composer. On the Web site Wikipedia, we're told that his wife Alma was a gifted musician and composer. After they got married, Mahler told Alma in no uncertain terms that her role should be only to tend to his needs. In fact, it is said that on the day of their wedding he said to her, "From now on the only music that will be played in our home will be my music." This man was envious of his own wife in the area of music. I'm sure that he would not have been envious of her in other areas. It's unlikely that he would have said to her, "From now on the only food that will be eaten in this house will be food that I have cooked." Or "the only cleaning that will be done in this house will be cleaning that I have done." No, his jealousy was focused on an area in which she might provide competition for him. In that area he wanted to be regarded as better than anyone else, including his wife.[2]

## What We Learn about Envy or Jealousy from Scriptural Lists of Sin

Not long ago, as I was reviewing some of the lists of sins in the New Testament, I was struck by the fact that you find the sin of envy or jealousy included in many of the lists. We find it in Mark 7:21–23, in Romans 1:29–31, and in Galatians 5:19–21. I think it is significant to note that though those lists don't include the names of every sin we could commit, many of them do include envy or jealousy.

This fact that envy or jealousy is mentioned in many lists of sin tells us that jealousy or envy is prevalent or common. The truth is that we have more of a problem with this sin than we want to admit.

In his book *Leading with Love*, Alexander Strauch writes:

None of us are immune from petty, self-centered envy. Even the most committed missionaries and servants of the Lord have struggled with this sin. George Muller was the founder of Ashley Down orphanage in Bristol, England. While co-pastoring with Henry Craik at a church in Bristol, England, George Muller saw that the people enjoyed the other man's ministry more than his own. Henry Craik was not only an excellent Bible teacher, but he was also a first-rate classical and Hebrew scholar. . . . Muller was a man of extraordinary faith and prayer. He confessed his envious feeling toward his co-worker and confronted his sin.

Of his struggle with envy toward Henry Craik, he wrote: "When in the year 1832, I saw how preferred my beloved friend's ministry was to my own, I determined, in the strength of God, to rejoice in this, instead of envying him. I said, with John the Baptist, 'A man can receive nothing, except it be given him from heaven' (John 3:27). This resisting the devil hindered separation of heart."

2. Adapted from http://en.wikipedia.org/wiki/Gustav_Mahler.

George Muller's and Henry Craik's friendship lasted for thirty-six years until Craik died. Although both were strong, multi-gifted men with different personalities, their long relationship was a public testimony to the power of Christian love. Muller was well known for his many lifelong friendships with people like Hudson Taylor, Charles Spurgeon, D. L. Moody, Robert Chapman, and others. Envious people, unfortunately, have few friends and many conflicts.

We need to be aware that envy is prevalent among the Lord's people and Christian leaders. Pastors can go to bizarre extremes to eliminate from the church gifted people who threaten them. Churches can envy other churches which are larger or are growing more rapidly. Missionaries can envy other missionaries who are more fruitful or better supported. Bible study leaders can envy more popular Bible study leaders; singers can envy other singers who sing more often or receive louder applause; elders can envy fellow elders who shine more brightly in leadership ability or knowledge; and deacons can envy fellow deacons who serve more effectively or are sought out for help more frequently.[3]

The fact that envy or jealousy is mentioned in many lists of sins tells us that jealousy or envy is serious and destructive. It was destructive in the cases of Cain and Abel, Joseph and his brothers, Saul and David, and the Jewish leaders and Jesus.

Proverbs 27:4 says, "Wrath is cruel, anger is overwhelming, but who can stand before jealousy?" A study of the emotions mentioned in this verse will quickly convince us that what this verse says about the destructiveness of all of them is played out in real life again and again. Even so, jealousy is described as being more powerful and devastating than either wrath or anger. All of them are strong emotions, but the text indicates that of the three, jealousy is perhaps the most dangerous. It says that no one can stand before envy or jealousy. Bruce Waltke says that anger and wrath are unbearable emotions and then adds that jealousy, a sidekick of these two unbearable emotions, is even more unbearable than they are. He says that the metaphor used in this verse depicts anger as a spiritual force that is destructive, irrational, and violent. "But," says

3. Alexander Strauch, *Leading with Love* (Littleton, CO: Lewis and Roth, 2006), 49–50.

Waltke, "anger unlike jealousy can be withstood. Balaam prophesied against Moab in spite of Balak's anger (Num. 23:11), but David fled from Saul's jealousy. . . . The proverb likens the person who arouses jealousy to a servant who is swept away."[4]

Concerning the incredible destructiveness of jealousy, Proverbs 6:34–35 tells us:

> For jealousy enrages a man,
> And he will not spare in the day of vengeance.
> He [the man consumed with jealousy] will not accept any ransom,
> Nor will he be satisfied though you give many gifts. (NASB)

In other words, when jealousy is aroused, the jealous man becomes enraged, which of course means that he is not happy. Jealousy and envy do nothing good to anyone, including the person who is experiencing the jealousy.

Mariano DiGangi writes about what envy did to a certain person. An "envious man was always wearing a sour expression. Day by day people would ask him, 'Why are you so depressed? Is it because something bad has happened to you? Or has something good happened to someone else?' Envy feels frustrated by the talents, happiness and success of others. It boils over. . . . But such is the generosity of love that it puts aside all envy and is glad to see others glad."[5]

So jealousy is destructive to the person experiencing it, and it is also destructive to the people of whom the person is jealous or envious. The proverb we are presently considering indicates that when a person's jealousy is aroused, he becomes unreasonable and even vicious and fixated on doing harm to the object or person that arouses his jealousy.

James 3:14–16 describes the destructiveness of jealousy or envy this way:

> But if you have bitter jealousy and selfish ambition in your hearts, do not boast and be false to the truth. This is not the wisdom that

---

4. Bruce Waltke, *The Book of Proverbs, Chapters 15–31* (Grand Rapids: Eerdmans, 2005), 375.

5. Mariano DiGangi, *Christian Love* (Philadelphia: Time and Eternity, 1966), 11.

comes down from above, but is earthly, unspiritual, demonic. For where jealousy and selfish ambition exist, there will be disorder and every vile practice.

Men tend to think lightly of envy, but God knows the truth. He knows just how destructive it can be. As we have just noted, envy has the power to destroy a person's joy and peace; it also has the power to devastate other people and his relationship with them by way of the jealous person's words and actions. And worse still, it certainly has the capacity to ruin a person's relationship with God; and according to 1 Corinthians 13, envy or jealousy will also destroy a person's usefulness for Christ. Make no mistake about it: God withholds His blessing in terms of usefulness from those who are jealous or envious.

And so in closing this chapter I remind you again of how having a love that does not envy or is not jealous is connected to the overall purpose of this book, and more importantly to the overall purpose for which God included 1 Corinthians 13 in the Bible. God wants every believer to glorify Him, and one of the ways we glorify Him is by bearing much fruit (John 15:1–8). In keeping with that desire of God, Paul is telling us in 1 Corinthians 13:4 that a most important factor in fulfilling that purpose is for us to have a love that is not envious or jealous.

## Review, Reflection, Application, and Discussion Questions

1. According to Paul, what are three very important qualities that should characterize every Christian's life?

2. What reasons are there for saying that the greatest of these qualities is love?

3. In addition to the ones mentioned in this chapter, what might be some other reasons why he says that love is the greatest?

4. Why is it important for us to have a clear definition of what envy and jealousy are?

5. What does this chapter say envy is? How would you define it to someone else?

6. List some biblical examples of envy (jealousy), and describe how each of those examples is an illustration of envy.

7. Reflect on Jonathan Edwards's definition of *envy* and take it apart phrase by phrase in terms of what he is actually saying.

8. Study Esther 3:1–7:10 and note everything you see in the account of Haman that helps us to understand what envy is and how it is manifested.

9. Study 1 Samuel 18:1–31:13 and note everything you see in the account of Saul that helps us to understand what envy is and how it is manifested.

10. What may we learn about envy or jealousy from the lists of sins in the New Testament?

11. What do we learn from Proverbs 27:4 about the seriousness of jealousy or envy?

12. What is the teaching of Proverbs 6:34–35? Why do you think these verses indicate that jealousy and envy are more serious than anger and wrath?

13. What does James 3:14–16 teach about the destructiveness of jealousy? Think of specific examples of what these verses say the consequences of selfish ambition and jealousy are.

14. From your knowledge of historical or contemporary experience, where have you observed envy or sinful jealousy being manifested, and how has it been destructive in the world, at work, in the home, or in the church? How might a husband or wife or parents or children or church members show envy or jealousy toward each other?

15. How does this chapter answer the question "Why should we be devoted to manifesting a love that is not envious?"

16. In what specific ways have you personally manifested a love that is not envious as described in this chapter to people in your church

and in your family and to people outside your church? Describe specific examples.

17. In what specific ways have you failed to manifest a love that is not envious to people in your church and in your family and by other Christians outside your church?

18. As a result of studying this chapter, are there ways in which you should and will, by God's grace, seek to develop more of the love that is not envious? Be specific.

19. And now an important reminder that you will find after every chapter in this book: please remember as you reflect on the love principle presented in this chapter that the purpose of evaluation and application is:

    a. not to discourage or destroy us;

    b. but to motivate us to see our constant need of the cross and how much we owe to Jesus—without Him we'd never make it, but praise God we are not without Him;

    c. and to motivate us to understand our constant daily need of grace—that our salvation never has been and never will be by the works we have done, but always by the work Christ has done and is doing for us; I want our studies in 1 Corinthians 13 to be a reminder that we need to live a cross-centered life; we need the application of the cross work of Jesus every day of our lives; remember there's not a day in our lives when we are so good that we don't need the cross and there is never a day in our lives when we are so bad that what Christ did on the cross is not sufficient to provide forgiveness for us (Rom. 3:24; 5:20; Eph. 1:7; 1 John 1:7; 2:1–2);

    d. and to cause us to understand that we must and can, by His grace, on a daily basis put off from our lives the "unlove" that is displeasing to God and put on in our lives the love that is beautifully described in 1 Corinthians 13, so that we might become more and more like our Savior and more prolific in bearing fruit for Him as others see the grace of God at work in our lives, changing and transforming us (Eph. 4:22–24; 1 Tim. 4:7).

# 7

# THE FLIP SIDE OF ENVY AND JEALOUSY

I n the last chapter we discussed the fact that real love isn't jealous and it does not envy. At this point, I want to turn Paul's negative statement about what love isn't into a positive statement about what love is. To do that, I want to answer the following questions: What is the counterpart of envy? What characteristic of love is opposite of jealousy?

## The Flip Side of Envy

When we look at 1 Corinthians 13:4 from a positive perspective, it says that *a person who has God's kind of love will be a person who has an attitude of contentment or satisfaction with what he has*. If love is the opposite of jealousy and a jealous person is not a satisfied person, then a person who really loves must be a satisfied and contented person. In other words, real love means that we will not be like the person described in Proverbs 30:15–16, which says:

The leech has two daughters;
  "Give" and "Give," they cry.

> Three things are never satisfied;
>     four never say, "Enough":
> Sheol, the barren womb,
>     the land never satisfied with water,
>     and the fire that never says, "Enough."

This proverb indicates that some people are like:

a. The leech that is always saying, "Give, Give"
b. The person who never says "Enough" in terms of what he has
c. The grave or the earth or the fire that always wants more

Such people are constantly thinking about what they don't have; they are constantly thinking that they need more and deserve more; they are constantly focusing on their own wants and desires.

Paul says that the person who really loves God and others won't be like that. He won't be in a state of constant dissatisfaction. He won't constantly be thinking that he needs and deserves more, wishing he had something newer and bigger and better, or thinking that he must have more money, a better position, more honor, success, prestige, a newer automobile, more things, more love and respect from people, or more talent or abilities. Let's face it—some people are like a broken record saying, "I want . . . ," "I need . . . ," "I deserve . . . ." That's the way an envious person thinks, and that destroys the person's ability to love others, because he is all wrapped up in himself.

In Philippians 4:11–12, Paul says that he has learned to be content, whether he's abounding or being abased. Can an envious person honestly say that? Why not? Because he's not content. He's just not satisfied.

But Paul was satisfied. He says, "Not that I am speaking of being in need, for I have learned in whatever situation I am to be content. I know how to be brought low, and I know how to abound. In any and every circumstance, I have learned the secret of facing plenty and hunger, abundance and need."

When Paul said, "in any and every circumstance," he was talking about being content when he was praised or when he was being criticized. He learned to be content when people showed him respect, and when they didn't. He was content when things happened as he wanted them to happen and when they didn't! He was content when the road was smooth, as well as when the going got rough.

## The Ultimate Cure of Jealousy or Envy

How on earth could he say that and mean it? He could say it because he wasn't envious or jealous. An envious or jealous person could never say that, because an envious or jealous person isn't content. Paul could say these things because he had learned the secret of contentment: Jesus—not things, other people, circumstances, prestige, or money—was his strength and sufficiency. He realized that he was complete in Christ Jesus, his Lord and Savior. Because his completion was in Him, he knew that Jesus was enough. He didn't need anything more than Him.

You might ask, "What does that have to do with real love's not being jealous?" It has everything to do with it! When I find my sufficiency or completeness or satisfaction in Jesus, I am freed up to really love people. If that's where you find your satisfaction, you have no reason to be jealous of others who seem to have more honor, position, prestige, or money. You already have everything you need in Jesus.

When we find our sufficiency in Jesus, we don't have to depend on people or circumstances to be happy or content. We don't have to prowl around, constantly looking for someone to prop us up, because Jesus is already propping us up! If Jesus is filling us up, we don't need to constantly search for someone else to fill us up. As I fully realize that truth and really believe it, I am freed to take the focus off myself and so I really can love others.

So the implication is that we will be satisfied and content with what we have because what we have is an all-sufficient Savior and Lord. We have what He's ordained for us. And He *is* our sufficiency!

When commenting on this aspect of real love, Jonathan Edwards wrote:

> A Christian spirit disposes us to feel content with our own condition, and with the estate which God has given us among men, and to a quietness and satisfaction of spirit with regard to the allotments and

distributions of stations and possessions which God, in his wise and kind providence, has made to ourselves. . . . Whether our rank be as high as that of the angels, or as low as that of the beggar at the rich man's gate (Luke 16:20), we shall be equally satisfied with it, as the post in which God has placed us, and shall equally respect ourselves, if we are endeavoring to faithfully serve him in it.[1]

## Some Insights from Jerry Bridges on Overcoming Envy and Becoming Content

In his comments on Paul's statements about contentment, Jerry Bridges writes:

The words that are rendered as "content" or "contentment" in our English Bibles actually mean "sufficiency." The same word that is translated "contentment" in 1 Timothy 6:6 is rendered "all that you need" in 2 Corinthians 9:8. . . . This must be the secret Paul had learned (Philippians 4:11): *God's grace is sufficient* whatever the circumstance. And because God's grace is sufficient, we can be content. . . . Since early childhood I have suffered a vision impairment that is often frustrating, and a total hearing loss in one ear that is often embarrassing (as when people speak to me and I don't hear them, and thus appear to be ignoring them). But those are not my only physical problems. One day I stood before the bedroom mirror and named seven distinct things that were "wrong" with my body; things I had often fretted about and murmured over. That day I said, "Lord, I accept the fact that you made me the way I am, and that your grace is sufficient for all these limitations." I cannot say I have not fretted over these problems since then, but I can now say I know how to be content with them: by accepting that God's grace is sufficient. Although I do not always apply this wonderful fact, it is true and it is always available. The choice to accept it and experience contentment is mine. And the choice is yours in your particular circumstances.

This is the secret of contentment [and I would say, freedom from envy and jealousy]: to learn and accept that we live daily by God's

1. Jonathan Edwards, *Charity and Its Fruits* (London: Banner of Truth Trust, 1969), 116.

unmerited favor given through Christ, and that we can respond
to any and every situation by his divine enablement through the
Holy Spirit.[2]

## Another Perspective on the Flip Side of Envy and Jealousy

If we turn Paul's negative statement about love into a positive
statement, I believe we could say that the text is saying that having a
love that is not jealous or envious means *that a loving person will have
an attitude of rejoicing and thanksgiving when others succeed and prosper
in any legitimate God-honoring venture.* When we love others as we
love ourselves, we will do what Romans 12:15 tells us to do—we will
rejoice with those who rejoice. In his commentary on this text, William
Hendriksen makes this comment: "the opposite of rejoicing is envy and
over against weeping is gloating."[3] If we really love someone as we love
ourselves, we will respond the same way when others are blessed as we
do when we are!

Loving others as we love ourselves means that we will do what
1 Corinthians 12:25 tells us to do—to recognize God's purpose "that
there may be no division in the body, but that the members may have
the same care for one another." Paul says that if we are functioning
in the way God wants us to function, we will have the same care for
one another. We will be just as concerned about what is happening
in the lives of others as we are with what is happening to us!

When we love others as we love ourselves, we will do what
1 Corinthians 12:26 says: "If one member suffers, all suffer together;
if one member is honored, all rejoice together." Here Paul is using
the metaphor of the body to describe how we as Christians should
relate to and care for one another. As parts of each other, when one
rejoices, we all do! There is no "separate-ness" where the body of
Christ is concerned.

2. Jerry Bridges, *The Practice of Godliness* (Colorado Springs: NavPress, 1989), 105,
120–21.

3. William Hendriksen, *Romans* (Grand Rapids: Baker, 1981), 418.

## Biblical Examples of People Who Had a Love That Was Not Envious

The Bible contains many examples of people who had a love that was not envious—a love that rejoiced in the prosperity of others. One example is Jonathan, King Saul's son. Technically, Jonathan was next in line to become king of Israel, and yet he rejoiced in David's success. He rejoiced in David's popularity and accomplishments even to the extent that he was willing to support and defend David when it became obvious that David, not Jonathan, would become the next king of Israel (1 Sam. 18:1–5; 19:1–4; 20:1–4, 16–17, 30–34).

Another example of the positive aspect of having a love that is not envious (jealous) is Timothy. We read about him in Philippians 2:20 where Paul tells the Philippians, "For I have no one like him, who will be genuinely concerned for your welfare." Timothy had a love that allowed him naturally and genuinely to care for people.

John the apostle is another example of this kind of genuine love. His nonenvious kind of love is illustrated in 3 John 3–4:

> For I rejoiced greatly when the brothers came and testified to your truth, as indeed you are walking in the truth. I have no greater joy than to hear that my children are walking in the truth.

Who were these children? They were certainly not his literal children! They were other believers—people to whom he had ministered. Notice the phrase "no greater joy." It was not that he simply had joy. It was more than that. He was as excited that they were walking in the truth as he would have been if they had been his own children!

Paul himself provides us an example of this selfless love. In 2 Corinthians 11:28–29 he says:

> And, apart from other things, there is the daily pressure on me of my anxiety for all the churches. Who is weak, and I am not weak? Who is made to fall, and I am not indignant?

He anguished over it when other believers were weak. He agonized over them when other believers were led into sin.

I'll mention one more Pauline example of this kind of love that is not jealous—a love that rejoices when others prosper. This is one of the most powerful examples I can think of! It's found in Philippians 1:14–18, as Paul writes this letter from prison:

> And most of the brothers, having become confident in the Lord by my imprisonment, are much more bold to speak the word without fear. Some indeed preach Christ from envy and rivalry, but others from good will. The latter do it out of love, knowing that I am put here for the defense of the gospel. The former proclaim Christ out of rivalry, not sincerely, but thinking to afflict me in my imprisonment. What then? Only that in every way, whether in pretense or in truth, Christ is proclaimed, and in that I rejoice.

Though at the time he wrote these words his freedom to move about and preach was limited, Paul tells us that he is rejoicing because Christ is being proclaimed, because others are preaching about Him boldly. Some are doing it, he says, with good will, but others who are preaching boldly are doing it for the wrong reasons. Paul informs us that he rejoices and would continue to rejoice that Christ is being preached by those who love him and respect him, but he also says that he rejoices that those who envy him are also preaching Christ, even though their motive for doing so is less than pure and would even add increased hardship on Paul. My friends, that's love! Paul is happy for those who are preaching who have a good attitude toward him, but he is also happy for those who have the opportunity to preach who have a bad attitude toward him.

So what does it mean to have a love that is not jealous? It means to have a love that rejoices and gets really excited when others are prospering, honored, blessed, or respected even though we are not.

In his comments on what it means to have a love that is not jealous, Jonathan Edwards wrote:

> The spirit of envy is the very contrary of the spirit of heaven, where all rejoice in the happiness of others; and it is the very spirit of hell itself—

which is the most hateful spirit—and one that feeds itself on the ruin of the prosperity and happiness of others, on which account some have compared envious people to caterpillars, which delight in devouring the most flourishing trees and plants. And as the envious disposition is the most hateful in itself, so it is the most uncomfortable and uneasy to its possessor. As it is the disposition of the devil, and partakes of his likeness, so it is the disposition of hell and partakes of its misery. It is like a powerful eating cancer, preying on the vitals, offensive and full of corruption. It is the most foolish kind of self injury; for the envious make themselves trouble most needlessly, being uncomfortable only because of the prosperity of others when that prosperity does not injure them. . . . But they are unwilling to enjoy what they have because others are or may enjoy what they are enjoying.

Then Edwards goes on to say, "Let then the consideration of the foolishness, the baseness, the infamy of so wicked a spirit cause us to abhor it, and shun its excuses, and earnestly to seek the spirit of Christian love . . . which will lead us to rejoice in the welfare of others, and which will fill our own hearts with happiness."[4] Edwards says that Christian love, the kind that is not jealous, will lead us to rejoice in the welfare of others, and will cause our hearts to be filled with happiness. And I would add that it will also make us the kind of person that God will use to make a powerful impact for Christ in our families, churches, and world.

## Review, Reflection, Application, and Discussion Questions

1. What about your love? Can you honestly say that your love passes the jealousy test?

2. Can you say that you are never bothered by the thought that others seem to be more successful and respected and prosperous than you are?

4. Edwards, *Charity and Its Fruits*, 127.

3. Can you say that you are never disturbed by the thought that someone else may be equal to you in honor, position, respect, success, possessions, or effectiveness?

4. Can you say that you are never bothered by the thought that someone may eventually become equal to you or superior to you in honor, position, respect, success, possessions, or effectiveness?

5. Can you say that you are never bothered by the thought that someone else is receiving or may receive as much or even more of the honor, position, respect, or success that you think belongs to a person or a movement with which you are identified and aligned?

6. Can you say that you are never concerned with the thought that someone may be ahead of you or above you or superior or equal to you or may become equal to or above you in honor, position, respect, success, or effectiveness, especially in an area that is of great value to you?

7. Can you say that you are never bothered by the thought that another church or organization is receiving or may receive as much or even more honor, position, respect, or success that you think belongs to a person or a movement with which you are identified and aligned?

8. Can you honestly say that you are always satisfied and content with the honor, position, or status or role or treatment or finances that the providence of God has allotted to you?

9. Can you honestly say that you always get as much satisfaction out of seeing someone else prosper as you do when you succeed or are honored?

10. Use the specific Bible verses given in this chapter to describe what a nonenvious love will look like in actual practice. Then evaluate yourself in terms of "I do this always" (4); "I do this frequently" (3); "I do this sometimes" (2); "I do this seldom" (1); "I never do this" (0).

11. And now an important reminder that you will find after every chapter in this book: please remember as you reflect on the love

principle presented in this chapter that the purpose of evaluation and application is:

a. not to discourage or destroy us;

b. but to motivate us to see our constant need of the cross and how much we owe to Jesus—without Him we'd never make it, but praise God we are not without Him;

c. and to motivate us to understand our constant daily need of grace—that our salvation never has been and never will be by the works swe have done, but always by the work Christ has done and is doing for us; I want our studies in 1 Corinthians 13 to be a reminder that we need to live a cross-centered life; we need the application of the cross work of Jesus every day of our lives; remember there's not a day in our lives when we are so good that we don't need the cross and there is never a day in our lives when we are so bad that what Christ did on the cross is not sufficient to provide forgiveness for us (Rom. 3:24; 5:20; Eph. 1:7; 1 John 1:7; 2:1–2);

d. and to cause us to understand that we must and can, by His grace, on a daily basis put off from our lives the "unlove" that is displeasing to God and put on in our lives the love that is beautifully described in 1 Corinthians 13, so that we might become more and more like our Savior and more prolific in bearing fruit for Him as others see the grace of God at work in our lives, changing and transforming us (Eph. 4:22–24; 1 Tim. 4:7).

# 8

## LOVERS DON'T BRAG

During the nineteenth century, one of the men God used in an unusual way to bring people to Christ and to build them up in Him was a man by the name of D. L. Moody. God used D. L. Moody to found a Christian training school that is still in existence today—the Moody Bible Institute. He also used him to plant a church that is still thriving today—Moody Memorial Church. And He also used him as an evangelist to bring thousands of people to Christ in the United States and in England.

The interesting thing was that at the beginning of his ministry, Moody was relatively ineffective, but then he heard a preacher by the name of Moorhouse preach a series of messages on the subject of love. Moody says that as he heard these sermons on love, he was so moved that he could not hold back the tears. "It was like news from a far country; I just drank in. I tell you there is one thing that draws everything else in the world, and that is love."

Moody says that having heard these messages on love, he decided to do a concentrated study of the doctrine of love:

I took up the word "Love" and I do not know how many weeks I spent in studying the passages in which it occurs, till at last I could not help loving people! I had been feeding on love so long that I was anxious to do good to everybody I came in contact with. I got full of it. It ran out my fingers. You take up the subject of love in the Bible and you will get so full of it so that all you will have to do is open your lips and a flood of the Love of God will flow out. There is no use trying to do church work without love. A doctor, a lawyer, may do good work without love, but God's work cannot be done without love.[1]

According to the apostle Paul in 1 Corinthians 13 and many other places, D. L. Moody was absolutely correct when he said, "God's work cannot be done without love." As previously mentioned and by way of review, in 1 Corinthians 12–14 Paul is writing to professing Christians who had some erroneous ideas about how to make an impact for Christ. They had the idea that to make an impact for Christ you had to have some extraordinary spiritual gifts—extraordinary abilities in the areas of speech, linguistics, prophecy, superior insights, knowledge, faith, being able to give, and courage to the point where you would suffer martyrdom.

In 1 Corinthians 12:31, Paul wants to show them and us that there is a more excellent way, a superior way, a more important way to make an impact for Christ. That way is the way of real love. So in 1 Corinthians 13:1–3 he emphasizes the superiority or preeminence of love when it comes to having an effective ministry for Christ.

And then in verses 4–7 Paul goes on to give them and us a description of what this love that will make us powerful witnesses for Christ looks like in practice. In these verses Paul delineates fifteen characteristics of the kind of love that will make us fruitful for Christ.

In previous chapters we've considered the first three. We've noted that God's kind of love is:

- Long-suffering
- Kind
- Not jealous or envious

1. William Moody, *The Life of Dwight L. Moody* (Chicago: Revell, 1900), 139–40.

In this chapter, we will carefully examine and apply the fourth characteristic of real love. In verse 4 Paul says that the love that will make us
powerful and useful servants of Christ "does not boast."

## Loving Cancels Bragging

When the text says that love doesn't boast, it means that, as servants
of Christ, our love does not brag (NASB), vaunt itself (KJV), or parade
itself (NKJV). In other words, it doesn't show off.

In the last chapter when we considered what love looks like in actual
practice, we noted that real love doesn't envy what others possess, but rather
rejoices when others prosper. Now, when Scripture says that love does not
boast, we notice the flip side of the coin—namely, that real love doesn't go
around bragging about what we possess. Real love doesn't do that which
might provoke others to become envious or jealous.

When we are jealous, we tend to put others down, or to try to make
them less in the estimation of others, or at least in our own minds.
Conversely, when we brag, we are trying to build ourselves up in the
estimation of other people or at least in our own minds.

Envy and jealousy are similar to bragging or vaunting oneself in
that in both of them the emphasis is on *self*!

John MacArthur wrote this about the Corinthian believers:

> The Corinthian believers were spiritual show-offs, constantly vying for
> public attention. They clamored for the most prestigious offices and
> the most glamorous gifts. They all wanted to talk at once, especially
> when speaking ecstatically. Most of their tongues speaking was coun-
> terfeit, but their bragging about it was genuine. They cared nothing
> for harmony, fellowship, edification or anything else worthwhile.
> They cared for flaunting themselves. "What is the outcome then,
> brethren? When you assemble, each one has a psalm, has a teaching,
> has a revelation, has a tongue, has an interpretation" (I Corinthians
> 14:26). Each did his own thing as prominently as possible, in total
> disregard for what others were doing.[2]

2. John MacArthur, *1 Corinthians* (Chicago: Moody, 1984), 342.

In an answer to a question about boasting, Richard Phillips said:

Many of us have been socialized enough not to brag in obvious ways that are sure to alienate others. But ours is a whole way of life based upon self-glory and pride and vanity of spirit. It is not enough for us to have; we have to advertise what we have, and especially how much more we have than others. So the rich man buys a house much larger than he needs. Why? To boast in language everyone understands. The woman graced with beauty boasts in her manner of dress and in how she carries herself. This is why one of the most powerful motivators in the workplace is status. Former automobile mogul, Lee Iacocca, tells in his autobiography about a place he once worked where the real status symbol was a gold key to the executive bathroom. You, and everybody else, knew that you had really made it when you got this key. Many, many men and women came in early and stayed late, neglected their families on weekends, for the sake of a bathroom key in which they would be able to boast!

Prideful boasting is deeply embedded in our sin nature, which is why boasting is one of the sins so strongly demonstrated by children. Satan tempted Eve with the boast, "You will be like God" (Gen. 3:5). That is what pride and boasting are all about: our self-enthronement in the place of God. This was the motive behind the Tower of Babel; they said, "Come, let us build ourselves a city, with a tower that reaches to the heavens, so that we may make a name for ourselves" (Gen. 11:4). C. S. Lewis identifies boastful pride as the prime sin; he aptly called it "the anti-God state of mind."

From the Bible's perspective, such boasting is pathetic and evil. We are so busy trumpeting our virtues and strengths, when in fact we are covered in shame because of sin and are daily shown to be weak, needy creatures. Indeed, the problem with pride is not that it seeks to bring us glory. We were created for glory, being made in the very image of God. Adam and Eve were glorious in the Garden. "They were naked," Genesis says, "and felt no shame" (2:25). In itself, glory is good, appropriate, something we should rightly pursue. The problem with our self-glorying is the problem with all sin; it is a good thing made evil because it is used not for its right end but to seek a wrongful end. Our glory is intended to promote the glory of the One who created us; that is what Adam was to do and to be, the image-bearer of God's glory. The problem with our pride and boasting is that it steals glory from God, to whom all boasting rightly is due.[3]

That's the way Phillips describes what many people do in the twenty-first century, and that's what many of the Corinthian believers did in the first century. They were boasters, people all wrapped up in themselves. Theirs was a way of life that was devoted to serving and exalting self, even if that meant using religion and religious activities as a way of making themselves look good in the eyes of others. Theirs was an unloving, selfish manner of interacting with people, which was contrary to the way of love that would make them a positive godly influence in the lives of others. And according to the apostle Paul, people who have real love won't act that way.

## What Love Won't Do

Now I want to become really specific about this and give you some concrete examples of what real love won't do:

- For one thing, real love won't do what the man in Luke 18:11–12 did: "The Pharisee, standing by himself, prayed thus: 'God, I thank you that I am not like other men, extortioners, unjust, adulterers, or even like this tax collector. I fast twice a week; I give tithes of all that I get.'"
- Real love won't do what the people whom Jesus described in Matthew 6:1, 16 did: "Beware of practicing your righteousness before other people in order to be seen by them, for then you will have no reward from your Father who is in heaven. . . . And when you fast, do not look gloomy like the hypocrites, for they disfigure their faces that their fasting may be seen by others. Truly, I say to you, they have received their reward."

3. Richard D. Phillips, "A Question about Boasting," *Tenth Presbyterian Church*, July 22, 2001, www.tenth.org/qbox/qb_010722.htm.

- Still further, if we have real love we won't do what the people described by Jesus in Matthew 23:5–7 did: "They do all their deeds to be seen by others. For they make their phylacteries broad and their fringes long, and they love the place of honor at feasts and the best seats in the synagogues and greetings in the marketplaces and being called rabbi by others."
- Moreover, if we have real love we won't do what Ananias and Sapphira did in Acts 5: They gave a certain amount and pretended they gave more. They weren't really concerned about the poor. They just wanted others to think well of them.
- Then too, if we have real love we won't try to impress people with our:
  - Power
  - Knowledge
  - Education
  - Material possessions
  - Beauty
  - Skills
  - Importance
  - Position
  - Background
  - List of associates
  - Family accomplishments

What was that I heard? The crashing sound of someone's ego imploding? What's wrong? Am I stepping on someone's toes here? I know I'm stepping on mine! But I'm not finished. There's more!

- Still further, if we have real love, we won't stretch or exaggerate the truth.
- If we have real love, we won't overdress or underdress in an attempt to call attention to self.
- If we have real love, we won't live beyond our means in an attempt to impress people with our importance.

- If we have real love, we won't tell people only the flattering part of what happened to us or what we did and leave out the less flattering parts. We will tell them the whole story.
- If we have real love, we won't try to take credit for the ideas we know we have received from others.
- If we have real love, we won't use unnecessarily big words that few people understand.
- If we have real love, we won't constantly make people aware of how many books we've read and how many verses we've memorized.
- If we have real love, we won't constantly make people aware of how poor we are or how badly we've been treated or how much we have suffered or sacrificed.

## Looking at Love Positively

There! You have some specific examples of the kind of bragging or vaunting that real love won't do. Now I want to do a turnabout and mention some examples of what real love *will* look like in the area of not bragging or boasting. From a positive perspective, a love that does not boast will look like the example Paul gave us throughout the New Testament. For example, it will look like Galatians 6:14: "But may it never be that I would boast, except in the cross of our Lord Jesus Christ" (NASB). It will look like 2 Corinthians 4:5 where Paul said, "For we do not preach ourselves but Christ Jesus as Lord, and ourselves as your bond-servants for Jesus' sake" (NASB). It will look like what he did in the book of Philippians. In chapter 1, Paul refers to Jesus Christ or Christ Jesus nineteen times! And we find him doing the same thing in the rest of this epistle as well as in his other epistles. Paul was a sanctified man, a man whose mind was marinated in the love of his Savior. The passion of Paul's life is stated well in Philippians 1:18–21:

> Yes, and I will rejoice, for I know that through your prayers and the help of the Spirit of Jesus Christ this will turn out for my deliverance,

as it is my eager expectation and hope that I will not be at all ashamed, but that with full courage now as always Christ will be honored in my body, whether by life or by death. For to me to live is Christ, and to die is gain.

For Paul, life was not all about himself; it was all about Him (Christ).

When a person has real love, he will follow the example of Paul as we have it in 2 Corinthians 10:13: "But we will not boast beyond limits, but will boast only with regard to the area of influence God assigned to us." In context, what Paul is doing here is comparing the way he functions with the way that some intruders who came into the Corinthian church and tried to win a following were functioning. These impostors were men who claimed to be apostles (2 Cor. 11:13). These men were going around commending themselves, talking about themselves, saying that they had done and had experienced things that were unverifiable in an attempt to impress people. These men loved themselves, they loved their own reputations, they loved fame, they loved power, but they didn't really love people. These men were guilty of gross exaggeration and made claims that could not be validated. And part of what these men did was to try to tear down the reputation of and respect for the apostle Paul. These men saw Paul as a competitor, and in an attempt to build themselves up, they made incredible claims about what they knew, about what they had done.

But Paul says, "I won't get into that kind of contest—I won't boast beyond limits," using the words "boast beyond limits [or measure]" because that's what these men were doing. Simon Kistemaker says that Paul means that he will not talk of accomplishments, which no one can measure, and that he will talk only about that which God wants him to talk about. In fact, Kistemaker says, this means that Paul is committed to boasting about the Lord, not about himself.[4] In other words, when it comes to ministry, Paul is saying that he will not talk about anything that is not absolutely true and verifiable, and he will not talk about anything unless it exalts the Lord.

4. Simon Kistemaker, *2 Corinthians* (Grand Rapids: Baker, 1997), 348.

Practicing real love in God's style doesn't mean that we should never share anything positive about what we possess or what we have done or what has happened to us. It doesn't mean that it is wrong to give a personal testimony in which we describe how the Lord has used us and what the Lord has done for us. We know that's true because of the many examples where Paul did that very thing (Acts 20:17–27, 33–35; 1 Cor. 15:10; 2 Cor. 2:15–17; 4:1–2, 8–10, 16; 6:4–10; 11:21–30; 12:7–10, 11–16; 1 Thess. 1 and 2; 2 Tim. 4:6–7).

## Important Guidelines for Sharing Positive Experiences

What does it mean to practice real love and share some things about us and our experiences and still not be bragging? It means that when we're sharing information about ourselves, we will talk about our weaknesses and defeats as well as our victories and successes. It means that we must not be puffed up with pride in our accomplishments. It means that we must honestly view, and speak of, our accomplishments through the lens of what God has done in and through our frail efforts. It means that we should be concerned about speaking in such a way that He will be honored and glorified rather than speaking in such a way that people will be impressed with our greatness (Acts 18; Rom. 7:18–19; 1 Cor. 2:3; 2 Cor. 1:10–11; 2:4; 7:5–6; Gal. 4:19–20; 1 Thess. 3:1).

Having a love that does not brag will mean that when we do share positive experiences, we do it for an unselfish reason: for the purpose of encouragement or instruction or for the purpose of exalting God and making Him glorious in the eyes of others. In other words, we'll follow the counsel of Ephesians 4:29, which says, "Let no corrupting talk come out of your mouths, but only such as is good for building up, as fits the occasion, that it may give grace to those who hear." Having a love that does not brag means that we will make every effort to magnify Christ rather than self in our conversations (1 Cor. 15:8–10; 2 Cor. 4:5; 12; Gal. 6:14).

Loving without bragging will also mean that the majority of our sharing will not be about us or me or mine. If you read the writings of Paul, you will find he sometimes speaks of his own experiences, but the majority of his communication is not primarily about himself, but about Jesus Christ.

Loving without bragging means that we will frequently talk about the victories and successes and accomplishments and good qualities of others. Paul did this in many of his letters (Rom. 16; 1 Cor. 16:15–16; 2 Cor. 8; Phil. 2:19–30; Col. 4:12–13).

For the sake of time and space, I've chosen to reference these passages rather than exegete them. But if you'll actually take the time to read them, I think you will find they will encourage your heart, and their illustrations will clarify each of these points. They will give you a deeper understanding and appreciation of these topics.

## The Greatest Example

Thus far, I've mainly used Paul's example to describe what a real love that doesn't brag will look like, but before I finish this chapter, I want to mention the greatest example of a love that doesn't brag. Who is it? Peter? John? No. The greatest example I could use is the example of Jesus Christ, our Lord.

The fact that Jesus had a love that did not brag was illustrated throughout the entirety of His life. For instance, this was emphasized at the time of His birth. Jesus was the only man who ever lived who could have completely arranged the circumstances of His own birth and early life. When He was born, Jesus chose to be born to a peasant lady who married a peasant man (Luke 2:1–14). Still further, this nonboasting love of Jesus was illustrated throughout His ministry. We're given many examples where people, or even demons, sought to broadcast the works and divinity of King Jesus, yet He bade them be quiet and not speak of these things. It wasn't time for these things to be made known.

Even in the circumstances surrounding His death, He illustrated this divine love without bragging. Peter tells us that when He was reviled, He did not revile in return; while suffering He uttered no threats, but quietly kept entrusting Himself to Him who judges righteously (1 Peter 2:23). In Acts 8:32 Philip said that Jesus was led as a sheep to slaughter; and as a lamb before its shearer is dumb, so He did not open His mouth.

Concerning the way Jesus conducted His life, John MacArthur has written:

> Jesus was God incarnate, yet never exalted Himself in any way. "Although He existed in the form of God, [He] did not regard equality with God a thing to be grasped, but emptied Himself, taking the form of a bond servant, and . . . being found in appearance as a man, He humbled Himself" (Phil. 2:6–8). Jesus, who had everything to boast of, never boasted. In total contrast, we who have nothing to boast of are prone to boast. Only the love that comes from Jesus Christ can save us from flaunting our knowledge, our abilities, our gifts, or our accomplishments, real or imagined.[5]

So what does it look like to have a love that doesn't brag or boast, that doesn't vaunt itself? Ultimately it means to be like Jesus.

- We are to love one another as Jesus loved us (John 13:34–35).
- He gave us an example that we should follow (John 13:15).
- We are to walk in the same manner Jesus did (1 John 2:6).

And how did Jesus live? He lived a life of love—a life motivated first and foremost by an overarching love for God, His Father. His life was also lived in such a way as to demonstrate His intense love for others—a love that was long-suffering, kind, not jealous, and not boastful. The love of Christ perfectly manifested itself in all the ways mentioned by Paul in 1 Corinthians 13.

## Why Believers Can and Should Love This Way

When the Bible calls on us to live a life of love, it is calling us to love God and others the way that Jesus loved. And why should we want to have that kind of love? There are many answers to that question. I will mention only a few:

First, in answering this question, we need to again remember the identity of the people to whom Paul was originally writing. Paul mentions

5. MacArthur, *1 Corinthians*, 342.

several times that these people were "in Christ Jesus," or in other words, that they were Christians. In the early verses of this book he mentions that they were set apart or sanctified in Christ Jesus, that they had been called by God, that they were people who called on the name of Jesus Christ, that they were people who had received the grace of God in Christ Jesus. They were people who had been spiritually enriched by Christ Jesus. They were people who believed and had embraced the apostolic testimony about Jesus Christ, and were eagerly awaiting the second coming of Christ. These people had been called into fellowship with Christ, and because they had been united by faith to Jesus Christ it would be only natural for them to want to live and love the way Jesus lived and loved. How could they not want to have that kind of love? That they had been united to Christ by faith was the greatest motivation for wanting to be more loving. What was true of them will certainly be true of all who are "in Christ."

Second, after reading what I just wrote in the last paragraph, one person said, "That's all very nice, but what relevance does all of that have to the question why we should be concerned about developing the kind of love Paul describes in 1 Corinthians 13?" Apparently, the person who asked that question didn't get the point I was making, and perhaps there are others reading this book who are still a bit perplexed about why being united to Christ should be the ultimate reason for wanting to develop and demonstrate a 1 Corinthians 13 type of love. Let me then clarify why being in Christ is the greatest motivation. The relevance is this: in this passage Paul is not telling the Corinthians (or us, for that matter) how to become Christians. He's not saying that anyone should try to develop this kind of love in an attempt to be saved or earn the favor of God. The truth is that no one could ever do that because even at best our love is imperfect.

No one who reads 1 Corinthians 13 should ever entertain the idea that Paul is telling us to try to earn the favor of God by being loving, because Jesus as our substitute has already perfectly loved God and won the favor of God on behalf of all who have put their faith and trust in Him—these people, as Paul said of the Corinthians, are already in Christ; they are already sanctified. These people have been called by God, and have already received the grace of God. They have been spiritually enriched by Christ Jesus, and already are in fellowship with God and on their way to heaven.

So the people whom Paul is exhorting to live a life characterized by the kind of love described in 1 Corinthians 13 are people to whose account God has already credited all the righteousness of Christ, including His righteous and perfect love. When we put our faith in Christ, God looks upon us as though we had lived a life of perfect obedience and love. As Paul says in Ephesians 1:5–6, God has accepted us because of Christ. We have been redeemed, and accepted by God; we have, by His grace, become children of God and part of the family of God. We have been forgiven, and have been translated out of the kingdom of darkness and into the kingdom of His dear Son. We are loved by God and will never be separated from Him. Because of Jesus, we have an inheritance that is undefiled and that does not fade away—we have a heavenly Father. Because we are united to Christ, He has come to dwell in us (Eph. 3:17; Col. 1:27), and His indwelling presence will inevitably manifest itself in the way we live and love. Again I ask, why should we want to have that kind of love? The answer: because it's our very nature as Christians to want to be like the Christ who indwells us by the presence of the Holy Spirit.

Third, there may be someone who still doesn't get the connection between being in Christ and possessing all the blessings that are in Him (Eph. 1:3) and being motivated to want to develop a life characterized by the love described in 1 Corinthians 13. By way of clarification, I appeal again to Paul, who, as we have seen, was a stellar human example of the love described in 1 Corinthians 13. Paul had a love for people that was basically long-suffering, that was kind, that was not jealous, that did not brag; his was a love for God that motivated him to give up a promising career, to travel all over the Mediterranean world, to experience hardship, reproach, slander, mistreatment, and rejection for the sake of reaching people for Christ. Paul really loved Christ and he loved people!

What motivated Paul to live that life of love? To answer that question we don't have to guess. We can turn to his own explanation in 2 Corinthians 5:13–15:

> For if we are beside ourselves, it is for God; if we are in our right mind, it is for you. For the love of Christ controls us, because we have concluded this: that one has died for all, therefore all have died; and

he died for all, that those who live might no longer live for themselves but for him who for their sake died and was raised.

In these words Paul is saying that what motivates him to love God and others the way he does is the immense love that Christ has shown for him in living for him and dying for him on the cross. What he is saying is that an understanding of the way Christ has loved him compels or constrains him to die to self and to live for Christ.

In these words Paul echoes the words of John in 1 John 4:10–11, 19:

> In this is love, not that we loved God but that he loved us and sent his Son to be the propitiation for our sins. Beloved, if God so loved us, we also ought to love one another. . . . We love because he first loved us.

So there we have the most important reason why we should be motivated to live a life of love. The question is, how can we not want to love others in this way when we consider the way God has loved us? How can we not love others in the 1 Corinthians 13 way when we remember what Romans 5:6, 8 says:

> For while we were still weak, at the right time Christ died for the ungodly . . . but God shows his love for us in that while we were still sinners, Christ died for us.

How can we not love others in the 1 Corinthians 13 way when we remember the love of Christ that caused Him to live for us and then pay the penalty for our sins by dying in our place on the cross?

In these words Paul is saying that he is motivated to live a life of total dedication to Christ and for the benefit of others by the same glorious realities that Isaac Watts so beautifully described in the hymn "When I Survey the Wondrous Cross." In a sense what Paul is saying is: "When I survey the wondrous cross on which the Prince of glory died, my richest gain I count but loss, and pour contempt on all my pride. Forbid it, Lord, that I should boast, save in the death of Christ my God. All the vain things that charm me most, I sacrifice them to his blood.

Were the whole realm of nature mine, that were a present far too small; love so amazing, so divine, demands my soul, my life, my all."

There we have the most important reason why we should be motivated to a life of love. How can we, who have been so loved by Christ, not want to love others in the 1 Corinthians 13 way when we consider the way God has loved us? Because of the way Jesus loved us, we should and can have a love that is long-suffering, a love for others that is kind, that is not jealous, that does not brag—a love that entails all the other characteristics mentioned in 1 Corinthians 13. So our ultimate motivation for wanting to be the loving person described in this passage is that *Jesus has loved us this way.*

There is, however, a secondary reason why we should be motivated to develop and sustain the kind of love described in 1 Corinthians. That is the reason Paul gives in 1 Corinthians 13:1–3 where he says that without this kind of love our ministries and efforts for Christ will profit nothing. Or to put it in a positive light, we should be motivated to develop and sustain this kind of love because loving God and others with all our hearts, souls, and strength is the key to making an impact in the lives of others that will be good for them and will bring glory to Christ. If we attempt to serve Him and people without that love we will, in the words of 1 Corinthians 13:1, be as a sounding brass and clanging cymbal.

In Ephesians 3:17–19 Paul prayed for the Ephesian Christians:

> That Christ may dwell in your hearts through faith—that you, being rooted and grounded in love, may have strength to comprehend with all the saints what is the breadth and length and height and depth, and to know the love of Christ that surpasses knowledge, so that you may be filled with all the fullness of God.

Brethren, let's make that prayer of Paul our prayer for ourselves and for others. Let's pray that we might more fully know Christ so that we might love each other with the fullness of a love that is long-suffering, is kind, is not jealous, and does not brag. And as that happens, we can count on what Paul mentioned at the end of his prayer in Ephesians

3:21: God will get "glory in the church [and in us] and in Christ Jesus throughout all generations, forever and ever." As we develop and sustain this 1 Corinthians 13 type of love, we can count on bearing much fruit, which in turn will fulfill the purpose of our creation and redemption, namely, that we might bring greater glory to God (John 15:8).

## Review, Reflection, Application, and Discussion Questions

1. This chapter asserts that envy, jealousy, and boasting are similar to one another. What does that statement mean? How are envy and jealousy related or similar to boasting?

2. What does C. S. Lewis call "the ultimate evil"? What is his reason for saying that?

3. Review the biblical examples of boasting mentioned in this chapter—look up the Scripture passages and then glean everything you can about ways to boast. Try to put the point of each of these passages into a contemporary setting. How do we who live in the twenty-first century do the same thing that these people were doing?

4. Reflect on the list of possible things we may brag about in an attempt to impress people. Evaluate yourself in terms of whether you have ever tried or perhaps still do try to impress people with your power, knowledge, education, material possessions, beauty, skills, importance, position, background, associates and relationships, acquaintances, family accomplishments. Identify and describe actual ways (create scenarios) in which we might try to impress people with any of these things.

5. Review the list of things mentioned in this chapter that we won't do if we have real love. Again evaluate yourself in terms of whether and how often you do the things you shouldn't do: "I never do this" (4); "I seldom do this" (3); "I sometimes do this" (2); "I frequently do this" (1); "I regularly do this" (0).

6. Review the positive examples of what it means to have a love that doesn't boast. Look up the passages that are mentioned and identify how they illustrate the point that is being made.

7. What specific directions (guidelines) were given in terms of talking about your own accomplishments?

8. Describe how (in what ways) Jesus was the greatest example of having a love that does not boast. What specific things can we learn from Jesus about not bragging or trying to impress people?

9. Do a mental review of your life for the past week and identify times and places where you may have violated the love principle of 1 Corinthians 13:4.

10. For you, what is your greatest motivation for practicing the love principle of this chapter?

11. And now my usual reminder: Please remember as you reflect on the love principle presented in this chapter that the purpose of evaluation and application is:

   a. not to discourage or destroy us;

   b. but to motivate us to see our constant need of the cross and how much we owe to Jesus—without Him we'd never make it, but praise God we are not without Him;

   c. and to motivate us to understand our constant daily need of grace—that our salvation never has been and never will be by the works we have done, but always by the work Christ has done and is doing for us; I want our studies in 1 Corinthians 13 to be a reminder that we need to live a cross-centered life; we need the application of the cross work of Jesus every day of our lives; remember there's not a day in our lives when we are so good that we don't need the cross, and there is never a day in our lives when we are so bad that what Christ did on the cross is not sufficient to provide forgiveness for us (Rom. 3:24; 5:20; Eph. 1:7; 1 John 1:7; 2:1–2);

d. and to cause us to understand that we must and can, by His grace, put off from our lives the "unlove" that is displeasing to God and put on in our lives the love that is beautifully described in 1 Corinthians 13 and become more and more like our Savior and become more prolific in bearing fruit for Him as others see the grace of God at work in our lives, changing and transforming us (Eph. 4:22–24; 1 Tim. 4:7).

# 9

## Talk Is Cheap . . . or Is It?

### Talk Is Cheap?

You've probably heard the expression "talk is cheap" and may have even used it before. Some may disagree with the statement because they've heard that some famous person—like former president Bill Clinton—receives hundreds of thousands of dollars for a half-hour speech! I recently read that he's made several million dollars in the last five years or so for speaking at various functions. So if you want to get Mr. Clinton to speak at your next meeting, you'd better recognize that his talk won't be cheap!

When used in that sense, talk may not be cheap, but the original meaning of the phrase wasn't referring to the price paid to certain speakers. It was referring to people who make promises and then don't keep them—who probably never intended on keeping them in the first place! The phrase refers to people who, for the sake of promoting a product, will make all kinds of erroneous claims about what that product will do. I can't tell you how many times I have fallen for such claims and actually purchased a certain product because of the supposed benefits it would give me. The product might be vitamins or some other miracle pill, or it might be some piece of equipment or the newest electronic gadget.

The phrase "talk is cheap" refers to people who say they will do one thing and then actually do another. In a spiritual sense, it can be applied to the talk of some people who say to Christ, "I love You and all I have is Yours. I'll do anything for You. I'll go anywhere for You," and then, when push comes to shove, they never do what they said they would do.

Talk is cheap when it applies to people who say they really love people—but then they don't act in a biblically loving way toward the people they claim to love. In other words, they say something with their lips and then do the opposite of what they declare!

God knows our propensity to do this kind of thing, especially in the area of loving others, and so He inspires the apostle to write a brilliant description of what it really means to love someone in 1 Corinthians 13:4–7. In this passage, God, as it were through the apostle Paul, says to us, "You say you love Me; you say you love others. Well, let Me show you how real love for Me will manifest itself in your relationships with people; let Me show you what real love for others will look like in actual practice."

In verses 4–7 Paul mentions fifteen of the characteristics of real love for others. It's as though this matter of love is like a beautiful diamond with fifteen different facets. Paul encourages us to look at the same diamond from fifteen different perspectives, and as we do, we'll catch a glimpse of how truly effective genuine, ministry-empowering love can be.

Thus far in our studies of what real love looks like, we've considered the first four characteristics in verse 4. In previous chapters we've seen that real love is long-suffering; real love is kind; real love is not jealous; and real love does not show off or boast.

Now we come to the fifth characteristic of real love.

## "Love Is Not Arrogant"

If you were to ask people to define real love, I doubt that most of them would include humility as one of love's main characteristics, but God does. The word translated "arrogant" or "proud" literally means to be puffed up, to be inflated, and to be filled with hot air. What God is saying is that an unloving person has a puffed-up opinion of himself. That is, he has an inflated opinion of his own importance, which of course means that he thinks others should share that high opinion and should treat him accordingly.

## Love and Arrogance Don't Go Hand in Hand

I think it can be rightly said that if one is arrogant, he cannot be a loving person, and if a person is loving, he will not be arrogant. The two simply can't exist together. Arrogance and love are not compatible. Where you have one, you don't have the other, because they are opposites. A loving person is concerned about other people, whereas an arrogant person is all wrapped up in himself.

That's not to say that a humble person cannot exhibit occasional lapses into the sin of pride. Pride and arrogance hits us all between the eyes from time to time. What I'm talking about here is a pattern of continued arrogance as a way of life, a way of thought, an attitude of the mind as well as the heart.

A study of the book of 1 Corinthians indicates that some of the professing Christians in Corinth had a huge problem with arrogance, which means that they were unloving toward other people—especially those who disagreed with them or treated them with less honor than they felt they deserved. Apparently, arrogance was a big problem among the Corinthians.

To help us get a grasp on this issue of loveless arrogance I want us to take a look at a few of the passages in 1 Corinthians where Paul uses the word *arrogance*. My reason for doing this is that, as we study these passages, it will be easy to see why Paul says that love is not arrogant. It will also validate what I said earlier, that love and arrogance cannot coexist. Finally, as we study these passages, we're going to obtain a firmer understanding of what arrogance really is, as well as crystallize our concept of how arrogance conflicts with what real love is.

## The Use of the Term *Arrogant* in 1 Corinthians

One of the passages where Paul uses the word *arrogant* is 1 Corinthians 4. In fact, in this chapter we find Paul using this Greek word three times: once in verse 6 (as "puffed up") and two more times in verses 18 and 19. When we look at the context of these verses, we get a picture of the way in which arrogance and love differ.

In verse 1 we catch a glimpse of the arrogance of some Corinthians who were questioning whether Paul was really a servant of Christ and whether he was actually presenting the truth of God. Verse 2 finds them perhaps questioning Paul's trustworthiness. In verse 3 they were constantly looking for faults in others and were being critical and judgmental. Verse 4 finds their arrogance manifested in condemning anyone who didn't agree with them. In verse 5 the Corinthians thought that they had the ability to read the hearts of people, to determine what they were thinking, to judge their motives. They didn't give each other the benefit of the doubt. Verse 6 tells that they went beyond what was written in the Scriptures. In fact, they usurped the role of God by accepting and propounding ideas not substantiated by Scripture. They were actually elevating their own ideas above the clear principles of Scripture, and in doing so, they were relying on their own insights rather than God's Word! Now, that is the ultimate of arrogance! These people were so sure they were right even when there was no biblical basis to substantiate their claims and even when what they thought was contrary to Scripture. This, of course, led to fighting and arguing because they had no standard except their own opinion for determining what was true or false, right or wrong. Each of them was convinced that his own thinking was correct and that whoever disagreed was incorrect.

When we turn to 1 Corinthians 1:10–12, we find Paul describing just what this kind of loveless arrogance had produced. In 3:3–8 he continues to enlarge on what a loveless arrogance was producing. According to Paul, it was producing jealousy, strife, schisms, cliques, factions, and hero worship in which one servant of Christ was pitted against another, and in which sides were being chosen. In so doing, the very cause of Christ was being hindered.

In his commentary on this passage, Simon Kistemaker writes:

The crux of what Paul is saying relates to the division in the Corinthian church: one party favors Paul and the other party Apollos. Strutting about like ruffled roosters, members of each party arrogantly set themselves against one another. Were it not so serious, it would be comical to watch the individual Corinthians fostering the factionalism in the church (1:12; 3:4). Let no one trumpet his preference for one leader, whether Paul or Apollos, but let each believer strive to learn from them what the Scriptures have to say. They must learn from their leaders to listen to the teachings of God's Word. In numerous places the Scriptures warn people against arrogance (e.g., see Job 40:12; Proverbs 8:13; Galatians 6:3). The Corinthians must learn meekness and understand that everything they possess they have received from God. They hear God speaking to them from the pages of Scripture.[1]

In 1 Corinthians 4:7, Paul continues to deal with their arrogance problem by asking them three questions, all exposing their lack of love and the presence of arrogance:

- Question 1: *Who makes you different from anyone else?* One of the marks of arrogance is that a person thinks he is different, superior to other people. He believes he is in a class by himself. As a result, he thinks that he deserves more credit and more respect than other people. In essence, Paul says, "Let's assume you *are* different. Assume you *are* more gifted or more skilled or more intelligent than someone else. Who made you different? Do you have these superior gifts because you decided to make yourself different?" The person who loves God and others would say, "I didn't make myself different. God did! He gave me whatever gifts I have and gave them to be used for His glory and for the benefit of other people."
- Question 2: *What do you have that you haven't received?* The obvious and correct answer to this question is "nothing," because as John 3:27 says, "A person cannot receive even one thing

1. Simon Kistemaker, *1 Corinthians* (Grand Rapids: Baker, 1993), 136.

unless it is given him from heaven," or as James 1:17 says, "Every good gift and every perfect gift is from above, coming down from the Father of lights." However, an arrogant person doesn't think that way. Oh, if you press him he may admit that whatever latent abilities he has were given to him, but that's not the thought that dominates his mind. He does not think of himself in terms of being a receiver, a beneficiary, except in terms of thinking that he deserves what others give to him. Apparently some people in Corinth forgot this truth. They acted as if they had generated their own abilities and therefore should be regarded differently from other people who may or may not have had these *superior* abilities.

- Question 3: *Why do you boast as if you had not received it?* Again, the obvious and correct answer to this question would be, "I have no reason for boasting." Paul asks this question because apparently there were some people in Corinth who were going around bragging about their abilities and at the same time criticizing others. Instead of giving God the glory for whatever gifts that they or anyone else had, they were acting as if somehow they were responsible for the good things they possessed.

The reality is that since every good and perfect gift is a gift from God and not based not on any merit of our own, it is absolutely foolish for us to puff ourselves up with arrogant pride for our gifts! The truth is that if we have a good mind, a good body, or certain skills and abilities, we had nothing to do with it. Since we are receivers and not originators, it is ludicrous for us to boast about our good points.

Instead, whatever abilities or gifts a person possesses, he has received from God. It is, therefore, illogical for us to put other people on a pedestal, almost worshiping them. Similarly, it is illogical for us to put other people down because they lack certain gifts and abilities.

Let me say one more thing about this topic. The fact that all our latent gifts and abilities have come from God means that we should focus on using whatever we have received for God's glory and for the good of other people. Instead of becoming puffed up by our spiritual or natural gifts, we should focus on giving God the glory for whatever gifts and abilities we have, and then, out of love for God, we should use those gifts for the benefit of others. If we have such gifts, we should be grateful to God for them—not so that we may be better served for having them, but that we may better serve others. According to Paul, this was not what some of the Corinthians were doing. Instead of glorifying God and showing genuine love for Him and others, they were showing pride and arrogance in themselves.

And just what were they boasting about? We don't know for sure, but from what Paul has written, we can imagine quite a few things, can't we? They may have been boasting:

- about how loving they were;
- or perhaps about how tolerant they were;
- about the fact that their church was not judgmental, that their church allowed people freedom and liberty;
- that their church was not authoritarian; that their church didn't try to run the lives of people;
- that their church allowed people to make up their own minds; that their church welcomed sinners; that their church was culturally relevant. Remember, Corinth at this time was one of the most wicked cities in the world. It was the Sodom and Gomorrah of the first century AD.

## More Evidence to Support the Fact That Arrogance Is the Opposite of Love

Moving on through the rest of 1 Corinthians 4, we find Paul continuing to deal with this problem of loveless arrogance. Apparently he considered this a major problem in the Corinthian church.

In verses 8–13 Paul tells them clearly that their arrogance was producing in them an attitude of self-sufficiency, complacency, spiritual indifference, spiritual pride, worldliness, compromise, and a lack of zeal.

In these verses Paul uses a bit of sarcasm or irony to make his point, especially in verses 8–10. Kistemaker states that the

> Corinthians think that they have filled their spiritual and material demands; they have no need of anything or anyone else . . . they considered themselves successful in church and society and, in effect, fostered the misconception that they were superior to everyone else. . . . Paul resorts to using phrases that circulated among the Stoic philosophers of that day. These philosophers prided themselves on being self-sufficient, and the Corinthians appeared to be influenced by their teaching. Instead of seeing themselves as citizens of God's Kingdom, the Corinthian Christians act as if they are rulers in the kingdom. They claim to be king rather than subjects of the king.[2]

Continuing on in verses 14–19, Paul indicates that their arrogance led to a lack of concern or compassion for others who were suffering hardships. It also led to a lack of love and respect for others whom God had used to bless them. God used the apostle Paul to bring many of them to Christ, yet it would appear that some of them were being critical, forgetting how much they owed Paul.

Paul continued to deal with their arrogance in verses 18 and 19 where he says, "Now some have become arrogant, as though I were not coming to you. But I will come to you soon, if the Lord wills, and I shall find out, not the words of those who are arrogant but their power" (NASB). The arrogance of some of the Corinthians was manifesting itself in a lack of respect for Paul (see 9:1–3; 2 Cor. 10:9–10). These verses indicate that some of these folks (probably those who presented themselves as leaders) were big talkers—probably people like the Mr. Talkative that Bunyan describes in *Pilgrim's Progress*. In fact, when Bunyan described Mr. Talkative, he quoted 1 Corinthians 4:20.

Bunyan says that as Christian and Faithful were progressing in the Christian life, they met a man whose name was Talkative. Bunyan describes Mr. Talkative as a man who is all talk but no walk, words but no action.[3] That's probably what Paul means when he says that he wants

---

2. Ibid.

3. John Bunyan, *The Pilgrim's Progress* (Pretoria: Word of the Cross, 2007), 99–110.

to find out not just the words of these people, but their power. Like
Talkative, the Corinthians were people who enjoyed bragging about
their own knowledge and importance. It was obvious that they were
critical and demeaning toward Paul, that they showed a lack of love
and respect for those to whom God had given authority in the church.
Instead of helping them in their ministry, they were competing with
them, making their ministry more difficult. Real love just doesn't treat
others that way: arrogance does.

Turning to 1 Corinthians 5 we get some additional insights about
the contrast between arrogance and love. Paul describes another aspect
of their arrogance and their lack of love in verses 1 and 2:

> It is actually reported that there is sexual immorality among you, and
> of a kind that is not tolerated even among pagans, for a man has his
> father's wife. And you are arrogant! Ought you not rather to mourn?
> Let him who has done this be removed from among you.

Paul reprimands the Corinthians for allowing themselves to be puffed
up with pride when such a grievous and flagrant sin was carried on
right under their noses by those within their own congregation—and
they tolerated it! He told them that even the pagans would abhor such
a sin as this one!

Paul notes that they overlooked the sin of this man and allowed
him to continue as a member in good standing, even though the Lord
Jesus had previously told them (Matt. 18) what to do when someone
sins and continues in sin. They obviously thought this was no big deal.
And that, my friends, according to God's Word, is loveless arrogance.
To ignore this situation was not only an act of arrogance, but also an act
of lovelessness, because ignoring what was occurring was disobedience to
Christ and damaging to the perpetrators and to the rest of the church.

Concerning the arrogance of these people, Simon Kistemaker says,
"They have been haughty in that they think they are free to decide
not to do anything about this wickedness."[4] They have been lovelessly
arrogant, because they think they are free to do nothing about this sin

---

4. Kistemaker, *1 Corinthians*, 156–57.

even though Jesus and the apostle Paul had said otherwise. And again I say, to refrain from dealing with this issue is arrogance and is also a lack of love.

John MacArthur writes, "These people were so self-satisfied and self-confident that they excused or rationalized the most wicked behavior in the congregation. Their arrogance blinded them to the clear truth of God's standards. Perhaps they felt so secure that they thought they could sin without consequence."[5] He goes on to say that their judgment took priority over what they had been taught. They obviously didn't care what God's Word said. They felt they didn't have to obey. It was unbridled arrogance that allowed them to think that they could willy-nilly do what they wanted and not suffer the consequences, even though God had said otherwise.

According to the Bible, failing to apply appropriate church discipline is not an act of love, but an act of arrogance. As I said earlier, the church might have considered their passivity as a positive value, but in reality they were totally wrong. They were using their own standards concerning what love was. Paul, in no uncertain terms, told them in this passage, as well as in 1 Corinthians 13, that they were dead wrong to excuse this kind of behavior!

Paul didn't advocate taking action against this person just to get him out of the church! Instead, he urged them to take action because the goal of church discipline, as described in Matthew 18 and in 2 Thessalonians 3:11–13, is to restore the sinning party to full fellowship in the church and with his Lord! Obedience to this biblical principle is an act of love when done with the right spirit, and when motivated by compassion and when carried out in a right manner. Revelation 3:19 says, "Those whom I love, I reprove and discipline, so be zealous and repent."

Paul therefore informed the Corinthians that their failure to deal appropriately with the situation was an unloving thing in terms of the man himself. First Corinthians 11 and many other passages make it clear that if sinners will not deal with their own sins through repentance and change, God will deal with them. If they are really believers and they will

5. John MacArthur, *1 Corinthians* (Chicago: Moody, 1984), 123–24.

not examine themselves, Scripture says, the Lord will discipline them and His judgment may be very severe (1 Cor. 11:28–32; Rev. 2:4–5, 14–16, 20–24; 3:3, 19–20). The warning is that if those who are living in consistent sin will not repent and change and if the church as God's agent will not confront that sin, then God will take steps to deal with it and that what God does may be very painful.

Yet Scripture reminds us that even though God's discipline may be very unpleasant, it is still the loving thing to do in that He disciplines so "that we may not be condemned along with the world" and "that his spirit might be saved in the day of the Lord Jesus" (1 Cor. 11:32; 5:5; see also Heb. 12:4–11). Because of the purpose of discipline as expressed in these verses, what the Corinthians were doing by ignoring the man's sin was an act of arrogance (disobedience to God's already revealed Word) and "unlove" because it is a loving thing (i.e., for their benefit) to lovingly confront people who are living in sin and try to help them to change.

There are, however, other reasons why confronting this man about his sin and calling him to repentance was the loving and obedient thing to do. It would have been the loving thing to do for the sake of other believers in the church. In the metaphor Paul uses in verse 6, he informs them that their neglect (passivity) is really an indication that they don't really love other believers. He says, "Do you not know that a little leaven leavens the whole lump?" Paul is saying, "I'm astonished! It's hard for me to believe that you are glossing over what is occurring. Aren't you aware of or concerned about the effect that your neglect is going to have on other believers? Don't you care for the rest of the people? Don't you love the other people in the church?"

Another reason why their neglect of lovingly confronting this man about his sin was not only an act of disobedience and therefore arrogance, but also an act of "unlove," is that it was related to the impact that their passivity would have on people outside the church. For them to allow this man who was living in open sin before other church members and before unbelievers to continue in good standing in the church even though he was consistently and unrepentantly living an immoral life was sending a message to the world that Christians are no different from the world. Paul alludes to the fact that even the world was astonished at what the Corinthian church was allowing to happen without any exercise of discipline: "Immorality of such a kind as does not exist even among the Gentiles [unbelievers], that someone has his father's wife" (v. 1 NASB). Paul is distressed because the Corinthian church was sending a message to unbelievers that the salvation that Christ provides and the gospel that the church proclaims was powerless to change lives and unconcerned about holiness. And he was convinced that sending a message like that to the world is an extremely unloving thing to do for the sake of Christ and for the sake of unbelievers outside the church.

This is why Paul writes to the Corinthian church: "But now I am writing to you not to associate with anyone who bears the name of brother if he is guilty of sexual immorality or greed, or is an idolater, reviler, drunkard, or swindler—not even to eat with such a one". (1 Cor. 5:11). He is indicating that we are supposed to live in such a way that nonbelievers will see that we are different—that we live by a different standard from anyone else. The very fact that the Corinthian church condoned this sinful behavior said to the world, "We are no different." In fact, even to the pagans, their acceptance of this particular sin would perhaps be shocking!

Paul considered the passivity of the church of Corinth to be an act of arrogance and "unlove," because he knew it was sending a muffled and distorted message to the world about the power of the gospel and the purpose of Christ's death that was stated clearly in Titus 2:14: "[Christ Jesus] gave himself for us to redeem us from all lawlessness and to purify for himself a people for his own possession who are zealous for good works." Jesus Christ didn't give Himself for us so that we might freely and continually engage in the worst kinds of sins, but rather Christ gave Himself for us so that we might have the power and inclination "to renounce ungodliness and worldly passions and to live self-controlled, upright, and godly lives in the present age" (Titus 2:12).

So because these were Paul's convictions, he considered the laxity of the Corinthian believers to be an act of arrogance and a lack of love. He really believed that God's way was not only the right way, but also the best way to receive blessing from God and impact the world with the gospel. Therefore, for the church to fail to do what the altogether wise and loving God commanded was the pathway to disaster.

In reference to understanding this "love not being arrogant" teaching, there is one more compelling passage in 1 Corinthians 8:1–3 where Paul uses the word *arrogant*:

> Now concerning food offered to idols: we know that "all of us possess knowledge." This "knowledge" puffs up, but love builds up. If anyone imagines that he knows something, he does not yet know as he ought to know. But if anyone loves God, he is known by God.

In one sense, Paul is saying the same thing here that he says in 1 Corinthians 13:2, where we read that if we have the gift of prophecy and understand all mysteries and have all knowledge but do not have love, we are nothing. It's possible to have a lot of knowledge—accurate, important, biblical knowledge—but if you don't have love, that knowledge is useless and any ministry you might have will amount to nothing.

That's also the point Paul is making in 1 Corinthians 8:1–3. He is saying that you can have accurate knowledge—knowledge of the truth—but instead of that knowledge of the truth being helpful and useful, your knowledge of the truth or rather what you do with that knowledge or what you allow that knowledge to do in you and for you can actually be destructive and harmful.

## Does Paul Disapprove of the Obtaining of Knowledge?

Obviously, from looking at what Paul writes about the importance of having accurate knowledge and knowing the truth in other places, we know that Paul was not opposed to the practice of obtaining knowledge. Titus 1:1–2 reads:

> Paul, a servant of God and an apostle of Jesus Christ, *for the sake of the faith of God's elect and their knowledge of the truth, which accords with godliness, in hope of eternal life,* which God, who never lies, promised before the ages began . . .

And Colossians 1:9:

> And so, from the day we heard, we have not ceased to pray for you, *asking that you may be filled with the knowledge of his will in all spiritual wisdom and understanding.*

What's going on here in 1 Corinthians 8:1–3 is that Paul recognized that there were two kinds of knowledge:

1. First is what we could call theoretical or abstract or factual knowledge, and this kind of knowledge doesn't necessarily make a person more godly;
2. Second is an experiential or practical knowledge that promotes godliness in a person's life.

Romans 1:19–21 speaks of people who know God but don't honor Him or give Him thanks. Their knowledge of God doesn't affect their lives at all. Well, I believe that's the kind of knowledge Paul is talking about in 1 Corinthians 8:1–3. He's talking about people who know facts, who know some spiritual truth, but it doesn't make them more holy or godly or more loving. These people, as the context indicates, knew a lot of truth. They understood that there is only one God and that there are no other gods. They were able to comprehend the worthlessness of idol worship, but in context it didn't make them wiser or more caring in their relationships with people. All it did was feed their pride and make them more arrogant. It fed their pride and caused them to be puffed up because they knew some things that others did not know. This knowledge puffed them up so that they were inconsiderate and judgmental and in so doing they were not only arrogant, but also unloving to others. They were using their knowledge in such a way that was ruining others. They had actually become a stumbling block for other people.

Titus 1:1 talks about another kind of knowledge. In this verse Paul says that he had been commissioned by God not simply to promote the knowledge of the truth, but to promote the knowledge of the truth that leads to godliness. Colossians 1:9 says that Paul didn't simply pray that the Colossians would be filled with knowledge, but that they would be filled with a knowledge that would help them to walk in a manner worthy of the Lord.

According to Paul, the Corinthians had a theoretical knowledge, but they were not using that knowledge in a loving way. In their arrogance they were using their knowledge in such a way that people were actually being hurt rather than helped, destroyed rather than edified. In other words, their arrogance fed by their superior knowledge was motivating them to tear others down, to be inconsiderate, to be uncaring, and to be judgmental.

So what is real love? So far, we have seen that it is a love that is long-suffering, a love that is kind, a love that is not jealous, a love that does not brag, and a love that is not arrogant. It means to have a love that uses its knowledge in a godly manner and for godly purposes. It means to have a love that will motivate you to use your knowledge of the truth in a humble, wise, caring, and patient way that is truly concerned about what is best for the other person. It means to handle and present truth in a humble and compassionate way.

## Knowledge of the Truth Combined with Humility and Compassion

How can we present the truth in humility and compassion? To do that we must present the truth in such a way that we don't come across to people as if we have the final word on everything. Instead, we must present truth to people as a learner and not as one who is omniscient. We must present truth to people in such a way that they get the idea we are journeying right along with them rather than that we have completely arrived.

Teaching others with humility and compassion means that we will be patient, long-suffering, and gentle with people who have not had the advantages we have. We will be willing to sit where they sit, to come alongside them so that in a loving manner we can share what we've been given of the truth and knowledge for the purpose of helping and not demeaning or destroying.

If we are to teach others with humility and compassion, we will avoid making big deals out of things that are not big deals. If we are communicating truth in a lovingly humble manner, we will avoid being nitpickers. And we will refrain from insisting that everyone dot all their i's and cross all their t's the way we do. Communicating truth in a loving, humble fashion will mean that we will make sure that we teach them God's standard instead of our preferences and opinions.

According to 1 Corinthians 8:9–13, being lovingly humble in manner will mean that we will be careful not to flaunt our liberty. It means that there will be times when we must deny ourselves and yield our rights to others so that we may minister to them in humility and compassion.

Paul agrees that some of the Corinthians had knowledge, but their knowledge was destructive to them (fostered their arrogance) and destructive to others (it was ruining and destroying them). Paul instructed them that using their knowledge in that way was evidence that there was something wrong with their love for God and others. What he was telling them was that real love won't act or behave the way they were behaving when dealing with other people who knew less than they knew or believed things that they didn't believe. He was also indicating that their lack of love was hindering their ministry for Christ in the lives of people.

What was true of some of the Corinthians may also be true of us. It is possible for us to have knowledge, to know the truth and comprehend biblical facts. And it is also possible for us to get puffed up by that knowledge. Moreover, it is very possible for our knowledge of the truth to make us hard, cold, uncaring, domineering, critical, judgmental, and pushy.

## The Right Use of the Knowledge of the Truth

To be sure, Paul isn't telling us that we should abandon the truth or that the truth is unimportant. He's not even saying that we should water down the truth. What he is saying to the Corinthians and to those of us who are concerned about the truth (those who believe that, as Jesus said, it is the truth that sets men free) is that we must stand for the truth and if necessary be willing to die for the truth.

When we stand for the truth and preach and teach the truth, we first must make sure that what we're standing for *is* the truth. Then we must also be humbled by that truth and make sure we present it in a loving manner in accordance with Ephesians 4:15. And we must make sure that we present the truth in love in accordance with 2 Timothy 2:24–25, which says that we "must not be quarrelsome, but be kind to all . . . with gentleness correcting those who are in opposition, if perhaps God may grant them repentance leading to the knowledge of the truth" (NASB). We must stand for and present the truth, but as we do that we must make sure that we are demonstrating the power of that truth as we manifest a love that is long-suffering, kind, and freed from envy, a love that doesn't brag, and a love that is accompanied by deep humility rather than arrogance.

Yes, as we said at the beginning of this chapter, talk is cheap. This was true of some of the Corinthians, and it can be true of some of us. The Corinthians would have said they loved God and loved others. But the way they related to others and ministered to them went beyond what was written. And the way they went above and beyond and around the truth proved that their professed love was really a myth. There were many Mr. Talkatives at Corinth, who talked a good talk but didn't walk a godly walk, and the result was that their ministry in the lives of other people for Christ was seriously hindered.

And so it will be with us, dear brothers and sisters in Christ, when we function as they did. Let's learn the lesson Paul taught the Corinthians. Let's remember that talking about how much we love God and others, about how committed we are to the truth, and about how much we want to impact others for Christ is not enough. All those things are good, but not good enough unless we walk in love. If we don't do that, our ministries will be as a sounding brass or a clanging cymbal. Our ministries will profit nothing.

### Review, Reflection, Application, and Discussion Questions

1. This chapter is titled "Talk Is Cheap." Why do you think I chose to give this chapter that title?

2. In what ways have you personally participated as either the sender or receiver in the "talk is cheap" phenomenon?

3. What does the word translated "arrogance" literally mean? What picture does that bring to your mind?

4. What would be another more commonly used English word for the word *arrogance*?

5. Why is it that love and arrogance are incompatible?

6. Review all the passages in 1 Corinthians where the word *arrogance* is used, and note everything you learn from these passages about what arrogance is and how it is manifested (displayed).

7. As you reflected on the arrogance of some of the professing Christians, what was the most shocking or surprising or alarming aspect or manifestation of their arrogance?

8. Memorize 1 Corinthians 4:7 and reflect on the three questions found in it. What are the answers to these questions?

9. How should believing the truths in 1 Corinthians 4:7 affect the way we view ourselves and our relationships with people?

10. How should believing the truths in 1 Corinthians 4:7 affect the way we view other people?

11. How are these truths actually affecting you in your daily experience?

12. What is it that the Corinthians may have been arrogant about?

13. Explain how church discipline is an act of love and why failure is an act of disobedience and "unlove."

14. Explain what you think Paul meant when he said, "Knowledge makes arrogant."

15. What are the two kinds of knowledge?

16. When rightly understood, what effect should knowledge have on a person?

17. And now my usual reminder: Please remember as you reflect on the love principle presented in this chapter, as I want you to do with

our study of all the love principles, that the purpose of evaluation and application is:

a.  not to discourage or destroy us;

b.  but to motivate us to see our constant need of the cross and how much we owe to Jesus—without Him we'd never make it, but praise God we are not without Him;

c.  and to motivate us to understand our constant daily need of grace—that our salvation never has been and never will be by the works we have done, but always by the work Christ has done and is doing for us; I want our studies in 1 Corinthians 13 to be a reminder that we need to live a cross-centered life; we need the application of the cross work of Jesus every day of our lives; remember there's not a day in our lives when we are so good that we don't need the cross, and there is never a day in our lives when we are so bad that what Christ did on the cross is not sufficient to provide forgiveness for us (Rom. 3:24; 5:20; Eph. 1:7; 1 John 1:7; 2:1–2);

d.  and to cause us to understand that we must and can, by His grace, put off from our lives the "unlove" that is displeasing to God and put on in our lives the love that is beautifully described in 1 Corinthians 13 and become more and more like our Savior and become more prolific in bearing fruit for Him as others see the grace of God at work in our lives, changing and transforming us (Eph. 4:22–24; 1 Tim. 4:7).

# 10

# Rudeness Is Out; Courtesy Is In

## A Loving Example

In April of 2008 I received a letter from Doug Nichols, the founder of a missionary agency that sends missionaries to many parts of the world. One of the main destinations is the Philippines. In that letter he wrote:

> Thousands of prisoners struggle just to stay alive in the jails and local and national prisons of the Philippines.
>
> Will and Joanie Feurenstein, an Action missionary couple, minister the gospel and compassionate care to the forgotten in the major security national prison fifteen miles south of Manila.
>
> Several thousand men there have indicated that they have trusted Christ in faith! Some of these believers have planted gardens in the prison compound to supplement their limited diet. When they began to harvest the first vegetables, they wanted to present the "first fruits" to the Lord. As they prayed, they decided to give this nourishing produce to sick and elderly prisoners in their same prison in Christ's name.

As a political prisoner and communist leader witnessed this tangible
demonstration along with other good works of the gospel of Christ,
he stated, "I want to know the God who leads people to reach out to
the oppressed as you do."[1]

This letter illustrates the truth that Paul emphasizes in 1 Corinthians
13. The statement by the prisoner and communist leader that he wants
to know the God who leads His people to reach out to the oppressed
as these Christians did makes it clear that showing real love to people is
a powerful instrument for making an impact for Christ.

As we have noted in the preceding few chapters of this book, Paul
not only gives us a general statement about the excellence or preeminence
of love, but also goes into great detail describing what this powerful
and impactful love will look like in our relationships with other people.
Thus far we've noted in verse 4 that real love is being manifested when
a person is long-suffering, kind, not jealous or envious, not boastful,
and not arrogant.

In this chapter we move on to the sixth characteristic of real love.
First Corinthians 13:5 tells us: Love does not act unbecomingly.

## General Definition of This Aspect of Love

The Greek word used here is also found in Romans 1:27 where
it says that men were "committing *shameless* acts." This could also be
translated "indecent acts." This concept of "shameless or indecent acts"
in the context of Romans 1 includes homosexuality, but it also includes
doing other things that are not appropriate or proper (e.g., being shame-
fully greedy, full of envy, creating strife, being deceitful, being a gossip,
being a slanderer, being insolent, arrogant, boastful, being disobedient
and disrespectful to parents, being untrustworthy or unmerciful).

The word is also used in 1 Corinthians 7:36 in reference to a father
who acts in an unbecoming way toward his single daughter. In the context, it refers to a father who is being unreasonable toward a daughter

1. E-mail letter from Doug Nichols, founder and international director emeritus, Action
International, April 11, 2008.

who is old enough to marry and wants to marry, but the father forbids her to get married without a good reason for doing so. Paul indicates that this father is being inconsiderate and acting inappropriately.

The word found in 1 Corinthians 13:5 is also used in Revelation 16:15 where it says, "Behold, I am coming like a thief! Blessed is the one who stays awake, keeping his garments on, that he may not go about naked and be seen exposed!" In the kjv, the verse says, "lest he walk naked, and they see his shame." In this context, the man has become lethargic about spiritual things and doesn't put on the appropriate spiritual clothing as described in many passages. For example, Ephesians 4:22–32 says he should put on (get dressed up in appropriate spiritual clothing) self-control, generosity, industriousness, wholesome speech, compassion, tenderheartedness, and forgiveness. Colossians 3:12–14 says much the same, except that it also adds that he should get dressed up in humility, gentleness, patience, and forbearance. So the man in Revelation 16:15 was naked, inappropriately dressed, because he had not put on these qualities, which form the appropriate clothing for Christians.

John MacArthur says that "the principle here has to do with poor manners, with acting rudely. It does not care enough for those around it to act becomingly or politely. It cares nothing for their feelings or sensitivities. The loveless person is careless, overbearing and often crude."[2]

As a general summary, I think we could accurately say that what Paul wants us to understand about real love from this phrase is that the person who is showing real God-honoring love will not be inconsiderate, crude, rude, or discourteous. Real love means that the person will avoid embarrassing or putting another person to shame, and he will do his best to avoid treating other people in inappropriate ways, which means that he will make sure that he treats people considerately, respectfully, and with dignity.

Some people do think that acting unbecomingly is behavior we should avoid, but that it is certainly not as serious as many of the other things that Paul mentions in 1 Corinthians 13. I ran the idea that acting unbecomingly was a lesser offense by a pastor friend of mine, and he

2. John MacArthur, *1 Corinthians* (Chicago: Moody, 1984), 343.

said, "How can people say that when it is listed right alongside other forbidden qualities in 1 Corinthians 13?" I had to say, "I don't know, but that's what some people do say. I am not sure that I understand what others mean when, it seems to me, they minimize the seriousness of being rude, but I am sure that acting in an unbecoming or rude fashion is a violation of God's will for us. I know that and believe that because of what 1 Corinthians 13:5 asserts, and because of what other verses of Scripture teach."

In my judgment, while not minimizing the fact that some sins have more serious consequences in the lives of others than other sins, it's still true that sin is sin and therefore what we have here is a serious matter that should not be taken lightly as I have seen many people do. Honesty compels me to admit that there have been times when I have behaved unbecomingly (rudely) and wanted to quickly excuse myself by saying that the other person shouldn't be so sensitive. Indeed, as I see it, behaving unbecomingly (rudely) should be taken seriously, because it usually comes from the same root as arrogance, bragging, or failing to be long-suffering or kind or being envious—namely, a focus on self rather than a focus on loving God and esteeming and loving others more than we do ourselves.

## Bad Examples Are Very Common

The Bible is replete with illustrations of people who were inconsiderate and inappropriate in terms of their behavior toward other human beings. The fact of the matter is that you can turn to almost any portion of Scripture and find illustrations of inappropriate and shameful behavior. If we wanted to, we could just stay in 1 Corinthians and we'd find illustration after illustration of people who were acting unbecomingly.

Of this church John MacArthur has written: "The Corinthian Christians were models of unbecoming behavior. Acting unseemly was almost their trademark. Nearly everything they did was rude and unloving. Even when they came together to celebrate the Lord's Supper they were self centered and offensive. 'Each one takes his own supper first, and one is hungry and another is drunk' (1 Corinthians 11:21). During worship services each one tried to outdo the other. . . . Everyone talked at once and tried to be the most dramatic and prominent."[3]

I believe John MacArthur is right. As you read through 1 Corinthians, you'll find illustration after illustration of unbecoming behavior. So if you want to know what it means to be rude and inconsiderate, just study the book of 1 Corinthians.

If we want to find illustrations of inconsiderate behavior, we don't even have to open our Bibles. All we need to do is open our eyes and look around us. In fact, all we need to do is reflect on our own experience because there probably isn't a person reading this book who can't tell of times when he or she has been treated discourteously. If truth be told, there's not a person reading this book who hasn't been guilty of violating the love principle we're talking about today. Probably all of us are ready to admit that we need help in the area of being more considerate of others.

In his book *Respectable Sins* with the suggestive subtitle *Confronting the Sins We Tolerate*, Jerry Bridges lists inconsiderateness (what Paul is calling "behaving unbecomingly") as one of those sins. Bridges writes, "The inconsiderate person never thinks about the impact of his actions on others. The person who is always late and keeps others waiting is inconsiderate. The person who talks loudly on his cell phone to the disturbance of others nearby is selfishly inconsiderate. So is the teenager who leaves her mess on the kitchen counter for someone else to clean up. Anytime we do not think about the impact of our actions on others we are being selfishly inconsiderate."[4]

## A Word about Our Approach to Presenting the Truth of This Love Principle

As I develop and illustrate what it means to have a love that acts unbecomingly, over against a love that is courteous and considerate, I will give some examples of what real love won't do, but primarily I

---

3. Ibid.
4. Jerry Bridges, *Respectable Sins* (Colorado Springs: NavPress, 2007), 105.

want to do that only as a means of illustrating what real love should and will do. Primarily, I want you to come away from this chapter with an excitement about the positive rather than negative aspects of the love principle we are focusing on. In particular, I've decided to present the main content of this chapter under two headings. First, I want to present some general principles based on several Scripture verses that will provide a biblical framework. I will then move on to give some specific examples of how these principles will work out in the nitty-gritty of life. So batten down the hatches, and let's dig in. May our God help each of us through this exercise to develop more of this kind of love that doesn't act unbecomingly.

## General Scriptural Principles Teaching the Importance of a Love That Does Not Act Unbecomingly

One of the general principles that ought to guide the way we relate to others is found in 1 Corinthians 10:32–33 and Romans 15:1–2 and in many similar passages. In the 1 Corinthians passage Paul writes:

> Give no offense to Jews or Greeks, or to the church of God; just as also I try to please everyone in everything I do, not seeking my own advantage [profit], but that of many, that they may be saved.

In the Romans passage he says essentially the same thing:

> We who are strong have an obligation to bear with the failings of the weak, and not to please ourselves. Let each of us please his neighbor for his good, to build him up.

Now, certainly, we know from Paul's other writings, as well as from his example, that he never compromised the truth in an attempt to please people. Certainly he was not wishy-washy when it came to standing for the truth, and he is not admonishing us to be that way. Paul, I'm convinced, was talking more about the manner in which we present the truth than he was about the content of the message we present. He was talking about the importance of wisdom as we relate to people. He was talking about putting Proverbs 15:2, which says that "the tongue of the wise makes knowledge acceptable" (NASB), into practice in real-life situations.

In the writings of Paul and his example, as described in the book of Acts and other portions of the New Testament, there is absolutely no reason for thinking that these statements in Romans and 1 Corinthians meant that Paul was afflicted with what secular counselors call codependency, a condition in which people find their strength and sufficiency in and are obsessed with an idolatrous desire to please people and have others think well of them. In the strictest sense, as the phrase is used today, Paul was not a "people-pleaser." Paul was a man who found his completeness and sufficiency in Jesus Christ. He already had a full sufficiency tank, and Jesus Christ kept that tank in his life full. He was, as he stated in Colossians 2:10, complete in Christ. Because that was true he could honestly say, "I am concerned about pleasing others, and I am living and speaking and relating to them in a becoming way, avoiding rudeness and seeking to refrain from doing anything that would unnecessarily offend others. I live this way not for my own benefit (not because I need or want anything from them), but because I truly want to bring great benefit to them, with the greatest of all benefits being that they repent of their sins and believe on the Lord Jesus Christ."

In his comments on this passage, Simon Kistemaker writes:

A Christian must seek to live blamelessly wherever he finds himself. We should not think that Paul failed to press the claims of Christ out of fear of being offensive. On the contrary, he boldly told both the Jews and the Greeks to turn to God in repentance and to put their faith in Jesus Christ (Acts 20:21). However, presenting Christ's Gospel effectively also requires tact, courtesy, and persistence. . . . Paul never asked anything for himself. . . . He stood ready to aid anyone, whether Jew or Gentile, or Christian, who asked for help. But in everything he did, he sought to glorify God by pointing the people to Jesus Christ. Accordingly, he could write that he did nothing for his own profit, but worked for the benefit of others.[5]

5. Simon Kistemaker, *1 Corinthians* (Grand Rapids: Baker, 1993), 358–59.

As we seek to put some meat on the bones of what it means to have a love that does not behave badly or rudely, Romans 12:17 would inform us that we should "do what is honorable in the sight of all" or, as the NASB puts it, we should "respect what is right in the sight of all men." The word translated "respect" literally means to "plan ahead to do what is right in the sight of all men." William Hendriksen renders this verse, "Always see to it that your affairs are right in the sight of everybody."[6] And then he goes on to say that Paul's words reflect the truth found in Proverbs 3:3–4:

> Let love and faithfulness never leave you;
>     bind them around your neck,
>     write them on the tablet of your heart.
> Then you will win favor and a good name
>     in the sight of God and man. (NIV)

In his explanation of the Romans text, Hendriksen comments:

> Paul wants the addressed to live such lives of thorough consecration to God and genuine love for all, including even the persecutors, that outsiders will not be given opportunity to complain or accuse (see 1 Timothy 5:14), and that the slanderer will be put to shame (1 Peter 3:16) . . . He wants them so to conduct their affairs that the public conscience (Romans 2:15) will approve. . . . Calvin has summarized the meaning of verse 17 as follows: "What is meant is that we ought diligently to labor, in order that all may be edified by our honest dealings . . . that they may, in a word, perceive the good and sweet odor of our life, by which they may be allured to the love of God."[7]

In the context, Paul is talking about how to overcome opposition, evil, and hostility. He is talking about how to love people—to win them for Christ. He says that unless it violates the Scriptures, we should do what others consider right behavior. That's what real love does. In other words, Paul is telling us to adapt ourselves to them and that whenever we can, without abandoning the truth, we should refrain from doing

6. William Hendriksen, *Romans* (Grand Rapids: Baker, 1981).
7. Ibid., 420.

or saying anything that offends people. In other words, for the sake of Jesus Christ and for the sake of winning others to or edifying others in Christ, show them a love that does not behave unbecomingly.

Colossians 4:5–6 emphasizes the same principle:

> Conduct yourselves wisely toward outsiders, making the best use of the time. Let your speech always be gracious, seasoned with salt, so that you may know how you ought to answer each person.

Paul says to "make sure that you conduct yourself wisely toward unbelievers and avail yourself of every opportunity to magnify Christ by the way you live and relate and speak to people. And remember that doing so will require being gracious in the way you talk and will also require thoughtfulness and adaptability in the way you answer everyone. Remember," says Paul, "that people are different and so you must not only know what to answer, but how to answer them." In other words, he exhorts us in these verses to manifest to people a love that doesn't act unbecomingly or rudely. Among the other things he is saying is that we, as Christians, should be considerate and thoughtful in our dealing with all people.

And of course, what Paul says here is right in line with what James writes: "Who among you is wise and understanding? Let him show by his good behavior his deeds in the gentleness of wisdom. . . . But the wisdom from above is first pure, then peaceable, gentle, reasonable, full of mercy and good fruits, unwavering, without hypocrisy" (3:13, 17 NASB). James wants us to know that walking wisely involves being peaceable (being careful to not do anything that would unnecessarily stir up conflict). Walking wisely will involve being gentle (being like a gentle breeze rather than a hurricane). Walking wisely will consist of being reasonable (being willing to listen to the other person's opinions or concerns or perspectives, being willing to yield on preference issues, not being domineering, being respectful, not making foolish and inordinate demands). Walking wisely will comprise being full of mercy (underscore the word *full*), meaning we must not have just a little bit of mercy, but must be full to the extent that we can't contain any more mercy. In other words, we should be known as people who really care about others who are encountering struggles and difficulties. Walking wisely will include being a person whose life and service are filled with good fruit, especially the fruit of the Spirit as in Galatians 5:22–23. Walking wisely will involve consistency and persistency (unwavering) and genuineness (motivated by a heart that loves God and people) and not doing things to be seen of men and win their approval. Paul's statement in 1 Corinthians 10:32–33 is a good description of what it means to be without hypocrisy. He did not do what he did for his own advantage, but for the advantage or profit of others.

I could go on multiplying other texts that fill out what Paul means when he says that real love does not act unbecomingly, but I think we've looked at enough Scriptures to see that the teaching of the first part of 1 Corinthians 13:5 is not an isolated concept in the Bible. Previously I wrote that the Bible is replete with examples of people who violated this teaching. That is certainly true, but it's also true that the failure of these people cannot be attributed to ignorance because, as we have seen, God, in many places, has told them that they should not behave in a rude and unbecoming way. Make no mistake about it: God wants His people to be considerate and thoughtful and respectful, and He has much to say about the meaning and importance of those qualities.

## Specific Examples of What a Considerate Love Looks Like

Earlier in this chapter I said that I wanted to first present some biblical principles that would give us a general understanding of what Paul's statement that "love doesn't act unbecomingly" means. And then I said I wanted to follow that by giving some specific examples of what these general principles will look like in practice. What does this kind of love look like in our lives? Now that we've laid out some general biblically based principles about the kind of love that is not rude, I want to give some specific examples of what this kind of love looks like in actual practice.

Having this kind of love will mean that you will follow the example of Hudson Taylor as you relate to the people with whom you live. Hudson Taylor is recognized as one of the most effective missionaries who have ever lived. He loved Christ supremely and he also loved people fervently. When he came to China, he soon came to the conclusion that if he was going to reach the Chinese for Christ, he should do as much as he could to become Christian Chinese. That meant, of course, as a minimum learning their language, but it also meant that as much as possible he would live like them. He decided that he would not oppose their customs unless their customs opposed Scripture. To reach them he began to wear Chinese rather than British-style clothing and encouraged all the other missionaries who worked with him to do the same. Since the Chinese men had their foreheads shaved and wore a queue in the rear of their heads, Hudson adopted this hairstyle and encouraged all the other missionaries who worked with him to do the same. To reach the Chinese and not offend them he took a Chinese name by which he was known to the Chinese population. He adopted the Chinese practice of eating with chopsticks and with practice became quite skillful at using them. He and his wife Maria knew that reaching the Chinese would require a total change of lifestyle, which would be accompanied by practicing the customs and courtesies of the Chinese. When, for example, they were in public, Maria would "no longer walk arm in arm (as had been their British custom) with her husband, but would walk several paces behind him."[8]

For all of this, Taylor and his fellow missionaries were criticized by other missionaries from Great Britain, but they were convinced that loving people meant they should not unnecessarily violate the customs of the people and thus be offensive to them, unless adapting themselves would violate Scripture. For us, following the example of Hudson Taylor (who incidentally was following the example of Paul and, even more, the example of Jesus Christ—John 1:14; Heb. 2:14–18) doesn't mean that you and I must do exactly what Hudson Taylor did unless, of course, we are living in a Chinese culture such as the one Taylor and his associates were living in at the end of the nineteenth and the beginning of the twentieth century. But it does mean that we should practice the kind of manners that are in keeping with the culture in which we live

8. Jim Cromarty, *It Is Not Death to Die: A New Biography of Hudson Taylor* (Ross-shire, Scotland: Christian Focus, 2008), 204–7.

and in keeping with the people with whom we associate—unless to do so would violate Scripture. It does mean that we should be considerate and respectful and courteous to everyone. To do otherwise is to act unbecomingly and thus fail to manifest the kind of love that Paul says will help us to become powerful witnesses for Jesus Christ.

Putting this kind of love into practice means that you will be very careful about teasing or making fun of people. A love that acts becomingly will not treat anyone the way some men treated Job in the book of Job. As we read through the book of Job, we find Job hurting badly—he has lost cattle and sheep, his barns have been destroyed, his sons have been killed, his wife has lashed out against him, and his health has seriously deteriorated to the point where he is constantly in pain from the top of his head to the bottom of his feet. When his so-called friends come to visit him, Job hopes that they will show him some compassion and provide some encouragement. Instead of doing that, they actually laugh at him and refuse to pay attention to what he is saying (Job 30:1). He talks, he explains, he solicits help, but instead they will not believe what he has to say or even pray with him or bring him any comforting truths from God. Instead, Zophar, one of his so-called friends, lashes out at him with some abusive, disrespectful words in which he accuses Job of being wicked, godless, a hypocrite, an oppressor of the poor, a thief who has stolen what belongs to someone else, a person who is getting from God the punishment he deserves (Job 20:5–29). And then when Zophar finishes his tirade, Eliphaz has a go at it and accuses Job of irreverence toward God, of being greatly wicked, of stripping men naked, of being extremely selfish and unwilling to show any mercy to poor and needy people, of making life difficult for widows and orphans (Job 22:1–30). And then when Eliphaz has had his say, Bildad, another supposed friend, joins in and makes additional attacks in which he viciously calls Job a maggot and a worm (Job 25:1–6).

None of these men showed any courtesy or consideration or compassion or respect for Job. Instead Job hears what they are saying as laughter or mockery, which probably means that they said what they said in a mocking, judgmental, demeaning, rude tone of voice. Probably it was not just what they said that Job considered laughable, but also the way they said it.

Proverbs 29:9 illustrates "unlove" by telling us about those times when a person communicates wise instruction and then someone responds with rage or with laughter and even refuses to be quiet. Perhaps the refusing to be quiet means that the listener either tried to drown out what the wise man said by talking over him or by arguing with him or by making fun of what he said with such snide remarks as "That is the dumbest thing I've ever heard. What you've just said is just stupid! That is really a harebrained idea. That is just ridiculous. You've got to be kidding!"

Mark 5:22–42 provides us with another example of an unbecoming love. In this instance, Jesus has come by invitation into the house of a synagogue official whose daughter had just died. As He enters the house, He encounters a room full of people who have gathered to mourn her death. Matthew indicates that they had brought with them some flute players (Matt. 9:23). Mark tells us that the people were making a great commotion and were weeping loudly even to the point of wailing (Mark 5:38).

When Jesus sees and hears them, He tries to calm them down by telling them that there is no need for such a commotion because the child is just sleeping. He didn't, of course, mean that she wasn't really dead, but that her present condition was only a temporary problem from which He would awaken her. When Jesus said that, He was not being flippant but was very serious. However, instead of taking Him seriously and respecting what He said, instead of being courteous and considerate and actually asking Him, "What do you mean, she is only sleeping? Please explain yourself," Mark indicates that they began laughing at Him (Mark 5:40). Note the word *began*, indicating that their fake mourning very quickly turned into raucous laughter in an attempt to embarrass Jesus and belittle Him and also with no thought about how their laughter might affect the mother and father who really and accurately believed that their daughter was dead.

What's the point that I want us to get from these examples? The point is that if we love people, we will make sure that we do not act rudely as all these examples illustrate, but rather that in all our dealings with people, whether they are seriously hurting or whether they are not in any immediate distress, if we love them we will always treat them with respect and courtesy.

Putting this kind of love into practice means that you will be careful and tactful in the way you talk to, admonish, rebuke, or correct someone. "The tongue of the wise commends knowledge, but the mouths of fools pour out folly" (Prov. 15:2). "The heart of the righteous ponders how to answer, but the mouth of the wicked pours out evil things" (Prov. 15:28).

Putting this aspect of love into practice means that you will be careful about the tone of voice you use in talking to people—even and especially your family! Proverbs 16:21 reminds us, "Sweetness of speech increases persuasiveness." Proverbs 16:24 says, "Gracious [pleasant] words are like a honeycomb, sweetness to the soul and health to the body."

Colossians 4:6 says, "Let your speech always be gracious, seasoned with salt, so that you may know how you ought to answer each person." And in Ephesians 4:29, 31–32 we read:

> Let no corrupting talk come out of your mouths, but only such as is good for building up, as fits the occasion, that it may give grace to those who hear. . . . Let all bitterness and wrath and anger and clamor and slander be put away from you, along with all malice. Be kind to one another, tenderhearted, forgiving one another, as God in Christ forgave you.

Putting this characteristic of love into practice means that you will change the practices and habits that annoy people, unless to do so is contrary to the revealed will of God.

> Give no offense to Jews or to Greeks or to the church of God, just as I try to please everyone in everything I do. (1 Cor. 10:32–33)

> For though I am free from all men, I have made myself a slave to all, so that I may win more. (1 Cor. 9:19 NASB)

> Let no one seek his own good, but that of his neighbor. (1 Cor. 10:24 NASB)

Putting this facet of love into practice means that we will not be overbearing and harsh toward people over whom we have authority.

> Masters, . . . stop your threatening. (Eph. 6:9)

> [Exercise] oversight not under compulsion, but voluntarily, according to the will of God; and not for sordid gain, but with eagerness; nor yet as lording it over those allotted to your charge, but proving to be examples. (1 Peter 5:2–3 NASB)

> Not that we lord it over your faith, but are workers with you for your joy. (2 Cor. 1:24 NASB)

Putting this aspect of love into practice means that you will not be disrespectful to those who have God-given authority over you.

> Slaves, obey your earthly masters with fear and trembling, with a sincere heart, as you would Christ, not by the way of eye-service, as people-pleasers, but as servants of Christ, doing the will of God from the heart, rendering service with a good will as to the Lord and not to man. (Eph. 6:5–7)

> Those who have believing masters must not be disrespectful on the ground that they are brothers; rather they must serve all the better. (1 Tim. 6:2)

Putting this kind of love into practice means that you will not demean or belittle people who are less gifted, talented, educated, or wealthy than you are. You must not look down on anyone!

> Honor everyone. Love the brotherhood. (1 Peter 2:17)

> For who regards you as superior? What do you have that you did not receive? (1 Cor. 4:7 NASB)

> But now God has placed the members, each one of them, in the body, just as He desired . . . It is much truer that the members of the body which

seem to be weaker are necessary; and those members of the body which
we deem less honorable, on these we bestow more abundant honor, and
our less presentable members become much more presentable. . . . God
has so composed the body, giving more abundant honor to that member
which lacked. (1 Cor. 12:18, 22–24 NASB)

Give preference to one another in honor. (Rom. 12:10 NASB)

Putting this characteristic of love into practice means that you will
not be fickle and undependable.

Be devoted to one another in brotherly love. (Rom. 12:10 NASB)

[God has composed the body] so that there may be no division in
the body, but that the members may have the same care for one
another. And if one member suffers, all the members suffer with it;
if one member is honored, all the members rejoice with it. (1 Cor.
12:25–26 NASB)

Do not merely look out for your own personal interests, but also for
the interests of others. (Phil. 2:4 NASB)

Putting this facet of love into practice means that you will not
make promises that you don't keep.

He swears to his own hurt and does not change. (Ps. 15:4 NASB)

Therefore, laying aside falsehood, speak truth each one of you with
his neighbor. (Eph. 4:25 NASB)

Do not lie to one another, since you laid aside the old self with its
evil practices. (Col. 3:9 NASB)

So take heed to your spirit, that you do not deal treacherously
[by making promises that you don't keep]. You have wearied the
LORD with your words [by making promises that you don't keep].
(Mal. 2:16–17 NASB)

Putting this facet of love into practice means that you will not neglect your work or home responsibilities.

> He must be one who manages his own household well. (1 Tim. 3:4 NASB)

> They must first learn to practice piety in regard to their own family . . . for this is acceptable in the sight of God. . . . But if anyone does not provide for his own, and especially for those of his household, he has denied the faith. (1 Tim. 5:4, 8 NASB)

> Encourage the young women to love their husbands, to love their children, to be sensible, pure, workers at home, kind, being subject to their own husbands, so that the word of God will not be dishonored. (Titus 2:4–5 NASB)

> Whatever you do, do your work heartily, as for the Lord rather than for men. . . . It is the Lord Christ whom you serve. (Col. 3:23–24 NASB)

Putting this kind of love into practice means that you will not slander people or spread evil reports about them.

> He does not slander with his tongue, nor does evil to his neighbor, nor takes up a reproach against his friend. (Ps. 15:3 NASB)

> Let all slander . . . be put away from you. (Eph. 4:31 NASB)

> Do not speak against one another, brethren. . . . There is only one Lawgiver and Judge, the One who is able to save and to destroy; but who are you to judge your neighbor? (James 4:11–12 NASB).

Putting this aspect of love into practice means that you will not take what people do for you or give to you for granted.

> Appreciate those who diligently labor among you . . . Esteem them very highly. (1 Thess. 5:12–13 NASB)

Render to all what is due them: . . . custom to whom custom . . . honor to whom honor. (Rom. 13:7 NASB)

Honor all people. (1 Peter 2:17 NASB)

Putting this quality of love into practice means that you will listen to people and think carefully about their suggestions. "The way of a fool is right in his own eyes, but a wise man [and I would add a loving man] is he who listens to counsel" (Prov. 12:15 NASB).

Putting this facet of love into practice means that you will dress modestly and in keeping with the culture in which you live unless to do so would violate Scripture (Prov. 7:10; 1 Tim. 2:9–10; 1 Peter 3:5–6).

Putting this kind of love into practice means that you will not make unreasonable and excessive demands of others. You will not be a bully who pushes and orders people around (Matt. 5:9; Rom. 14:19; Eph. 4:2–31; Tim. 3:3; 2 Tim. 2:24–25; Titus 1:7–8).

Putting this kind of love into practice means that you will not expect or demand that people do things you are not personally willing to do (John 13:1–17; 1 Cor. 11:1; Phil. 4:9; 2 Tim. 3:10).

Putting this kind of love into practice means that you will not be rude and discourteous to other drivers, as you drive down the highway or around town (Matt. 7:12; 1 Cor. 13:5).

Putting this kind of love into practice means that you will not abuse others verbally or physically (Prov. 15:1; 16:21, 24; 20:15; Eph. 4:2; Col. 4:6).

John MacArthur has written about this aspect of real love:

Love is much more than being gracious and considerate, but it is never less. To the extent that our living is ungracious and inconsiderate it is also unloving and unchristian. Self-righteous rudeness by Christians can turn people away from Christ before they have a chance to hear the Gospel. . . . The messenger can become a barrier to the message. If people do not see the "gentleness of Christ" (2 Corinthians 10:1) they are less likely to see Him in the Gospel we preach.[9]

9. MacArthur, *1 Corinthians*, 344.

### Let's Get Personal

This sixth characteristic of the kind of love God wants us to have will contribute to making us more powerful witnesses for Christ. What about you? Did I step on some toes with the list I've just given you? Did these items make you squirm just a little as you read them? Good. Consider yourselves convicted by the Holy Spirit, repent, and put these positive changes in place of the negative behaviors.

Let me ask you a few more questions while we're at it. Would other people describe you as a courteous and considerate person? What about your spouse? Would she (he) describe you this way? Is that the way your children think of you? Your parents? Your fellow Christians? Your fellow employees?

May God help each of us to examine ourselves, to repent wherever we need to repent, and to change wherever we need to change. We don't do these things to gain the favor of God, because we already have that. We do these things because we want to live a life that is pleasing to our Savior and will impact others for Him. A wonderful consequence of all this is that as we develop and manifest this kind of love, we will be blessed and we will be a blessing to others.

## Review, Reflection, Application, and Discussion Questions

1. What is a general definition for the word translated by the NASB as "unbecoming"? What are some of the ways in which the word in the original language of the New Testament is translated?

2. What are some of the synonyms for this word?

3. From a positive perspective, what is this phrase saying that love is?

4. What do you think about the idea that acting unbecomingly is not as serious as some of the other things Paul mentions in 1 Corinthians 13?

5. What are some of the unbecoming (rude) ways in which some of the Corinthians were behaving?

6. Was Paul afflicted by the condition that counselors in our modern world call *codependency*?

7. What did Paul really mean when he said that he tried to please all men?

8. What does James say about the wisdom that is from above (from God)?

9. According to James, what does it mean to walk wisely?

10. Review the list of ways in which a love that is not unbecoming will manifest itself. Can you think of any ways that should be added to the list?

11. Review the list of ways in which a love that is not unbecoming will manifest itself, and rate yourself as to how often you manifest such love: always (4); frequently (3); sometimes (2); seldom (1); never (0).

12. What does the inventory you took indicate about your courtesy or considerateness quotient? In which items are you strong and in which areas do you need improvement?

13. What practical things can you do to strengthen this aspect of love in your life?

14. And now my usual reminder: Please remember as you reflect on the love principle presented in this chapter that the purpose of evaluation and application is:

    a. not to discourage or destroy us;

    b. but to motivate us to see our constant need of the cross and how much we owe to Jesus—without Him we'd never make it, but praise God we are not without Him;

    c. and to motivate us to understand our constant daily need of grace—that our salvation never has been and never will be by the works we have done, but always by the work Christ has done and is doing for us; I want our studies in 1 Corinthians 13 to be a reminder that we need to live a cross-centered life; we need the application of the cross work of Jesus every day of our lives; remember there's not a day in our lives when we are so good that we don't need the cross, and there is never a day in our lives when we are so bad that what Christ did on the cross is not sufficient to provide forgiveness for us (Rom. 3:24; 5:20; Eph. 1:7; 1 John 1:7; 2:1–2);

d. and to cause us to understand that we must and can, by His grace, put off from our lives the "unlove" that is displeasing to God and put on in our lives the love that is beautifully described in 1 Corinthians 13 and become more and more like our Savior and become more prolific in bearing fruit for Him as others see the grace of God at work in our lives, changing and transforming us (Eph. 4:22–24; 1 Tim. 4:7).

# 11

## THE "SEEKING NOT ITS OWN" LIFESTYLE

Some time ago I read a book that included the biographies of some very fruitful Christians from the past. It included biographies of David Brainerd, who ministered so effectively during the eighteenth century among the American Indians; Henry Martyn, who ministered so successfully in India and Persia; and Robert Murray McCheyne, who ministered so powerfully in Scotland.

What made these men such effective servants of Christ? This question could be answered in many ways, but I was challenged by a statement about McCheyne that I believe is a large part of the reason why he was so mightily used of God. I hope that you are as challenged and encouraged by it as I was, and that you will pray with me that God will make us more like McCheyne, who so wonderfully reflected our Lord Jesus Christ:

> The secret of his success . . . was his faithfulness to the Word of God with tenderness for the souls of men. He went about his work with an air of reverence, which made men feel that the majesty of God was in his heart. There were few who could exhort the guilty in more

searching or tremendous terms; there were few who could address the troubled in more gentle or persuasive terms. Andrew Bonar once told him how he had chosen for a text the words with regard to the doom of those who forget God and are sent to hell (Psalm 9:17). McCheyne at once asked him: "Were you able to preach with tenderness?" He knew that there is an enormous difference between a voice that scolds and a heart that yearns. . . . It is not by threats and thunder, but by love and pathos that hearts are made to melt; it is not by words that scorch and condemn, but by a heart that bleeds to bless that souls are won. McCheyne himself preached on eternal destiny as one whose heart was wrung with a sense of anguish. He did not spare his hearers a word of truth; still less did he spare his own feelings a stab of pain. . . . J. H. Jowett once said that his severities were terrific because they were so tender. . . . Both the motive and the power in all such preaching may be discerned in his sermon on a broken heart and a contrite spirit. "It is not," he said, "a look into your own heart, or the heart of hell, but unto the heart of Christ, that breaks the heart. Oh pray for a broken heart."[1]

McCheyne believed that it is not merely standing for and proclaiming the truth that influences people for Christ, but rather proclaiming the truth with a heart that bleeds with love and pathos and brokenness. And as we've previously said in reference to similar statements from other mighty servants of God, he was essentially saying the same thing the inspired apostle Paul was saying in 1 Corinthians 13.

In previous chapters we discussed some of the marks of a person who has real love:

1. Long-suffering
2. Kindness
3. No jealousy or envy of others who are more prosperous and successful
4. No bragging or boasting
5. No arrogance or pride
6. No unbecoming or rude behavior

1. Marcus Sloan, *They Were Pilgrims* (London: Banner of Truth Trust, 2006), 172.

In this chapter we pick up on the seventh characteristic of real love in the middle of verse 5 where Paul says that the kind of love that will honor God and make us a powerful influence for Christ in the lives of others is *a love that will not seek its own nor insist on its own way.*

## Defining the "Not Seeking Your Own" Lifestyle

One of the passages that will help us to understand what Paul means by this statement is found in Philippians 2, where Paul explains what it means to be a person who doesn't seek his own. In Philippians 2:3–4 Paul first explains what it means to not seek your own by way of a propositional statement:

> Do nothing from rivalry or conceit, but in humility count others more significant than yourselves. Let each of you look not only to his own interests, but also to the interests of others.

In this text Paul describes the way Christians should live. More specifically, he is describing what should motivate our behaviors and attitudes toward others.

"Do nothing," he says. What that means is that we are never (without exception, not even one thing) to do anything from selfish motives. The same word is found in Philippians 1:17 where Paul speaks of certain preachers who preach Christ out of selfish ambition rather than from pure motives. On the surface these preachers seemed to be doing kingdom-of-God work, but in reality they were doing kingdom-of-self work. They were operating the way that Diotrephes was working in 3 John 9–11. On the surface Diotrephes, who was a leader in the church, was giving of his time and energy in what he would have claimed was for the glory of Christ and the good of other people, but in reality he was doing it to exalt himself. James 3:14 also describes the subtle way in which zealous service in spiritual matters can be done from selfishness when he uses the same word and speaks of those who have ambition, but says it is selfish ambition. And here in Philippians 2:3–4 Paul indicates that it is possible to be doing what appears to be the right thing while all the while be mainly, if not exclusively, concerned with our own interests and motivated by pride.

In his comments on this text, James Montgomery Boice writes:

> The principle that Paul is stating here is one that is found through-out the New Testament. The unbeliever naturally puts himself first, others second, and God last. And he may think he merits that order. The Bible teaches that we should reverse the series. God is to be first; others must be second, and we must come last. The Bible says, "Bear one another's burdens, and so fulfill the law of Christ" (Galatians 6:2). "For though I am free from all men, yet I have made myself servant unto all, that I might gain the more. . . . I am made all things to all men, that I might by all means save some" (1 Corinthians 9:19, 22). "Be kindly affectioned one to another with brotherly love, in honor preferring one another" (Romans 12:10). "We, then, that are strong ought to bear with the infirmities of the weak, not to please ourselves. Let every one of us please his neighbor for his good to edification" (Romans 15:1–2).[2]

## The "Not Seeking Your Own" Lifestyle Exemplified

In other portions of Philippians Paul explains what these verses mean by way of several examples. What it means is supremely illustrated by the example of Christ as described in Philippians 2:5–8:

> Have this mind among yourselves, which is yours in Christ Jesus, who, though he was in the form of God, did not count equality with God a thing to be grasped, but made himself nothing [laid aside his privileges, emptied himself], taking the form of a servant, being born in the likeness of men. And being found in human form, he humbled himself by becoming obedient to the point of death, even death on a cross.

This is our greatest example of a love that did not seek its own.

2. James Montgomery Boice, *Philippians* (Grand Rapids: Zondervan, 1971), 119.

In this passage Jesus exemplified a love that didn't seek its own in reference to the Father. Frequently, during His earthly life span, He said that He had not come to do His own will, but the will of the Father (Matt. 26:39; John 4:34–35; 5:30; 17:4; Phil. 2:8). This "seeking not your own" way of living was manifested throughout His entire life, but especially or supremely in that He was obedient to the point of death, even the shameful and painful death on the cross.

A second way Jesus perfectly exemplified this "seeking not your own" way of living related to His ministry and concern for others. He came to serve rather than to be served (Matt. 20:28). He came to give rather than get. He came to minister to rather than be ministered to. He came to help rather than be helped. He took upon Himself the form of a bondservant and actually served others constantly and unselfishly, rather than taking upon Himself the form of a master or a king or a dictator who would do nothing for others but demand that they wait on Him hand and foot. His whole life was *others*-oriented in the sense that He was constantly going about doing good for them with the purest of motives—not to His own advantage, but for theirs.

Jonathan Edwards mentions four things that demonstrated the unselfish manner of Christ's love on our behalf.

1. Christ set His love on those who were His enemies (Romans 5:8, 10).

2. Christ's unselfish love was displayed in that He was pleased, in some respects, to look on us as Himself. His elect were, from all eternity, dear to Him as the apple of His eye. He looked upon them so much as Himself, that He regarded their concerns as His, and their interests as His own, and He has even made their guilt as His. . . . And His love has sought to unite them to Himself, so as to make them, as it were, members of His body (Matthew 25:40).

3. Such was the love of Christ to us, that He did, as it were, spend Himself for our sakes. He gave up His own ease, and comfort, and interest, and honour, and wealth; and became poor, and

outcast and despised, and had not where [sic] to lay His head, and all for us.

4. Christ's unselfish love was manifested without any expectation of ever being requited by us for His love. He knew that we were poor, miserable, and empty-handed outcasts, who might receive from Him, but could render nothing to Him in return.[3]

After reading of the "seeking not your own" way Jesus lived, someone might say, "Well, that was Jesus! Of course, *He* could have a love that didn't seek its own—a love that was totally unselfish and free from selfish ambition. But I'm not Jesus!" It seems as if Paul anticipates that objection, so he goes on to give us other examples of people who had a love that didn't seek its own.

In this book I will use only one of the examples that Paul uses to describe a "seeking not your own" way of living, and that example is Paul himself. Like his Lord and Savior Jesus Christ, Paul manifested this "seeking not your own" way of living in reference to God. While in prison for preaching the gospel, and with some measure of uncertainty about what would happen to him, he said that he didn't care whether he lived or died—his earnest desire was that "Christ will be honored in my body. . . . For to me to live is Christ" (Phil. 1:20–21). "If dying will magnify Christ more, then I want to die. If living will magnify Christ more in the eyes of people, then I want to live." For Paul, life was not all about him and for him; it was all about Christ and for Christ. His main concern in life was not to please himself but to please and exalt the Lord. He was first of all and foremost, as he said on numerous occasions, a bondservant of Christ Jesus (Phil. 1:1) who lived to do not his own will, but the will of God (2 Cor. 5:9; Eph. 1:1; Col. 1:1; 1 Tim. 1:1; 2 Tim. 1:1).

Like his Lord and Savior Jesus Christ, Paul manifested this "seeking not your own" way of living by the way he unselfishly served other people.

3. Jonathan Edwards, *Charity and Its Fruits* (London: Banner of Truth Trust, 1969), 178–80.

> Even if I am to be poured out as a drink offering upon the sacrificial
> offering of your faith, I am glad and rejoice with you all. Likewise you
> also should be glad and rejoice with me. (Phil. 2:17–18)

Here Paul draws an illustration from the offering system in the Old
Testament. Some of the offerings that the people brought to God
in the Old Testament involved the worshiper's bringing his offering
to the priest, who would then put parts of the offering on the altar.
After that was done, that which "remained after portions had been
burned belonged to the priest, and was eaten in the sanctuary precincts
(Leviticus 5:13)."[4]

With some of the offerings, portions were put on the altar and
consumed, but some of what was brought was also given to the priests
for their personal use. However, the procedure for drink offerings was
different. The drink offering involved the worshiper's bringing a container filled with oil or wine to the place of worship and then completely
emptying that container at the altar, retaining none of it for the priest's
or anyone else's use.

When Paul mentioned being poured out as a drink offering, he
meant that he was willing to be totally emptied (poured out) in a life
of service for others. He meant that he was willing to do whatever was
necessary; he was willing to make whatever personal sacrifices would
bring benefit to them in their relationship with Christ; he meant that
he was ready and willing to give of his energies, his resources, even
his life if doing so would advance their spiritual well-being. Like his
Savior and Lord, Paul lived a "seeking not your own" kind of life.
And that kind of living was an example of what it means to do nothing out of selfishness or vain conceit; that was an example of what
it means to esteem others better than yourself; that was an example
of what it means to manifest a love that seeks not its own. (See also
2 Cor. 4:7–15; Rom. 9:3–4; 14:7–8; Phil. 1:12, 18; 2:19–30; and
Col. 1:24; for other examples of what it means to live a "seeking not
your own" manner of life.)

---

4. Merrill Tenney, ed., *Zondervan Pictorial Bible Dictionary* (Grand Rapids: Zondervan,
1967), 601–2.

## What Does This Kind of Love Look Like for Us in Actual Practice?

Loving God and others with a love that doesn't seek its own means that we will be willing to make costly sacrifices for God and for people (Gal. 2:20; Eph. 5:2, 25).

Loving God and others with a love that doesn't seek its own means that we will be willing to do what the good Samaritan did (Luke 10:25–37).

Loving God and others with a love that doesn't seek its own means that we will not be opportunistic or manipulative (1 Thess. 2 and Philemon).

Loving God and others with a love that doesn't seek its own means that we will not operate out of a "give to get" philosophy (Luke 6:35).

Loving God and others with a love that doesn't seek its own means that we will attempt to see things from the other person's point of view and frequently be willing to submit when there is a disagreement, unless to do so would be harmful for the other person or the cause of Christ (Eph. 5:22; 1 Peter 3:7).

The story of the way a Christian Chinese rice farmer handled a problematic situation with a neighbor is an excellent illustration of what may be involved in living a "seeking not your own" manner of life. The fields on which this farmer grew rice were located high on a mountain. Every day he would pump water from a pond on his property into his rice paddies. And every day he would return to find that an unbelieving neighbor who lived down the hill had opened the dikes and drained the water out of his rice paddies into his own fields. For a while the Christian ignored the injustice, but at last he began to become upset. He wondered what he should do. He asked the perpetrator to stop doing this, but he refused. The Chinese man knew that his own rice would die if this continued. He thought about it and prayed about it. He talked to other Christians about it and together they came up with this solution. They decided that what he ought to do was to start the day by first watering his neighbor's field and then his own field. That is, he decided to show this man a love that didn't seek its own. The result was that the neighbor was so impacted by this demonstration of love that he sought to know why this man was so loving. When the man told him that it was because of Jesus Christ, the neighbor was willing to listen to the gospel and subsequently became a Christian himself. That's what a love that does not seek its own will look like.

Loving God and others with a love that doesn't seek its own means that we will be willing to help other people in those areas where they want help and in the way they want to be helped.

Loving God and others with a love that doesn't seek its own means that we will be willing to give other people our undivided attention when they want to talk.

Loving God and others with a love that doesn't seek its own also means that we will be willing to let other people have the last word.

Loving God and others with a love that doesn't seek its own means that we will be willing to allow others to do things differently than we do, without judging or condemning them.

Loving God and others with a love that doesn't seek its own means that we will be the first, and perhaps the last, to ask for forgiveness.

Loving God and others with a love that doesn't seek its own means that we will not get upset if someone else is honored or gets the credit for what we have done.

Loving God and others with a love that doesn't seek its own means that we will not be upset if we are never recognized or applauded for good works we have done.

Loving God and others with a love that doesn't seek its own means that we will be willing to do what is beneficial for other people even though it is hard and costly for us.

Loving God and others with a love that doesn't seek its own means that we will be devoted to seeking the good of other people. It means that we will do what Paul says in 1 Corinthians 10:24, "Let no one seek his own good, but the good of his neighbor."

Loving God and others with a love that doesn't seek its own means that we will do what Romans 12:1 says: "present your bodies as a living sacrifice, holy and acceptable to God, which is your spiritual worship."

Loving God and others with a love that doesn't seek its own means that we will, as Romans 12:2 says, be concerned about knowing and doing the perfect and acceptable will of God. We should make a conscious effort to conform our will to His, to be satisfied with His plans, and not our own.

Loving God and others with a love that doesn't seek its own means that we will act as Ephesians 6:5–7 says:

> Obey your earthly masters with fear and trembling, with a sincere heart, as you would Christ, not by the way of eye-service, as people-pleasers, but as servants of Christ, doing the will of God from the heart, rendering service with a good will as to the Lord and not to man.

Loving God and others with a love that doesn't seek its own means that we will have a liberal spirit that disposes us to obey Hebrews 13:16: "Do not neglect to do good and to share what you have, for such sacrifices are pleasing to God."

Loving God and others with a love that doesn't seek its own means that, if need be, we will be willing to do what Paul says he was willing to do in Acts 21:13: "Then Paul answered, 'What are you doing, weeping and breaking my heart? For I am ready not only to be imprisoned but even to die in Jerusalem for the name of the Lord Jesus.'" Jonathan Edwards says that having this kind of love means that we will be more concerned about the state of the church and the souls of men than we are about our own well-being.[5]

Loving God and others with a love that doesn't seek its own means that we should have the spirit of Paul, who spoke in 2 Corinthians 11:28–29 of the daily pressure of concern he had for the churches and for individual Christians who were weak and being led into sin.

Loving God and others with a love that doesn't seek its own means that we will not be mainly concerned about the "me and mine" concerns of life. We are not to be primarily focused on fulfilling our own needs and desires, on solving our own problems, but we will focus

5. Edwards, *Charity and Its Fruits*, 168–70.

mainly on the needs, concerns, and struggles of others and especially on God's concerns.

Concerning this aspect of living and loving in a "not seeking your own" fashion, Paul Tripp writes about how we are so prone to live a "seeking our own" kind of life:

It was one of my worst childhood moments. My brother Tedd had quite the prestigious model car collection, carefully displayed on shelves in his bedroom. He had assembled and painted them all himself and was quite proud of his handiwork. For some reason I don't now remember, Tedd had angered me. He made the mistake of breaking my law, so in a fit of anger, I hit him where I knew it would hurt. I ran into his room, took off my shoe, and smashed his collection. I knew what I was doing, and it felt good. Well, it felt good until my mom discovered what I had done.

This sad moment in the life of one child is a picture of every sinner. We all want to be accepted, served, and validated by people and circumstances around us. When this doesn't happen, our reactions range from mild irritation to violent anger. Married couples criticize one another, not because their spouse has broken God's law, but their own law. Parents get angry with their children, not because they are sinners, but because in their sin they mess up what their parents crave. Neighbors break relationship with each other because they don't like the way they have been treated or the way the neighbor keeps his yard. Businessmen work too hard and too long because they are never able to be satisfied and content. People move in and out of local churches as if they were malls because they didn't feel like they were getting what they needed. Siblings fight over the final bowl of cereal, who gets to hold the remote control, where people are going to sit in the car, and who gets to take his shower first. People at parties jockey to be the center of attention. A man will throw a good marriage away for a few moments of erotic pleasure, and a teenager will sell his soul for the acceptance of his peers.

We constantly think "me and mine," "bigger and better," and "now, not later." We hate it when someone is in the bathroom we want to use, when we're asked to do something we hadn't planned on, or when we are asked to go without. We think getting is a greater blessing than giving. We love it when we are able to prove ourselves right and another wrong. We dream of what our lives would be like if we were in control. We are often blind to opportunities to love, while we are too skilled at remembering an offense against us.

What's so heinous about all this is that when I am content to live in my little kingdom of one, it is God who gets squeezed out. He will not shrink himself to the size of my solitary kingdom. He will be God, and He will not be anything else. I was never meant to shrink the size of my life to a size smaller than the contours of His glory. I was never created to establish my own kingdom, but to give myself to wholehearted, sacrificial devotion to Him.[6]

Paul says that we are prone to live a life in which God and His kingdom get squeezed out. And I would add as a corollary that we also squeeze others out and live a "seeking our own" kind of life that is in direct conflict with the "love seeking not its own" kind of life that God wants us to live. Well, when we're in right relationship with the Lord, we won't want to live that way and we will be making progress in living a life of real service to other people.

Loving God and others with a love that doesn't seek its own means that we will not be primarily concerned about the physical and material aspects of life. The tangible aspects of life—what can be seen and touched and felt and tasted—must not drive our focus; rather, we must be focused mainly on spiritual realities and dimensions of life.

Loving God and others with a love that doesn't seek its own means that we will do what Paul says in Colossians 3:1–3:

If then you have been raised with Christ, seek the things that are above, where Christ is, seated at the right hand of God. Set your minds on things that are above, not on things that are on earth. For you have died, and your life is hidden with Christ in God.

6. Paul Tripp, *A Quest for More* (Greensboro, NC: New Growth, 2007), 87–89.

Recently, while studying a passage in the Old Testament, I came across a marvelous illustration of what it means to have a love that doesn't seek its own. The passage was 2 Samuel 15:14–22. David's son Absalom had gathered together a large number of skilled warriors in an attempt to overthrow his father as king of Israel. David was warned that Absalom had been successful in turning the hearts of many of the Israelites. David took this threat seriously and concluded that if he stayed in Jerusalem, Absalom would win. The city and the people in it would be destroyed. So he said to those who were faithful to him, "Let's get out of here." His faithful servants said they'd do whatever he told them to do.

Among those who were leaving was Ittai the Gittite. David told him that he didn't need to go and advised him to stay because his family would not be in danger in that they had moved to Jerusalem only the day before. When David told him this, Ittai responded, "As the LORD lives, and as my lord the king lives, wherever my lord the king shall be, whether for death or for life, there also will your servant be" (v. 21).

That, my friends, is an example of love that doesn't seek its own. What Ittai was saying, in essence, was, "Whether I live or die, whether it is pleasant or difficult for me to serve you, I will be loyal to you, my king. It doesn't matter what happens to me. I'm here to serve you."

I began chapter 10 with a letter from Doug Nichols that illustrates what real love is. Well, I received another e-mail from him in which he told another story of a love that seeks not its own. It was the story of a little boy whose sister was very sick and needed a blood transfusion from someone who had the same blood type. The problem was that she had a rare type of blood. The doctors investigated this and found that her little brother had the same blood type. So they asked him whether he would be willing to donate blood for his sister. The little boy said, "Sure, I'll be willing to give blood for my sister." They had him lie down and they put the needle in his arm and drew a pint of blood. Sometime after the blood had been drawn, the physician came in and thanked the little boy for being willing to donate the blood. The little boy lay on the bed with quivering lips and then, with tears in his eyes, asked, "Doctor, when am I going to die?" When the boy asked that question, the doctor realized that the naive little boy thought that by giving his blood, he was giving up his life. Quickly he reassured the little boy that he was not going to die. But then he said to the boy, "If you thought that giving the blood would cause you to die, why were you willing to do it?" "Well," said the boy, "I did it because she's my sister and I love her." Now, that's a story to illustrate my point. This little boy demonstrated what it means to have a love that doesn't seek its own.

And that's the kind of love God wants us to have—a love that does nothing out of selfishness or empty conceit, a love that makes us willing to esteem others better than ourselves, a love that causes us to be genuinely interested in the needs, concerns, and interests of others.

## Pursuing the "Not Seeking Your Own" Lifestyle

Certainly Jesus is the primary example of that kind of love. His immense and intense love for His Father motivated Him to perfect obedience, and His love for His people motivated Him to live for them and die and rise again for them and now to reign and rule for them.

While we will never in this world be able to perfectly love in the way Jesus did, we can still, by His grace and by the indwelling presence of His Spirit, do what Paul commands us to do in 1 Corinthians 14:1: "Pursue love." We are to pursue the kind of love he described for us in 1 Corinthians 13. God does not just zap this kind of love into our hearts. We must search for it, train for it, reach for it! It takes effort and sacrifice and prayer for us to be able to lay hold of this precious love.

To rightly understand and obey Paul's command for us to pursue love, we must understand several things. First of all, as we have previously mentioned, we must remember to whom 1 Corinthians was written. It was written to those who, according to 1:2–9, had called upon the name of Jesus Christ, who had acknowledged Jesus as Lord, who had been recipients of the grace of God in Christ Jesus, who had been enriched in Christ Jesus, who were looking forward to the second coming of Christ, who had been called into fellowship with Christ Jesus; it was written to those who were indwelt by the Holy Spirit (6:19). It was written to people who could develop this kind of love because, as believers, all of these things were true of them. So Paul is telling them and us that we can develop this kind of love because of the tremendous privileges and resources that we who have come to Christ have received.

The fact that the verb *pursue* is in the present tense indicates that love is something we must continue to go after. If you stop pursuing this kind of love, it will begin to diminish. There is never a time when we can stop trying to demonstrate this kind of love. This particular pursuit must go on until the time we die.

I was raised on a farm. And on a farm, I learned very quickly that harvesting a good crop doesn't just happen automatically. No, before harvest there is a lot of work that must be done. You have to plow the ground, secure the right kind of seed, plant it correctly, fertilize the ground, cultivate the crop, continue to cultivate, irrigate (if necessary), spray with insecticides, and protect the crop at all costs. If you don't do these things, you won't enjoy a good harvest. So it is with the crop of love. It will require a lot of care, tending, and hard work.

What's involved in pursuing? Pursuing involves understanding the characteristics of this kind of love. It involves constantly reminding ourselves of what this love looks like in practice. To pursue this kind of love means reflecting on the love Jesus had for us. It means putting out the effort to evaluate where we are succeeding and where we are failing, confessing to God our failures, and asking for His forgiveness. It involves depending on the Holy Spirit to enable us to love this way. We can't have this kind of love without Him. We must continue a commitment to practice loving in the 1 Corinthians way and to exercise discipline to actually behave toward others in this way. Pursuing love like this isn't easy. But the rewards are great!

## Motivations for Pursuing Love

That, in summary, is what it means to pursue love. So, in closing, allow me to mention briefly a few reasons why we should pursue love.

One reason is found in 1 Corinthians 12:31 and chapter 13 where Paul says that we should pursue love because it is the excellent way. The excellent way of what? It is the excellent way to make an impact for Christ, excellent because without it all our efforts to impact people for Christ will be worthless.

Another reason we should pursue love is that God has loved us. "And walk in love, as Christ loved us and gave himself up for us, a fragrant offering and sacrifice to God" (Eph. 5:2). We are to pursue love because we have been forgiven, loved, accepted, justified, and adopted as heirs of the kingdom.

A third reason for pursuing this godly kind of love was suggested by the words of Jesus in John 15:16: "You did not choose me, but I chose you and appointed you that you should go and bear fruit and that your fruit should abide." Part of that fruit we are to bear is the striving after and pursuing of love.

Yes, my friends, the way of love is the excellent way—excellent for all these reasons. You and I may not have the gift of tongues, or the gift of prophecy. We may not be able to understand all mysteries and have all knowledge. We may not have mountain-moving faith or the resources to give large amounts of money. We may or may not be called upon to literally die for the cause of Christ. But if our lives drip with the kind of love described by Paul in 1 Corinthians 13, I guarantee that we will be fruitful in impacting others for Christ and fruitful in bringing glory to God.

### Review, Reflection, Application, and Discussion Questions

1. What can we learn from the example of some preachers described in the first chapter of Philippians? What lesson can we learn from the man Diotrephes in 3 John 9–11?

2. What are the two primary ways in which Jesus exemplifies a love that doesn't seek its own?

3. Reflect on the four things that Jonathan Edwards said demonstrated the unselfish manner of Christ's love.

4. How would you answer someone who said, "Of course Jesus could manifest an unselfish love because of who He was, but I'm not Jesus and so I can't and shouldn't be expected to be as unselfish as He was"?

5. Identify and reflect on the different ways Paul manifested a love that did not seek its own.

6. Explain the significance of Paul's statement that he was glad to be poured out as a drink offering for others.

7. Review the list of ways in which this chapter says that a love that seeks not its own will manifest itself. Can you think of any ways that should be added to the list?

8. Again review the list of ways in which a love that seeks not its own will manifest itself. Rate yourself as to how often you manifest such love: always (4); frequently (3); sometimes (2); seldom (1); never (0).

9. What does the inventory you took indicate about the "seeking not your own" quotient in your life? In which items are you strong and in which areas do you need improvement?

10. What practical things can you do to strengthen this aspect of love in your life?

11. And now an important reminder that you will find after every chapter in this book: please remember as you reflect on the love principle presented in this chapter that the purpose of evaluation and application is:

    a. not to discourage or destroy us;

    b. but to motivate us to see our constant need of the cross and how much we owe to Jesus—without Him we'd never make it, but praise God we are not without Him;

    c. and to motivate us to understand our constant daily need of grace—that our salvation never has been and never will be by the works we have done, but always by the work Christ has done and is doing for us; I want our studies in 1 Corinthians

13 to be a reminder that we need to live a cross-centered life; we need the application of the cross work of Jesus every day of our lives; remember there's not a day in our lives when we are so good that we don't need the cross, and there is never a day in our lives when we are so bad that what Christ did on the cross is not sufficient to provide forgiveness for us (Rom. 3:24; 5:20; Eph. 1:7; 1 John 1:7; 2:1–2);

d. and to cause us to understand that we must and can, by His grace, on a daily basis put off from our lives the "unlove" that is displeasing to God and put on in our lives the love that is beautifully described in 1 Corinthians 13 so that we might become more and more like our Savior and more prolific in bearing fruit for Him as others see the grace of God at work in our lives, changing and transforming us (Eph. 4:22–24; 1 Tim. 4:7).

# 12

# Being Irritable Is More than a Trait—It's a Sin!

When you realize that this is the twelfth chapter of this book on the subject of love, you might begin to wonder why I'm spending so much time and effort explaining and applying this passage in 1 Corinthians 13. You may be asking, "What is so important about it?" After all, some people are of the opinion that this passage about love is cut-and-dried.

That is a good question and deserves an answer, so let me take a moment to give you several reasons why I've chosen to focus on this subject. First, I've chosen to spend the time and effort on this subject of love because I believe that while many people know that God has commanded us to love others as we love ourselves—and may even know that it is the second greatest commandment—I still believe it is one of the commands that we misunderstand and disobey as much as or more than any other.

Why do I think that? One reason is that I have spent countless thousands of hours counseling people who profess to be followers of Jesus Christ. And one fact stands out again and again—most of their problems result from an imperfect understanding and application of what it means to love each other. Some can give me a fairly good description of what the words in this passage mean. But repeatedly, I see them failing to apply what they know. It is my belief that people need to be taught these important principles regarding love. That's just what this book attempts to do.

Another reason for spending so much time on this subject is that I believe that most of us are not as loving as we should be. I know this is true of myself, and frankly I know that I'm not the only one who struggles with being the kind of lover of people that God wants me to be. I also know that one of the means that God uses to promote increased obedience on any subject is through the teaching of His Word on that subject.

Yet another reason I'm spending this amount of time and effort on this subject is the incredible emphasis that the Bible places on loving other people. In the Old Testament you'll find the Hebrew words for *love* used over 500 times, and in the New Testament the Greek words for *love* are found more than 370 times! Not all those references are about loving others in this regard. Some are wholly directed toward loving God. But a huge number of them concern the way we love one another. (For a few examples, see Matt. 19:19; 22:37–40; Luke 6:35; 10; John 13:34–35; 15:12; Gal. 5:13–14; 1 John 4:7–8, 20–21—thirty-five references in the book of 1 John alone.)

I've grown to love teaching people about 1 Corinthians 12:31–13:8 because, as Paul mentions in this passage, having a life saturated with real love is a key to having a fruitful life and ministry. It's a key to making an impact for Christ with other people. In fact, Paul says that having a life that drips with love is more important to our ministries than having incredible spiritual gifts and abilities.

For all these reasons, I've chosen to spend a lot of time explaining and applying the truths about love found in 1 Corinthians 13:4–8. As I do, I'm praying that God will use this book to fulfill the purpose for which 2 Timothy 3:16–17 says God gave us the Bible—to teach, to reprove, to correct, to train, and to make us competent for every good work.

Thus far, as we've looked at this passage, we've discussed seven of the characteristics of the kind of love that is pleasing to God and will make us a powerful influence for Christ in the lives of others. Just to recap, we've discovered that this kind of real love is long-suffering, is kind, is not jealous or envious, does not brag or boast, is not arrogant or proud, does not act unbecomingly, and does not seek its own.

In the next several chapters I want to move on to discuss several other characteristics of the kind of love that will cause us to have a powerful impact on others for Christ. Then I will conclude this book by making some practical suggestions about how to develop more of this kind of love.

## The Eighth Characteristic of Real Love

The eighth characteristic of real love as described in verse 5 of our passage is this: "Love is not provoked" (NASB). In other translations, it says that love is not irritable. Let's consider this aspect of love from three different perspectives:

1. The actual meaning of the word *provoked* or *irritated*
2. What the Old Testament says about being provoked or irritated
3. New Testament passages that will help us to understand what Paul means by being provoked or irritated

## Defining the Word

Let's define the actual meaning of the word Paul uses to describe what love *isn't*. The word *provoked* is a translation of the Greek word *paraxynō* from which we get the English word *paroxysm*. As defined in the dictionary, it can mean literally to have a fit of some kind, some kind of attack, a convulsion in which a person loses control of himself.

Perhaps you've heard it said of someone that he "flew off the handle." That phrase literally refers to an axe or a hammer that is attached to a handle and that, when being used, flies off the handle! And of course, when that happens, the person wielding the tool loses control of the axe or hammer. When that happens, someone may get seriously hurt.

Well, in a similar fashion, when a person flies off the handle in a trying situation, he is also prone to lose control of his emotions or even his actions, and someone may just as easily get hurt—physically or emotionally, or both! To put it another way, love doesn't fly off the handle; love doesn't have a fit.

## What Does the Old Testament Have to Say about Being Provoked or Irritated?

The Old Testament is replete with statements of what it means to be provoked and also has numerous illustrations of the kind of damage that can happen when someone has paroxysms. Although examples of this behavior can be found throughout the Old Testament, for the sake of time and efficiency I will limit myself to the book of Proverbs for this study.

Proverbs 12:16 says, "The vexation of a fool is known at once, but the prudent ignores an insult." The word *vexation* is characteristic of a person who gets excited in a bad way, a person who experiences the emotion of severe anger, a person who is very troubled and distressed. (This word is also used of Ahab in 1 Kings 21:4 when Naboth refused to give him what he wanted. It affected Ahab's emotions, his attitude, and even his behavior and judgment. It is also used in Proverbs 21:19 to describe a wife who is contentious. It would be better to live out in the desert where you don't have water or any comforts of life than to share a home with a contentious person.)

Proverbs 12:16 says that the fool's vexation is known "at once." This means that the person is quickly and easily upset, annoyed, or irritated—that he gets angry very quickly. He is easily offended, and it doesn't take much to set him off. Some would say that this kind of person has a short fuse. He is picky. Instead of being slow to anger, this person is quick to anger!

The text also says that his vexation "is known" at once. Basically, this indicates that when this person is annoyed or angry, he's quite obvious about his annoyance. He leaves no room for speculation. In fact, I take it that everyone knows he is upset! How do they know it? Perhaps they know it because of the expression on his face, his tone of voice, or his behavior. We're not told exactly how they know. But I believe we've all been around quick-tempered people enough to be able to tell when someone has lost control, or become upset and angry.

Note one more thing about this text. It calls this man a "fool." When this person becomes vexed and displays that vexation, he is being foolish. He makes a fool out of himself and he does foolish things. When that happens, not only is the person being foolish, but according to Paul in 1 Corinthians 13:5, he is also being unloving. He is not displaying the kind of godly love we are called to, because the Bible clearly says that love is not irritable or easily provoked. I don't know about you, but I find myself quite embarrassed for the one who behaves in this fashion.

Let's turn to Proverbs 29 and note several other examples of what it means to have a paroxysm—and the harm it causes. Proverbs 29:9 says, "If a wise man has an argument with a fool, the fool only rages and laughs, and there is no quiet." When you're around this kind of person, you are never sure when the other shoe will drop. You always feel a bit on edge as you wait for the explosion to happen. It's hard to relax in that environment. It's hard to be comfortable talking to such a person. He seems to be either criticizing you or making fun of you when you try to have a serious conversation.

A couple of verses later we read, "A fool gives full vent to his spirit, but a wise man quietly holds it back" (v. 11). The word translated "spirit" here refers to temper. A wise man holds his temper back, or quiets it—brings it under control. Verse 20 says, "Do you see a man who is hasty in his words?" These words describe what often happens when a person is easily annoyed. He is hasty with his words. Harmful, heated, demeaning, rash, reckless, destructive words come out of his mouth very quickly—words for which he most likely will have to ask for forgiveness in the near future. These are the kinds of words that ruin relationships. They ruin people. They ruin any positive impact that a person may have on another. These are the kinds of words that are hard to forget—or to forgive.

This text gives us a contrast. It indicates that it is a foolish thing to be a person who loses his temper, but it also says that it is a wise thing to be a person who controls his emotions and his words.

A fellow counselor has said that people often accuse him of wanting them to be robots or clones when he talks to them about controlling their harmful emotions. He tells them, "I'm not saying that you shouldn't feel emotion. Emotions are fine things—God-given parts of our individual makeup. But they're good only if we are in control of them and not the other way around."

Paul, of course, would agree with the writer of Proverbs that it is a foolish thing to lose your temper, to be easily, quickly, and openly provoked, but he would add to that by saying that not only it is a foolish thing to lose your temper, it is also an *unloving* thing to lose your temper. Along with that, Paul would probably say that it is not only a wise thing to control your temper and your words, but also a loving thing to do so, because love is not irritable, nasty, abusive, or easily provoked.

## Additional Passages That Teach the "Love Is Not Provoked" Concept of Love

Let's consider one primary passage and several secondary ones that will help us gain an understanding of what Paul meant when he said that real love isn't easily provoked. The primary passage is found in Titus 3:1–2:

> Remind them to be submissive to rulers and authorities, to be obedient, to be ready for every good work, to speak evil of no one, to avoid quarreling, to be gentle, and to show perfect courtesy toward all people.

In this passage, Paul uses four descriptive phrases about how Christians should function. These descriptions will help to paint an accurate picture of what it means to have a love that is not provoked.

The very first phrase describes what we often do when we are provoked at someone. We tend to speak evil of that person. If we are not self-controlled, it is our tendency to malign or revile the targets of our anger. The word *malign* is a translation of the Greek word *blasphēmeō*—to slander, revile, curse, to treat someone with contempt, or to speak evil of him or her. This word is also used in Luke 22:63–65 regarding what happened to Jesus shortly before His crucifixion. Jesus was mocked, blindfolded, beaten, and taunted. The guards teased Him, saying, "Prophesy! Who is it that struck you?" Yet Jesus did not revile them or malign them in return. Instead, He displayed a love that was not easily provoked.

The same word is also used in Matthew 27:39 to describe what certain people did to Jesus while He was on the cross. They hurled abuse at Him, wagged their heads, mocked Him, made fun of Him, taunted Him, misrepresented Him, twisted His words. They ridiculed Him, saying, "You who would destroy the temple and rebuild it in three days, save yourself! If you are the Son of God, come down from the cross." Yet Jesus didn't allow Himself to become provoked. He didn't have a fit or fly off the handle. He didn't become annoyed or yell back at them. Instead, Jesus displayed a love that was not provoked.

The passage in Titus says to speak evil of no one. That includes even those with whom you disagree most. It includes even those who are the worst of sinners. It includes those who will not do things the way you think they should be done. Love doesn't malign people.

As we look at the second phrase in the Titus passage, we find another aspect of what it means to have a love that is not provoked in the admonition to "avoid quarreling." In other words, we are not to be contentious toward others. People who are easily provoked often (usually) become argumentative, quarrelsome, or belligerent. In Paul's own words in 1 Timothy 3, they have a tendency to become pugnacious or a brawler. Their attacks on others are sometimes verbal and sometimes even physical!

However, a person who has real love will seek to be peaceful—not quarreling with anyone! This person will put Romans 12:18 into practice: "If possible, so far as it depends on you, live peaceably with all." Even though the context indicates that people are treating them like an enemy, people who have real love will do what Romans 14:19 says we should do: "So then let us pursue what makes for peace and for mutual upbuilding." We are to pursue peace with all men even though people don't do things the way we think they should be done. Let's face it, people won't always agree with us!

Being uncontentious means that the person who is practicing real love will have a desire to be a peacemaker and that his actions will correspond to that desire. Still further, being uncontentious means that the person who is practicing real love will not go around looking for a fight, will not be on the defensive or constantly finding fault. Instead he will be willing to go the extra mile, to turn the other cheek, to do anything short of abandoning the truth to make peace with all men. That's part of having a love that is not easily provoked.

That brings us to the third descriptive statement in Titus 3:2 that will help crystallize Paul's meaning in our 1 Corinthians passage. The Titus text says that our lives should be characterized by gentleness.

In a book on the fruit of the Spirit, George Bethune wrote, "Perhaps no grace is less prayed for, or less cultivated than gentleness. Indeed it is considered rather as belonging to natural disposition or external manners, than as a Christian virtue; and seldom do we reflect that not to be gentle is sin."[1] I believe he is right. I've been a Christian for more than five decades, and during that time I've been in a lot of prayer meetings. I've heard Christians pray for a lot of things—self-control, peace, victory, joy—but I can't remember ever hearing anyone pray for gentleness. In fact, I can't remember many people even acknowledging that they want it or that they don't have it!

Now, if Bethune and I are right in our assessment of this lack of prayer for and concern about gentleness, there are a number of reasons why that is extremely unfortunate:

- Gentleness is lacking in many of our lives.
- Numerous passages exhort Christians to be gentle or to put on gentleness (Gal. 6:1; Eph. 4:1–2; Col. 3:12; 1 Tim. 6:11; 2 Tim. 2:24–25).

1. George Bethune, *The Fruit of the Spirit* (Swengel, PA: Reiner, 1839), 100.

- Gentleness was found in the life of Jesus, and as Christians we are called to be like Jesus. We are to be gentle because He was gentle (Isa. 40:11; Matt. 12:18–20; 2 Cor. 10:1).
- Paul says in 1 Corinthians 13 that the kind of real love that will make us powerful influences for Christ is characterized by gentleness, which is the opposite of being provoked.

What is this gentleness that is the opposite of being easily provoked? What does it look like? The word Paul uses in Titus 3:2 is also found in Philippians 4:5 where it is translated, "Let your *reasonableness* [gentleness, forbearance] be known to everyone." Paul uses it in 1 Thessalonians 2:7 to describe the way a loving mother cares for her children. In 1 Timothy 3:3 the word is used in contrast with someone who is argumentative, nasty, and harsh in the way he deals with people.

Colossians 3:12 uses the word in association with compassion, kindness, and humility. The word was sometimes used to describe a moderate or gentle wind in contrast with a violent wind, and it is a word that was often used to describe a tame animal in contrast to a wild animal. The word is found in Paul's instructions about how we should deal with argumentative and resistant people—"the Lord's servant must not be quarrelsome . . . correcting his opponents with gentleness" (2 Tim. 2:24–25).

And of course, here in our 1 Corinthians 13 passage, it is important to note that having a love that is not easily provoked follows the statement that love doesn't seek its own, doesn't behave unbecomingly, is not arrogant, does not brag, is not envious, is kind and long-suffering. A person who is not provoked is a gentle person who is a submissive person, an unselfish person—a person who does not demand his or her own rights, and is not authoritarian or dictatorial. Possessing the qualities previously mentioned in 1 Corinthians 13:4–5 is foundational for being a person who is gentle and able to handle opposition and disagreement without being provoked. With those kinds of qualities in our lives, how could it be otherwise? Without them in our lives, it naturally follows that we will be people who are easily and frequently provoked or irritated.

We're still not finished with the insights that Titus 3:2 can give us about what it means to not be provoked. The last phrase describes the flip side of being provoked—it says that we are to be people who show perfect courtesy toward all people. A person who is provoked does the very opposite of that! That person is not a considerate person. He will certainly not show every consideration for all men.

Note carefully what Paul says in this Titus passage. He says that we should show perfect courtesy to all people—not just a little, but *perfect* courtesy. We are to show every consideration to others—even those who mistreat us.

On one occasion the missionary Hudson Taylor was waiting to get on a boat to take him across a river. While he was standing there, a wealthy man came up and pushed Taylor down into the mud. The man didn't recognize the person he had pushed because Taylor was dressed in the clothing of a peasant. He'd even adopted the hairstyle of the people to whom he came to minister. Someone told the man who he was, and the man apologized. The captain of the boat saw all of this and said that he would not allow the man on the boat because of what he had done. Taylor appealed to the boat captain to let him on the boat, and because of his appeal the captain did so. As they crossed the river, Taylor had an opportunity to share the gospel with the man. In doing this Taylor was showing consideration and perfect courtesy to this person.

In his comment on what Paul means here, William Hendriksen rightly said that Paul was encouraging Titus "to show all mildness (consideration) to all people, even to the people on the island of Crete, who were, as one of the Cretans had said, liars, evil brutes and lazy gluttons." This, says Hendriksen, "was an assignment impossible of fulfillment apart from God's special grace."[2] Paul wasn't encouraging Titus to show all consideration because of his personality or in his own strength, but because of God's special grace or favor or help.

Having said that, Hendriksen goes on to say that the reason why showing consideration to all men can and must be done is found in what Paul goes on to say in Titus 3:3–8. Verse 3 begins with the word *for* to indicate the reason we cannot and should not malign anyone, the

2. William Hendriksen, *The Pastoral Epistles* (Grand Rapids: Baker, 1957), 387.

reason we cannot and should not be contentious, the reason we can and should be gentle, the reason we can and should show consideration to all men regardless of how they treat us: that reason is our understanding of what we were before God saved us. In other words, Paul is asking, "How can we, who are so unworthy, so undeserving of God's goodness and mercy, not be moved to show consideration to others?" God has shown mercy to us even though we were wholly undeserving; we must therefore treat others in the same way God has treated us.

Titus 3:4–8 mentions some other reasons why we can and must avoid maligning people, why we can be uncontentious, gentle, and considerate toward all men. That is because of what God has done and is doing for us and in us. We can and should treat all men this way because:

- God saved us;
- He delivered us from our slavery to sin;
- He justified us;
- He washed us;
- He regenerated us;
- He renewed us;
- He gave us the Holy Spirit, who works and dwells in us.

The specific words Paul uses in the book of Titus to describe how Christians should relate to other people are a bit different from the ones he uses in 1 Corinthians 13:5, but the meaning is the same. In 1 Corinthians 13:5 Paul tells us we should have a love for people that is devoid of annoyance and irritability, and in Titus 3:2 he shows us what that kind of love will look like in actual practice. In both these passages, Paul tells us how to really love people. And in both these passages, he would have us know that God doesn't expect us to live and love this way because we are so great, so strong, so naturally loving, and so full of such incredible personal resources. Rather, he would have us know and believe that we can and should love in this way because of what God has done for us and is doing in us. *He* is the reason we can love in this way. It is by *His* strength that this can be accomplished!

## In Conclusion

I've heard some people who are quickly, easily, and openly provoked either justify or excuse their irritability and annoyance or minimize the seriousness of their irritability. How do they rationalize their bad behavior?

1. They justify it by blaming it on their circumstances or on other people.
2. They excuse or minimize it by saying that they get over it quickly.
3. They defend themselves by saying, "I just can't help it. That's just the way I am."
4. They minimize the seriousness of what they've done by saying, "What do you expect? That's the way my parents were!" In essence, the apple doesn't fall far from the tree. "It was their fault."
5. They justify it by saying that other people ought to know that they don't really mean it when they react badly, that they really do respect them and love them in spite of their anger and irritability. Often I've heard, "Other people ought to remember all the good things I do and say and just ignore this aspect of my behavior. Why do they focus only on the bad stuff?"
6. They excuse it by heaping insults upon themselves: "I'm just weak! I'm no good! Others may be able to be uncontentious, gentle, considerate, meek, and submissive, but I just can't be those things."

According to God's Word, being irritable or easily annoyed is not just a harmless weakness. It is a sin! We know that because the Bible again and again condemns irritability as one of the most destructive elements in human nature.

Concerning the justifications that people give for their irritability, John MacArthur writes:

We get angry when another person gains a privilege or recognition we want for ourselves, because it is our "right." But to put our rights before our duty and before loving concern for others comes from self-centeredness and lovelessness. . . . Love considers nothing its right and everything its obligation.

Telling our wives or husbands we love them is not convincing if we continually get upset and angry at what they say and do. Telling our children that we love them is not convincing if we often yell at them for doing things that irritate us and interfere with our own plans. It does no good to protest, "I lose my temper a lot, but it's all over in a short time." So is a nuclear bomb. A great deal of damage can be done in a very short time. Temper is always destructive, and even small temper "bombs" can leave much hurt and damage. . . . Lovelessness is the cause of temper, and love is the only cure.[3]

Love, says the inspired apostle, is not provoked (period, full stop). The text doesn't say, "Love is not provoked unless others don't agree with us, unless our parents set a bad example, unless we were born with a certain kind of personality, unless we don't feel well." No, there is absolutely no wiggle room in this statement by the Word of God. It is simply and categorically, "Love is not provoked." Until you and I begin to look on our irritability, annoyance, impatience, and nastiness with people as a sin for which we are responsible, we will never overcome it. We will never change.

So if you are a believer—if you have truly been saved, if you have been justified, if you have been regenerated, if you have been washed—the Holy Spirit indwells you and you do, therefore, have resources for change. Let me encourage you to stop excusing and minimizing these sins. Accept responsibility! Every time you become irritable, acknowledge it as sin and ask God to forgive you. Ask Him to help you avail yourself of the resources you have in Christ. Study the Word and apply His Word to your life. Read the right kind of literature. Begin to discipline yourself for godliness by practicing these godly principles (1 Tim. 4:7). You *can* change—but only through His power and not your own.

3. John MacArthur, *1 Corinthians* (Chicago: Moody, 1984), 346.

And of course, if you are not a believer, your greatest need is to come to Christ. Acknowledge your sin and your weakness, your inability to change. Surrender your life to Him and acknowledge Him as your Lord. I urge you to seek counsel from believers who can help you learn how to avail yourself of the resources that can be yours in Christ.

Does this mean that you will never fail—that you will never again be tempted to be exasperated and provoked? No, but it does mean that you can grow. It gives us hope that we actually *can* become more pleasant, more peaceful, calmer, gentler, meeker, and more considerate. Remember 1 Timothy 4:7: "Have nothing to do with irreverent, silly myths. Rather train yourself for godliness." As we grow in this kind of love, we will become more fruitful in making an impact for Christ in the lives of others.

## Review, Reflection, Application, and Discussion Questions

1. Why is it so important for us to spend time studying 1 Corinthians 13?

2. Including the focus of this chapter, what are the eight characteristics of love that we have studied thus far in the book?

3. What is a paroxysm?

4. What can we learn about what it means to be provoked from Proverbs 12:16? Explain the various words used in this verse that help us to understand what being provoked means.

5. What phrases in Titus 3:2 help us to understand what happens when someone is provoked? Identify the four key phrases. Explain the meaning of each of these terms. How does this verse help us to understand how we tend to respond when we are provoked or irritated?

6. Explain the quality of gentleness and describe what it looks like in practice.

7. What reasons does Titus 3:4–8 give that make being considerate to all men a necessity and a possibility for Christians?

8. How do people sometimes excuse or justify their irritability and annoyance? Can you think of ways not mentioned in this book that people do this? Have you been guilty of trying to justify your own bad behavior?

9. How often were you provoked in the last week? How often have you been provoked or irritated today?

10. How would you rate yourself in terms of your gentleness or irritability quotient? "I am never irritated or annoyed" (3); "I am seldom irritated or annoyed" (not more than once every two weeks) (2); "I am occasionally irritated or provoked" (probably once every week or every couple of days) (1); "I am very easily and frequently irritated or provoked" (probably at least once every day) (0). Check the accuracy of your rating by having other family members or friends rate you on this irritability inventory.

11. What were the circumstances in which you became irritated in the last week? Was it in connection with people? What people? Was it in connection with situations or things that were or were not happening?

12. How do you view your irritability when it occurs? Serious or no big deal?

13. What is your typical response when you become irritated?

14. What can you do to strengthen your gentleness quotient and reduce your irritability quotient?

15. And now my usual reminder: Please remember as you reflect on the love principle presented in this chapter that the purpose of evaluation and application is:

   a. not to discourage or destroy us;

   b. but to motivate us to see our constant need of the cross and how much we owe to Jesus—without Him we'd never make it, but praise God we are not without Him;

c. and to motivate us to understand our constant daily need of grace—that our salvation never has been and never will be by the works we have done, but always by the work Christ has done and is doing for us; I want our studies in 1 Corinthians 13 to be a reminder that we need to live a cross-centered life; we need the application of the cross work of Jesus every day of our lives; remember there's not a day in our lives when we are so good that we don't need the cross, and there is never a day in our lives when we are so bad so that what Christ did on the cross is not sufficient to provide forgiveness for us (Rom. 3:24; 5:20; Eph. 1:7; 1 John 1:7; 2:1–2);

d. and to cause us to understand that we must and can, by His grace, put off from our lives the "unlove" that is displeasing to God and put on in our lives the love that is beautifully described in 1 Corinthians 13 and become more and more like our Savior and become more prolific in bearing fruit for Him as others see the grace of God at work in our lives, changing and transforming us (Eph. 4:22–24; 1 Tim. 4:7).

# 13

## LOVERS DON'T KEEP RECORDS

On one occasion, two older people were sitting in their living room one morning when the wife asked her husband if he would like to have some breakfast. He said, "Yes, I would really like to have some eggs and some toast." She said, "Fine, I'll get it for you." As she was going to the kitchen, he said, "Now, don't forget the toast!" She went to the kitchen to fix his breakfast. A few minutes later she returned with a bowl of ice cream. As she handed him the bowl of ice cream, he said, "I knew you'd forget to put the cherry on the top!"

Both of those older people were a bit forgetful, and so are we about many things. Perhaps you have noticed that there are certain subjects or themes to which the Bible returns again and again. It doesn't seem to matter whether you're reading in the Old Testament or New Testament, the Gospels or the Epistles, you will frequently come across teaching on the same topics. Even in this book, you've read some truths over and over. Perhaps you've wondered why God repeats Himself so much in the Bible, or wondered why I seem to repeat myself so much. I believe God does this:

- To emphasize how important certain subjects are. If you know someone who is constantly talking about the same subject again and again, you've found someone who thinks that subject is very important. This, I believe, is one way God highlights the importance of these subjects.

- To counteract our tendency to forget things. With us it's true that "out of sight is out of mind." God knows we are prone to remember things we ought to forget and forget things we ought to remember. So He gives us these truths with repetition.

One of the themes God repeats again and again throughout the Bible is that we ought to love one another. We find the command to love one another mentioned many times in the Bible. God continually reminds us about this command because it is so terribly important. Christians are to be known by their love. He also does this because we are so prone to forget it altogether or forget its importance.

In His Word God not only tells us that we should love one another—He tells us how we should love one another:

1. "And a second [commandment] is like it: You shall love your neighbor *as* yourself" (Matt. 22:39).
2. "A new commandment I give to you, that you love one another: *just as* I have loved you, you also are to love one another" (John 13:34).
3. "For this is the message which you have heard from the beginning, that we should love one another; *not as Cain, who was of the evil one and slew his brother*" (1 John 3:11–12 NASB).
4. "We know love by this, that He laid down His life for us; and we *ought to lay down our lives* for the brethren. But whoever has the world's goods, and sees his brother in need and closes his heart against him, how does the love of God abide in him? Little children, *let us not love [merely] with word or tongue, but in deed and truth*" (1 John 3:16–18 NASB).
5. See the instructions in 1 Corinthians 13:1–8.

In 1 Corinthians 13:1–8 Paul gives us extended teaching on the importance or preeminence of love and also the ingredients or characteristics of the kind of love that will cause us to have an impact on other people. Thus far, we've examined eight characteristics of the kind of love that will please God and cause us to make an impact on others for Christ.

Let's now turn our attention to the ninth characteristic of this kind of impacting love described in the last phrase of verse 5: "Love does not keep a record of wrongs suffered."

## Let's Define the Words

This phrase is variously translated: in the KJV, love "thinketh no evil"; in the NASB, love "does not take into account a wrong suffered"; in the NIV, love "keeps no record of wrongs."

To help us get our arms around what Paul is saying about real love in this phrase, we need to explore the meaning of the two most important Greek words used here. One of the words is a noun and the other is a verb.

In the NASB translation of this phrase, Paul speaks of "a wrong suffered." The actual Greek word, *kakos*, translated "wrong," may have two different meanings. Sometimes the word is used in reference to what is morally, ethically, and/or openly sinful. For instance, Mark 7:21–23 says:

> For from within, out of the heart of man, come evil thoughts, sexual immorality, theft, murder, adultery, coveting, wickedness, deceit, sensuality, envy, slander, pride, foolishness. All these evil things come from within, and they defile a person.

*Kakos* is here translated "evil." We see the word translated similarly in another passage. First Timothy 6:10 says, "For the love of money is a root of all kinds of evil [meaning in context moral evil or sin]. It is through this craving that some have wandered away from the faith and pierced themselves with many pangs."

In other passages the related word *kakia* is translated "malice." *Malice* generally means "a fixed and unreasonable desire to harm and hurt others, to cause pain and see someone suffer." We see it translated thus in Ephesians 4:31 ("Let all bitterness and wrath and anger and clamor and slander be put away from you, along with all malice") and Titus 3:3 ("For we ourselves were once foolish, disobedient, led astray, slaves to various passions and pleasures, passing our days in malice and envy, hated by others and hating one another").

However, there are instances where this word is used in reference to that which is injurious, painful, unpleasant, distressing, grievous, or troublesome, but not necessarily sinful. In Luke 16:22–25 we read about the rich man who dies and being in torment in hell lifts his eyes and cries out for mercy. He asks Abraham to send Lazarus to minister to him with a drop of water for his parched tongue. Abraham tells the rich man to remember that during his life he had received many good things while Lazarus had received the bad things. The rich man had received "good things" in terms of being pleasurable or comfortable or enjoyable, and Lazarus had received "bad things" in terms of being unpleasant or painful or distressing. Matthew 6:34 tells us not to worry about tomorrow because each day has enough trouble (*kakia*, which in this context means hard, difficult, or distressing experiences such as not having enough food or clothing) of its own. In Acts 16:28 Paul told the Philippian jailer, "Do yourself no harm" (*kakos*, which in the context suggests that the man was about to hurt himself, probably committing suicide). In each of these passages the word translated "wrong" (*kakos*) in 1 Corinthians 13:5 is found, but translated as "bad things," "trouble," or "harm."

So when Paul speaks of someone doing wrong to you, he may refer to those times when someone does something to you that is morally wrong (like those times when people lie about you or to you, or when people actually cheat you or cheat on you, or when people attack you, or when they may abuse you, or when they steal from you, or when people may not keep promises they made to you, or when they misuse your property, or are rude and discourteous to you, or when they make life difficult for you, or when people explode at you, or yell at you, or when they manipulate or demean you). Then again, he may be referring to someone doing something to you that is hurtful or painful or troublesome, but not necessarily sinful. He may be referring to times when people ignore you, or may not show you the appreciation or praise you would like to receive, or when people do not cooperate with you in some effort, or when they disagree with you, or when they don't support you, or when people may actually rebuke or reprove you. Those instances may cause you disappointment and distress, but they may not be necessarily sinful.

So in our passage, Paul may refer to being resentful about something that is actually sinful behavior or something that is not necessarily a sinful act. In other words, he might be referring to a behavior or treatment that is not necessarily a violation of Scripture. This type of behavior is not necessarily sinful as much as thoughtless or inadvertently harmful or injurious.

The second word that we must define, if we are to understand the aspect of love that Paul is talking about in this phrase, is the Greek verb *logizomai*. Basically, this word means "to keep a list or record or to calculate." This was a word used to describe what a bookkeeper or an accountant would do.

What do accountants do? Part of what an accountant does is work with numbers and figures, keeping a list or record of all the income or expenses of a business. An accountant keeps a record of what is spent—purchases, expenditures, charges—and what others owe. He makes records involving accounts receivable and accounts payable. He balances checkbooks. He figures taxes and performs many other tasks to help manage a business or personal account.

Of *logizomai* Simon Kistemaker writes, "Here is a verbal portrait of a bookkeeper who flips the pages of his ledger to reveal what has been received and spent. He is able to give an exact account and provide an itemized list. Some people are keeping a similar list of wrongs that they have experienced. But love is extremely forgetful when it comes to remembering injury and injustice. When wrongs have been forgiven, they ought to be forgotten and never mentioned again."[1]

John MacArthur also describes the word *logizomai*: "[*Logizomai*] is a bookkeeping term that means to calculate or reckon, as when figuring an entry in a ledger. The purpose of the entry is to make a permanent

1. Simon Kistemaker, *1 Corinthians* (Grand Rapids: Baker, 1993), 460–61.

record that can be consulted when needed. In business that practice is necessary, but in personal matters it is not only unnecessary but also harmful. Keeping track of things done against us is a sure way to unhappiness—our own and those on whom we keep records."[2]

Alexander Strauch says that a loving person "does not keep a private file of grievances that can be consulted and nursed whenever there is a possibility of a new slight."[3]

## Some Specifics about the Kind of Records That Love Won't Keep

So what Paul is saying is that when it comes to the way you respond to the sinful ways people may treat you or simply let you down, not treating you in the way you'd like to be treated, you must not allow yourself to be an accountant or bookkeeper. Don't keep a tally. Being an accountant for the right kind of businesses is an honorable job, but there is a kind of accounting that a loving person must not do.

For example, I've heard counselor Jay Adams tell of a couple who came to him because their marriage was falling apart. The wife had been advised to come because she had developed an ulcer that had no apparent physical cause. When Jay asked the woman what was bothering her, she plopped a notebook down on the desk with page after page filled with things that her husband had done wrong for the last thirteen years. That woman had done the very thing that God says we shouldn't do—she had literally kept a detailed record of the real or imagined wrongs she had suffered, and it was ruining her health, her disposition, her marriage, her relationship with the Lord, and her usefulness in life.

Having a love that doesn't keep a record of the wrongs means that we won't do what one of my own counselees did when her husband failed to do something she wanted him to do. When she and her husband came for counseling, what he had done was as fresh in her mind as if he had done it on the same day she came for counseling. In this case,

2. John MacArthur, *1 Corinthians* (Chicago: Moody, 1984), 347.
3. Alexander Strauch, *Leading with Love* (Littleton, CO: Lewis and Roth, 2006), 72.

what he had done was really something that he shouldn't have done. He had really wronged her, but it had happened long ago when she was having a baby. Apparently he took her to the hospital and, in spite of the fact that she asked him to stay while she had the baby, he went home because their dog was about to have puppies. When he did that, the message she got was that the dog and puppies were more important to him than she and their baby were. At the time she came for counseling, the child was now a teenager, but she was still brooding over what her husband had done. She was so hurt by this that she began to keep a record of everything that he did or didn't do that seemed to say she wasn't important to him.

Consider another set of counselees. When this couple came for counseling, their home had become a war zone. The wife was extremely unhappy with their marriage and bitter at her husband. And he was experiencing the same emotions toward his wife. When asked what had brought them to this point, the woman began by telling me how badly her husband treated her. She started by telling of a time when she was having an operation and her husband was unwilling to take off work to be at the hospital during her surgery. To her that meant that his work was more important to him than she was. When that happened, she confronted him about what he had done. After spilling her heart to him, he still refused to acknowledge that he had done anything thoughtless or wrong and to ask for forgiveness. Instead he defended himself and made excuses. He blamed her by telling her that she shouldn't be so sensitive, and then accused her of being unreasonable and impossible to please. After that she began to notice many other things that he did or didn't do that she didn't like. From that moment on, she began to keep a mental record of the wrongs she was suffering. She began to notice every little nitpicking thing her husband did that she didn't like. She became a bookkeeper storing up items in her memory bank and meditating on them. The result of that kind of behavior was that her affectionate feelings toward him were completely destroyed, and the flames of bitterness and resentment were increased. Her attitude and actions toward him were poisoned. She had begun to punish him by words and actions. She became more critical of him and avoided him.

She disagreed with him more frequently and voiced her disagreement more freely. She became stubborn and resistant, and almost everything in their relationship was negatively affected. While that was going on with the wife, the husband was practicing bookkeeping as well. Much to his discredit, the husband began to respond in kind.

That's the way some people (even those in our churches) respond to wrongs that they have suffered. When people wrong them, some people do exactly:

- what 1 Corinthians 13:5 says that they shouldn't do when someone wrongs them;
- what Romans 12:17 says that they shouldn't do—they should never pay back evil with evil;
- what Romans 12:19 says that they shouldn't do—they should never take their own revenge;
- what Ephesians 4:26 says that they shouldn't do—they should never let the sun go down on their anger;
- what Ephesians 4:31 says that they shouldn't do—they should not hold on to their malice instead of letting it go;
- what Psalm 37:1 says that they shouldn't do—they should not fret because of evildoers or be envious of wrongdoers.

That's what it means to have a love that is not resentful or does not take into account or keep a record of wrongs that have been suffered. It means that we will not keep a record, that we won't fret about it, that we won't rehearse the wrongs committed against us, that we won't go around telling others about these wrongs or try to gain sympathy by being a victim.

## Answering Some Key Questions

Having defined the words, we now look at the application of the phrase. I'll do that by asking three questions.

First, *what happens when a person fails to love in this way?* "Husbands, love your wives, and do not be harsh with them" (Col. 3:19). If you fail to love in this way, you may be harsh with your wife. That kind of treatment is opposite to the right kind of love. Hebrews 12:15 says, "See to it that no one fails to obtain the grace of God; that no 'root of bitterness' springs up and causes trouble, and by it many become defiled." So if you fail to love in this way, the root of bitterness may spring up in your life and cause trouble.

What exactly is bitterness? The word literally means "to cut or prick." In the Bible, the word is sometimes associated with grapes or water that is poisonous (Deut. 32:32). Bitterness is said to bring intense grief or misery, sometimes with weeping or mourning. Bitterness is sometimes contrasted with that which is sweet, pleasant, or desirable.

Second, *how does bitterness, which is the inevitable result of keeping a record of wrongs suffered, manifest itself?* The following talking points are drawn from my own counseling experience with bitter people as well as from a helpful booklet on bitterness by Lou Priolo. As I mention each of them, ask yourself, "Is this true of me?"

- Bitterness not only causes conflicts but also causes an inability to resolve those conflicts.
- Bitterness may manifest itself in acts of vengeance, as it did with Herodias in Mark 6.
- Bitterness may manifest itself in withdrawal or avoidance.
- Bitterness may manifest itself in outbursts of anger.
- Bitterness may manifest itself in biting sarcasm or snide remarks.
- Bitterness may manifest itself in condescending communication.
- Bitterness may manifest itself in faultfinding and censoriousness over even small offenses.
- Bitterness may manifest itself in suspicion and mistrust.
- Bitterness may manifest itself in intolerance and a lack of forbearance.
- Bitterness may manifest itself in impatience.
- Bitterness may manifest itself in disrespect, as was true in all the previously mentioned counseling cases.

- Bitterness may manifest itself in rebellion toward, or abuse or misuse of, authority.
- Bitterness may manifest itself in depression. It can quickly steal your joy.
- Bitterness may manifest itself in a lack of friends and close associates; people avoid you or don't want to be with you.
- Bitterness may manifest itself in a lack of assurance of salvation or at least a lack of a sense of the presence of God or closeness to God.
- Bitterness may manifest itself in a sense of guilt and shame, as in Matthew 6:14–15.
- Bitterness may manifest itself in a lack of fruitfulness in your Christian life and ministry to others.

Third, *how can bitterness be prevented and defeated?* The only reliable source for the answers to this question is the Bible, the holy Word of God.

- First and foremost, to prevent and defeat bitterness you must make sure you are truly a Christian (1 Cor. 1:2, 4–5, 8–9; 3:23; 6:19–20; 13:5).
- Next, it must be our continual prayer that God would increase our ability to love in this way and to eradicate any trace of bitterness in our hearts (Rom. 5:5; Gal. 5:22–23; Eph. 3:16–18; Phil. 1:9; 1 Thess. 3:11–12).
- We must pursue love (Matt. 22:36–40; John 13:34–35; 1 Cor. 14:1).
- We must constantly remember how gracious and patient God has been and is being with us. It is hard to be bitter toward others when we consider how merciful He has been with us (Ps. 130:5; Matt. 18:21–35; Rom. 7:24; 1 Tim. 1:15; 1 John 1:9).
- It is so important to remember that there is never a day in our lives when we are so good that we don't need God's grace, and never a day in our lives when we are so bad that we are beyond the reach of God's grace.

- We must remember the serious implications and consequences of not practicing 1 Corinthians 13:5. Failure to love in this way will inevitably lead to bitterness, which opens us to all the ugly manifestations we previously mentioned (Ps. 37:8; Matt. 6:14–15; 18:32–34; Heb. 12:15).
- We must discipline ourselves to do what Romans 12:2; 2 Corinthians 10:4–5; and Philippians 4:8 tell us to do. Bitterness is always tied to what a person is thinking. We can't be bitter without thinking bitter thoughts. That means we must put off the kinds of thoughts and practices that produce bitterness and put on the kinds of thoughts and practices that produce love, mercy, and patience.
- We must understand what fretting or being a bookkeeper of the wrongs of others is. It is a sin, not a weakness or character flaw (Eph. 4:31; Col. 3:19).
- We must recognize that when we allow ourselves to become bitter we are really trying to replace God and are guilty of idolatry. In essence, what we're doing is telling God that He is doing a bad job in our lives (Ps. 37; Rom. 12:19).
- We must focus on the fact that our God is altogether sovereign, loving, and wise, and that He could have prevented the person who has wronged us from doing what he did. So instead of fretting and bookkeeping, we should be asking God what He wants us to learn through what has occurred (Gen. 50:20; 2 Sam. 16; Rom. 8:28).
- We must focus on the truth of Psalm 119:67, 71 and James 1:2–5—God is up to something and what He is up to is good.
- We must remind ourselves how God would have us respond to a person who wrongs us. Ask yourself, "Is this one of those times when we should practice Matthew 18:15 and Luke 17:3, or is this one of those times when we should put Proverbs 19:11 and Romans 12:19–21 into practice?" (See chapter 15 for a fuller explanation of what to do when we perceive that a person has wronged us.)
- We should be asking ourselves the question, "At this time, what would be the best way to glorify God and do good to the person who is wronging me?"

- We should reflect on the fact that, according to 1 Corinthians 13:1–3, this is giving us another opportunity to develop the kind of love that will cause us to make a powerful impact on others in and out of our family for Christ.

## In Conclusion

Ask yourself the same questions I ask myself. "Is what we've been talking about true in my life, true in my family? Can I honestly say that in my interactions with people I manifest a love that does not keep records of the wrongs they have done to me? Can I honestly say I do not brood or fret over the wrongs they have done to me? Can I honestly say that my life is free from resentment and the manifestations of bitterness that cause trouble and defile and destroy my usefulness for Christ in the lives of others?"

I don't know about you, but after asking myself these questions, I frequently arrive at the conclusion that I need more of this kind of love—the kind of love that doesn't keep a record of the wrongs suffered. I personally have had to ask God for forgiveness, and I'm asking God to help me be more faithful in putting the suggestions for preventing and overcoming bitterness into practice in my life. Please join me in doing the same.

### Review, Reflection, Application, and Discussion Questions

1. Including the focus of this chapter, what are the nine characteristics of love that we have studied thus far in the book?

2. What are the two primary ways in which the original word translated "wrong" is used in the Bible? Explain the difference between these two ways and what relevance this understanding has for applying the truth of this phrase to our lives.

3. What can we learn about what it means to be provoked from Proverbs 12:16? Explain the various words used in this verse that help us to understand what being provoked means.

4. What do the words "keep a record" refer to? What common practice do they describe? What is this phrase telling us that we must not do if we are to be loving people?

5. If we have a love that doesn't keep a record of wrongs we have suffered, what will we not do? Describe how and when we can disobey this phrase.

6. What happens when a person fails to love in this way?

7. How does a failure to love in this way manifest itself in specific ways? What does a failure to love in this way do or cause? Reflect on the list of consequences described in this chapter. Reflect on the consequences described in Hebrews 12:15.

8. In what ways have you seen Hebrews 12:15 work out in your own life, family, workplace, church, community?

9. How can bitterness be prevented? Reflect on the suggestions made in this chapter and add any others that you think will be preventive.

10. How do people sometimes excuse or justify their recordkeeping? Can you think of ways not mentioned in this book that people do this?

11. How would you rate yourself in terms of your not keeping records of wrongs suffered? "I never keep records" (4); "I very seldom keep records of wrongs" (3); "I sometimes keep records" (2); "I frequently keep records of wrongs" (1); "I almost always keep records" (0).

12. How often during this past week did you reflect on some wrong you experienced? How much time today have you spent reviewing wrongs that have been done to you?

13. Was the recordkeeping related to people? What people? Was it in connection with situations or things that were or were not happening? Was it in reference to God and what He allowed to happen or not happen?

14. How do you view your recordkeeping when it occurs? Serious? No big deal? Sinful? What good do you expect your recordkeeping to accomplish?

15. What is your typical response to your own recordkeeping?

16. What can you do to become a worse recordkeeper and reduce your potential for bitterness?

17. And now my usual reminder: Please remember as you reflect on the love principle presented in this chapter that the purpose of evaluation and application is:

   a. not to discourage or destroy us;

   b. but to motivate us to see our constant need of the cross and how much we owe to Jesus—without Him we'd never make it, but praise God we are not without Him;

   c. and to motivate us to understand our constant daily need of grace—that our salvation never has been and never will be by the works we have done, but always by the work Christ has done and is doing for us; I want our studies in 1 Corinthians 13 to be a reminder that we need to live a cross-centered life; we need the application of the cross work of Jesus every day of our lives; remember there's not a day in our lives when we are so good that we don't need the cross, and there is never a day in our lives when we are so bad so that what Christ did on the cross is not sufficient to provide forgiveness for us (Rom. 3:24; 5:20; Eph. 1:7; 1 John 1:7; 2:1–2);

   d. and to cause us to understand that we must and can, by His grace, put off from our lives the "unlove" that is displeasing to God and put on in our lives the love that is beautifully described in 1 Corinthians 13 so that we might become more and more like our Savior and more prolific in bearing fruit for Him as others see the grace of God at work in our lives, changing and transforming us (Eph. 4:22–24; 1 Tim. 4:7).

# 14

## The Kind of Love That Rejoices in Truth—Not Wrongdoing

### Loving People to Christ

In the nineteenth century Charles Spurgeon wrote a book that he called *An All Around Ministry*. As its title suggests, it was a book written to teach people how to have an effective ministry for Christ. In that volume Spurgeon writes:

> Assuredly we must abound in love. It is a hard thing for some preachers to saturate and perfume their sermons with love; for their natures are hard, or cold, or coarse, or selfish. We are none of us all that we ought to be, but some are specially poverty stricken in point of love. They do not "naturally care" for the souls of men, as Paul puts it. To all, especially to the harder sort, I would say, "Be doubly earnest as to holy love, for without this you will be no more than sounding brass or a tinkling cymbal." Love is power. The Holy Spirit, for the most part, works by our affection. Love men to Christ; faith accomplishes much, but love is the actual instrument by which faith works out its desires in the Name of the Lord of love. And I am sure that, until we heartily love our work, and love the people with whom we are working, we shall not accomplish much.[1]

1. Charles Spurgeon, *An All Around Ministry* (London: Banner of Truth Trust, 1960), 192–93.

In that statement Charles Spurgeon said a number of things about the importance of love if we are to be effective in ministry:

1. Without love you will be no more than sounding brass or a tinkling cymbal.
2. Love is power.
3. The Holy Spirit, for the most part, works by our affection.
4. It is a hard thing for some of us to abound in love.
5. Some of us have natures that are hard, cold, or selfish.
6. We must love men to Christ.
7. While faith is important, love is the actual instrument by which faith works out its desires.
8. Unless we love the people with whom we are working, we will not accomplish much.

That was Charles Spurgeon's conviction about the importance of love in ministry. When he wrote those words, he was addressing them primarily to pastors, but everything he said is true of all Christians! If we want our lives to count for Christ, if we want to make an impact for Christ in the lives of others, then we must *love* them to Christ.

Spurgeon was the greatest preacher of the nineteenth century, so he commands our respect and our attention. But we are not to adopt these truths just on his word. We're to adopt these truths because our holy Father said them through Paul in his first letter to the Corinthians!

## Who Would Disagree with Spurgeon?

Hardly anyone would disagree with the statement that if you want to make an impact for Christ, you must be a loving person. In fact, I've never heard anyone say, "Love isn't important in ministry. Don't be concerned about it." I've never heard anyone say to women, "If you want to be a positive influence for Christ in the lives of your husband and children, loving them just isn't that important." And I've never heard anyone say to men, "If you want to be a positive influence for Christ in the lives of your wife and children, loving them just isn't that important."

So if we are not being effective in ministry, the problem is not that we don't acknowledge the importance of love. The problem is that in spite of what we say, we don't practice real love in our relationships!

Paul knew that. That's what he was addressing in our passage. In 1 Corinthians 13 he not only tells us how important love is, but also goes on to describe in detail the nature or characteristics of the kind of real love that will make us powerful instruments for Christ in the lives of others.

Thus far in our exposition of real love, we've noted nine of the characteristics of the kind of love that will make us effective in ministry:

1. Is long-suffering;
2. Is kind;
3. Is not jealous or envious;
4. Is not boastful;
5. Is not arrogant;
6. Doesn't act unbecomingly;
7. Does not seek its own;
8. Is not provoked;
9. Does not keep a record of the wrongs it has suffered.

It's time now to move on to the tenth and eleventh characteristics of this kind of love, if we want to become powerful instruments for Christ in the lives of others. In the first part of verse 6 we have a description of the tenth of these characteristics: "Love does not rejoice at wrongdoing."

## Defining the Words—What Exactly Is Wrongdoing?

Another way to say this would be that love doesn't rejoice in iniquity or unrighteousness. Let's try to get our arms around this concept. What is Paul saying? What does he mean by "wrongdoing"?

In order to understand this, we need to examine a couple of passages where this word is used. This is an important principle in interpreting Scripture. Let Scripture interpret Scripture.

In Matthew 7:21–23 Jesus uses the same word. In this passage Jesus speaks of workers of lawlessness. Who are they? Here, workers of lawlessness are contrasted with those who actually do the will of the Father—who do what God wants. They don't merely talk about the will of the Father and then go and do something else. They actually do what He has commanded them to do. Therefore, righteousness is defined in terms of doing God's will, and unrighteousness is defined in terms of that which is contrary to God's will.

The word is also used in 2 Timothy 2:19: "But God's firm foundation stands, bearing this seal: 'The Lord knows those who are his,' and, 'Let everyone who names the name of the Lord depart from iniquity.'" In this same chapter, unrighteousness is variously described:

1. Irreverent babble, worldly and empty chatter, speech that promotes ungodliness (v. 16).
2. Speech that spreads like gangrene, speech that destroys the faith of other people, that causes people to question the truths of God's Word, that contradicts the truths of the Christian faith (vv. 17–18).
3. Foolish, ignorant controversies that produce quarrels, that focus on ignorant speculations, that are not based on solid fact (v. 23).

This word is also used in James 3:6: "And the tongue is a fire, a world of unrighteousness. The tongue is set among our members, staining the whole body, setting on fire the entire course of life, and set on fire by hell." Wow, that's strong. This passage says that the tongue is a world of unrighteousness, or iniquity. Note that James says the tongue is not just a little town of unrighteousness, not even just a little city of unrighteousness, not just a continent of iniquity, but a world of iniquity. What he wants us to realize is that the potential for iniquity that resides in an untamed tongue is enormous! It is a world of unrighteousness!

In fact, an untamed tongue is so powerfully unrighteous that James heaps up figures of speech to illustrate just what this unrighteous tongue can do. Verses 5–6 say that this tongue, which is a world of unrighteousness, is like a raging fire that can destroy a forest. It's not just like a little grass fire or the kind of fire in your barbecue grill.

From our experience living in California, Carol and I know the damage that fire can bring to an area. Almost every year fire destroys thousands of acres—as well as hundreds of houses and even lives. It might start small. Maybe someone dropped a cigarette butt or a lighted match. Perhaps someone started a little campfire and didn't put it out properly. First a bit of grass catches fire. Before long, it spreads to the underbrush and then to the trees, gathering speed and power with every second. Hundreds of firefighters are called in from all over the country. Huge planes, helicopters, and bulldozers are put into service to put out the fire. Why? Because they understand the damage that fire can bring to all it touches!

James understands this, too. He's saying that the tongue is so full of unrighteousness that it can do a tremendous amount of damage. Unrighteousness in the form of demeaning and speaking evil to and about someone else brings a tremendous amount of damage to other people. Well, Paul says in 1 Corinthians 13, love does not enjoy talking in that way to or about other people.

In verse 6 James says that the tongue is so full of unrighteousness that it can defile or corrupt the whole body, not just a part of it. Thus unrighteousness consists in bringing corruption or defilement to people—including yourself.

Verses 7–8 say, "For every kind of beast and bird, of reptile and sea creature, can be tamed and has been tamed by mankind, but no human being can tame the tongue. It is a restless evil, full of deadly poison." These verses say that the tongue has more potential for damage than the fiercest and most dangerous of all animals. It is more untamable than the most ferocious lion, than fierce tigers, than wild elephants.

This untamed tongue, James says, is like a restless, unsettled, unrestrained, volatile, or unstable evil. The word used here is the word that might be used to describe nitroglycerine, which is a very unstable and explosive liquid. The word *restless* conveys the idea of constant dissatisfaction or discontentment. The word *evil* speaks of the fact that the tongue can bring corruption and severe destruction. According to

James, wrongdoing or unrighteousness may involve being restless and unstable and volatile in your relationships with people.

In verses 9–10 James indicates that using the tongue to curse rather than bless men is an act of unrighteousness. What does he mean by cursing men? He doesn't mean by the word *curse* what many people think cursing involves. (In fact, the Bible never uses the word *curse* in the way we often use it today. It never uses it to describe what we call swear words or profane language. Now, don't misunderstand me; I'm not saying, and James wouldn't either, that what we call swearing is not wrong or unrighteous. It is wrong because the Bible says we should not take the name of God in vain, but that's not what James or the rest of the Bible means when it talks about cursing men.) In the context of James, he makes it clear that cursing someone is the opposite of blessing him (vv. 9–10). Jesus also makes that clear in Luke 6:28: "Bless those who curse you, pray for those who abuse you."

Cursing would involve doing the very things James says we should not do. It would involve speaking evil or unrighteously to one another, against one another, and about one another. Cursing involves complaining against and being judgmental and condemnatory toward one another.

Blessing, on the other hand, means that our speech will be righteous speech—that is, speech that is right in God's sight; it is speech that is intended to help. Blessing benefits people. It encourages them. It is given in accordance with the truth of Scripture. It will be speech that is characterized by purity, gentleness, reasonableness, mercy, and good fruits, speech that is peaceable and consistent and sincere and genuine. That's what it means to bless. When our speech is not in keeping with that description, Paul and James would say it is unrighteous speech.

To bring it all back to 1 Corinthians 13:6, let me remind you that when Paul uses the word *wrongdoing* or *unrighteousness*, he is referring to any action, any speech, any thought, any desire, or any event that is not right in the sight of God. Unrighteousness is anything that is contrary to God's will as it is revealed in the

Bible. Therefore, that's what I believe 1 Corinthians 13:6 means by "wrongdoing." But what does it mean when it says that love does not *rejoice* at wrongdoing?

## Defining the Words—What Exactly Is Rejoicing?

The word *rejoice* literally means to be joyful or glad or delighted or to find pleasure in something. In Luke 1:14 the word *rejoice* is associated with the words *gladness* and *joy*. In that passage, an angel tells Zechariah that he and his wife Elizabeth, who were old and had never been able to conceive, would become the parents of John the Baptist. Then the angel said, "And you will have joy and gladness, and many will rejoice at his birth." Obviously, "rejoicing" is associated with having joy and gladness.

In Philippians 4:4 Paul said that we are to rejoice in the Lord. That means we are to find our joy and pleasure and gladness in Christ Jesus.

Proverbs 2:14 tells us of those who delight in doing evil and rejoice in the perversity of evil. In this text the delight felt is because of evil and sin. Yet the character of the word is the same—gladness and joy are related to something that we find desirable.

When we turn to Proverbs 8:30–31, we find the same connection. Here wisdom is personified and says, "I [wisdom] was daily his [God's] delight, rejoicing before him always, rejoicing in his inhabited world and delighting in the children of man."

In 2 Thessalonians 2:12 we read of those who take pleasure in wickedness or unrighteousness. In other words, they find pleasure or joy or happiness in unrighteousness.

So when Paul says, "Love does not rejoice at wrongdoing [unrighteousness]," he means that real love will not be glad in or take any joy in evil or unrighteousness of any kind. He means that love will have no sympathetic attitude toward anything unrighteous. As Romans 12:9 says, we are to abhor that which is evil and cleave to that which is good.

John MacArthur says that love never takes satisfaction from sin, whether it be our own sin or the sins of others. Love will never make wrong appear to be right.[2]

## Some "Where the Rubber Meets the Road" Examples of This Principle

In a general sense, that is what Paul means when he says that love does not rejoice in wrongdoing. Now let's bring it down to where the rubber meets the road. Specifically:

1. Love does not rejoice in personally doing what the Bible would call evil or sin (Rom. 1:32).
2. Love does not enjoy doing evil to others. It does not enjoy treating others in an unjust fashion—the practice of oppressing others or putting undue pressure on people. It does not make unreasonable demands or engage in the practice of cheating others out of what is rightly theirs. It doesn't make promises that are not kept or fulfilled. Love does not rejoice in gossip or slander.
3. Love does not rejoice in encouraging others to do what is wrong in the sight of God.
4. Love does not enjoy watching others do evil (Rom. 1:32).
5. Love does not get pleasure out of seeing others have evil done to them.
6. Love does not enjoy exposing the sins and faults of others.
7. Love does not feel good about making fun of others—about doing what the enemies of Christ did to Him in Luke 22 and Matthew 27.
8. Love avoids doing what would make others feel uncomfortable or foolish or stupid.
9. Love is grieved by the wickedness that is going on in the world.

2. John MacArthur, *1 Corinthians* (Chicago: Moody, 1984), 349.

10. Love is saddened by the violence, cruelty, brutality, and crime that are so prevalent in the world and so freely displayed on television and in movies and books and magazines.
11. Love avoids being abusive in any way whether it be physical, verbal, or emotional.
12. Love doesn't take pleasure in pornography or sexual immorality.
13. Love doesn't engage in the practices God condemns.
14. Love does not glorify or justify evil, does not make wrong seem right, does not call evil good (Isa. 5:20).
15. Love can say with Job when something unpleasant happens to someone else, "I have [not] rejoiced at the ruin of him who hated me, or exulted when evil [trouble] overtook him" (Job 31:29).
16. Love does not hope someone will make a mistake, suffer loss, or fall into sin.

There! We have a good description of this tenth component of real love—the kind of love that is pleasing to God and makes us more effective in our ministry. It's time to turn our attention to the next characteristic—the flip side of the one we've just covered.

## The Flip Side of the Same Principle; Going for the Positive

The characteristic we've just studied was given to us in a negative: it tells us what we are not to do. The next aspect turns the negative into a positive and tells us what we as lovers of people are to do. We are not to rejoice at wrongdoing, but instead we are to do something else. According to the second part of verse 6, "Love rejoices with the truth."

To put both parts of the principle together, Paul makes it doubly clear what he means. We are not to rejoice at wrongdoing, but instead we are to rejoice in truth. The tenth and eleventh characteristics of real love are different sides of the same coin.

In his comments on this text, Simon Kistemaker writes, "Love and truth are inseparable partners residing in God Himself. God shares those characteristics with His people. He endowed them with love and truth, which, though tainted by sin, are renewed in Christ Jesus through the indwelling of the Holy Spirit."[3]

## But What Is Truth?

As mentioned previously, the word *love* is found some 370 times in the New Testament alone and the word for "truth" is used 99 times. I believe we are generally familiar with the concepts of both words. But what is the truth that believers are to rejoice in? What is this truth that Christians are to get excited about and delight in? The Bible uses the word *truth* in several ways:

1. Sometimes the Bible uses the word *truth* to refer to God's Word. Second Timothy 2:15 refers to the word of truth (see also John 8:32; 17:17). John 16:13 says that the Spirit will guide us into all truth. Colossians 1:5 says that the Colossians had heard and believed the word of truth. Second Timothy 3:8 refers to people who oppose the truth. Ephesians 1:13 tells us that we are saved because we believed and received the truth. James 1:18 urges us to receive with meekness the word of truth.
2. Sometimes the Bible uses the word *truth* in reference to Jesus, as it does in John 14:6 and John 1:14. John 1:17 tells us beautifully that grace and truth came by Jesus Christ. Ephesians 4:21 says that truth is in Jesus.
3. Sometimes the Bible uses the word *truth* to refer to honesty, sincerity, accuracy, or that which is true or in keeping with reality as over against falsehood or pretense. For example, in John 16:7 we read, "Nevertheless, I tell you the truth: it is to your advantage that I go away, for if I do not go away, the Helper will not come to you. But if I go, I will send him to you." Mark 5:33 tells us that a woman came to Jesus and told him the whole truth. Ephesians 4:25 says that we are to put away lying and speak the truth. First Timothy 2:7 assures us that Paul is

3. Simon Kistemaker, *1 Corinthians* (Grand Rapids: Baker, 1993), 461.

telling the truth; he is not lying. First John 1:8 says that if we say we have no sin, we deceive ourselves, and the truth is not in us. First John 2:4 tells us that whoever says "I know Him" but does not keep His commandments is a liar, and the truth is not in him. First John 3:18 urges us not to love in word only, but in deed and truth. Second John 1 speaks of people whom he loves in truth—truly loves. Romans 9:1–2 explains that Paul was telling the truth in Christ, that he was not lying, and that his conscience was clear.

4. Sometimes the Bible uses the word *truth* to refer to the progress or practice of truth as a synonym for righteousness. It is used as a synonym for living our lives in accordance with God's will, for living and thinking and desiring what is right in the eyes of God. This is the way that it is used in 2 John 4: "I rejoiced greatly to find some of your children walking in the truth, just as we were commanded by the Father." Also, 3 John 3–6 tells us similarly, "For I rejoiced greatly when the brothers came and testified to your truth, as indeed you are walking in the truth. I have no greater joy than to hear that my children are walking in the truth. Beloved, it is a faithful thing you do in all your efforts for these brothers, strangers as they are, who testified to your love before the church." Romans 2:8 reminds us of the importance of obeying the truth. Galatians 5:7 tells us that the truth is to be obeyed. James 5:19 speaks of people who wander or stray from the truth into sin. In Titus 1:1 we're told that truth is intended to produce godliness. First Peter 1:22 combines the ideas of obedience to the truth with love when it says, "Having purified your souls by your obedience to the truth for a sincere brotherly love, love one another earnestly from a pure heart."

## What Rejoicing in the Truth Means

So how does all this relate to our text in 1 Corinthians 13:6 that says, "Love rejoices with the truth"? To rejoice in the truth means that the truth is what turns on the person who really loves—the truth is what gets him really excited—what brings pleasure to him is to see the truth of God put into practice in the form of righteous living. Truth, or righteousness, is the source of a believer's sense of joy, gladness, and delight.

John MacArthur said:

> Love does not focus on the wrongs of others. It does not parade their faults for the entire world to see. Love does not disregard falsehood and unrighteousness, but as much as possible it focuses on the true and the right. It looks for the good, hopes for the good, and emphasizes the good. It rejoices with those who teach and live the truth. . . . Love appreciates the triumphs of ordinary folk. Our children are built up and strengthened when we encourage them in their accomplishments and in their obedience. Love doesn't rejoice in falsehood or wrong, but its primary business is to build up, not tear down, to strengthen, not weaken.[4]

Perhaps the best illustration and commentary on what Paul means when he says that love rejoices with the truth is found in Paul's own relationship with people as it is reflected in many of his writings:

1. When Paul writes to the Roman Christians, he concludes his epistle by spending almost a whole chapter (16) commending people, thirty-three of them, who have been instrumental in ministry to Christ.

2. When he begins his first letter to the Corinthians, he spends a considerable amount of time speaking about positive things he saw in their lives. When he concludes in chapter 16, he expresses his appreciation for the family of Stephanas, as well as Aquila and Priscilla.

3. When he writes to the Philippians, after a brief introduction, he mentions some positive things about them that have brought joy and encouragement to him. In chapter 2, he talks about Timothy, and about Epaphroditus. He begins chapter 4 by calling the church at Philippi his joy and crown and saying that he longs to see them. In Philippians 4:10–18 he writes: "I rejoiced in the Lord greatly that now at length you have revived your concern for me. You were indeed concerned for me, but you had no opportunity.

4. MacArthur, *1 Corinthians*, 351.

Not that I am speaking of being in need, for I have learned in whatever situation I am to be content. I know how to be brought low, and I know how to abound. In any and every circumstance, I have learned the secret of facing plenty and hunger, abundance and need. I can do all things through him who strengthens me. Yet it was kind of you to share my trouble. And you Philippians yourselves know that in the beginning of the gospel, when I left Macedonia, no church entered into partnership with me in giving and receiving, except you only. Even in Thessalonica you sent me help for my needs once and again. Not that I seek the gift, but I seek the fruit that increases to your credit. I have received full payment, and more. I am well supplied, having received from Epaphroditus the gifts you sent, a fragrant offering, a sacrifice acceptable and pleasing to God."

4. I could go on to mention other epistles where he did this same thing. Paul didn't only urge people to love others by looking for the good in their lives and then express appreciation to them. He actually did it himself—and did it freely, sincerely, and often.

## In Conclusion

At the beginning of this chapter, I mentioned what Charles Spurgeon said about the importance of love in ministry. He said that love is power and that we must love men to Christ. Then he closed by saying that unless we love people, we will not accomplish much for Christ.

According to God's Word as we've looked at 1 Corinthians 13:1–3, Spurgeon was right. He didn't overstate the case. It is not just any old kind of love that will bring men to Christ. It is the kind of love that is characterized by the qualities Paul mentions here. According to God's Word, the kind of love that will make us powerful witnesses for Christ is:

1. Long-suffering
2. Kind
3. Not jealous

4. Not boastful
5. Not arrogant or proud
6. Not discourteous
7. A love that doesn't seek its own
8. A love that isn't provoked
9. A love that doesn't keep a record of wrongs suffered
10. A love that doesn't rejoice or delight in unrighteousness
11. A love that does rejoice with the truth

Now, that's the kind of love that God wants us to have! And that's the kind of love that will make each of us more powerful for Christ. Sound impossible? It's not. It's the kind of love that you and I can have if we have come to Christ.

## Making the Impossible Possible

This love is not a natural love. No one is born with the capacity to love with this kind of love. Instead, it is a supernatural love. Paul says so in Romans 5:5: "God's love has been poured into our hearts through the Holy Spirit who has been given to us." Loving in this way is not our doing—something we can do in and of ourselves. It requires the supernatural pouring by the Holy Spirit. Peter says in 1 Peter 1:22–23 that the only people who can fervently love others in this way are people who have been born again and who have had their souls purified through obedience to the truth. The Bible says in Galatians 5:22 that this kind of love is the fruit of the Spirit. Therefore, the only people who can manifest this kind of love are people who have come to Christ. God actually gives us this supernatural power to love in this way.

Since this is absolutely true, I want to close by directing a word of counsel to you. First, I want to speak specifically to those of you who are not Christians. This kind of love may be completely foreign to you and your families. You know you ought to love in this way and perhaps you desire to love in this way, but you know you don't, and the truth of the matter is that you can't and won't love this way until you come to Christ. God holds you responsible to love this way, and the fact that you don't is sin. In fact, your very inability to love in this way demonstrates your need of the new birth—your need of God's forgiveness, of a new nature, of the indwelling presence of the Holy Spirit. There's great news for you! God will forgive your sins if you genuinely repent of them. He will give you a new nature, a new heart, and will put the Holy Spirit in you so that you will have access to the power of so great a love. So I urge you to come to Christ. I urge you to seek out a believer who can help you to know how to come to Christ. That's my counsel for those of you who know nothing of this kind of love.

But as I end this chapter, I also want to give two words of counsel to those of us who *have* come to Christ. First of all, I want to remind you that since this kind of love is a supernatural love and since the Holy Spirit does live in us, we can develop more and more of this kind of love. We have access to His vast resources. Ladies, you can become more loving wives and mothers. Men, you can become more loving husbands and fathers. All of us can be more loving people, because being more loving is not dependent upon our personality or on our background, or our strengths and virtues, or our present or past circumstances. It is dependent on availing ourselves of the infinite resources we have in Christ. We can, as Paul says in Philippians 4:13, do and be everything God wants us to be through Christ, who is our strength. We can be and do what God wants us to be and do because of 2 Corinthians 9:8: "And God is able to make all grace abound to you, so that having all sufficiency in all things at all times, you may abound in every good work."

The second piece of counsel I want to impart to those who are Christians is that when we fail to love this way (and we will and we do—the only one who always loved this way was Jesus), let's not excuse or minimize our lack of love. Instead, let's go to the cross, confess our sins, and thank God for the blood of Christ that cleanses from all sin (1 John 1:7). Thank Him for His promise in 1 John 1:9: "If we confess our sins, he is faithful and just to forgive us our sins and to cleanse us from all unrighteousness." Thank Him for the truth of 1 John 2:1–2:

My little children, I am writing these things to you so that you may not sin. But if anyone does sin, we have an advocate with the Father,

Jesus Christ the righteous. He is the propitiation for our sins, and not for ours only but also for the sins of the whole world.

Pray the prayer that Paul prayed in 1 Thessalonians 3:11–12:

> Now may our God and Father himself, and our Lord Jesus, direct our way to you, and may the Lord make you increase and abound in love for one another and for all, as we do for you.

Then, let's get up and do what Paul tells us to do in 1 Corinthians 14:1: "Pursue love."

## Review, Reflection, Application, and Discussion Questions

1. In this chapter we have studied the tenth and eleventh characteristics of true love. For the sake of memory, review the eleven aspects of real love covered so far.

2. What does Paul mean by "wrongdoing"? What is he referring to?

3. When Paul uses the word *rejoice*, what is he suggesting that love does not do? What does he mean by rejoicing in wrongdoing?

4. Review the list of things that love will not rejoice in.

5. Use the list as an inventory to evaluate your love quotient. Read each item and then rate yourself: "I never do that" (0); "I almost never do that" (1); "I sometimes do that" (2); "I frequently do that" (3).

6. How do people sometimes excuse or justify their taking pleasure in sin or evil?

7. How often did you take pleasure in sin in the last week? How often have you taken pleasure in sin today?

8. What were the circumstances in which you took pleasure in sin? Was it in connection with people? What people? Was it in connection with situations or things that were or were not happening?

9. How do you view your taking pleasure in sin when it occurs? Serious? No big deal? Sinful? What do you expect will come of it?

10. What is your typical response when you find yourself rejoicing in iniquity?

11. What can you do to strengthen your aversion-to-sin quotient and reduce your rejoicing-in-sin quotient?

12. When Paul says that "love rejoices in the truth," what is the truth in which love rejoices? What are the different ways the Bible uses the word *truth*?

13. In terms of what this chapter says it means to rejoice in the truth, how would you evaluate your rejoicing-in-truth quotient? Review the ways in which the Bible uses the word *truth* and then evaluate yourself in terms of how much you rejoice in each: always (4); frequently (3); sometimes (2); seldom (1); never (0).

14. Think about what you can do to sustain and strengthen your rejoicing-in-the-truth quotient.

15. And now my usual reminder: Please remember as you reflect on the love principle presented in this chapter that the purpose of evaluation and application is:

    a. not to discourage or destroy us;

    b. but to motivate us to see our constant need of the cross and how much we owe to Jesus—without Him we'd never make it, but praise God we are not without Him;

    c. and to motivate us to understand our constant daily need of grace—that our salvation never has been and never will be by the works we have done, but always by the work Christ has done and is doing for us; I want our studies in 1 Corinthians 13 to be a reminder that we need to live a cross-centered life; we need the application of the cross work of Jesus every day of our lives; remember there's not a day in our lives when we are so good that we don't need the cross, and there is never a day in our lives when we are so bad so that what Christ did on the

cross is not sufficient to provide forgiveness for us (Rom. 3:24; 5:20; Eph. 1:7; 1 John 1:7; 2:1–2);

d. and to cause us to understand that we must and can, by His grace, put off from our lives the "unlove" that is displeasing to God and put on in our lives the love that is beautifully described in 1 Corinthians 13 so that we might become more and more like our Savior and more prolific in bearing fruit for Him as others see the grace of God at work in our lives, changing and transforming us (Eph. 4:22–24; 1 Tim. 4:7).

# 15

## LOVE PROVIDES A STRONG ROOF

### Love Is Strength in Action

If you were to ask me to make a list of words or phrases that are least spoken or heard every day, I would include on that list the words "Please forgive me." For some reason we don't like to admit we have sinned. We hate taking responsibility for what we have done and asking for forgiveness.

We have a friend who is exemplary in this area. His wife has told of many occasions when he carefully looks her in the eyes and says to her, "Honey, I was wrong. Will you forgive me?" She admits that these simple words spoken from a sincere heart are enough to melt any resistance she has to forgiveness. Instead of prolonging an argument, she puts her arms around him and says, "Of course I will!"

It's amazing how rare it is for me to hear such accounts from the couples I counsel. Even among my friends and colleagues, I don't often hear such a testimonial. Why is it so hard for us to do what this dear friend does without hesitation?

That being said, if you were to ask me to make a list of words or phrases that are spoken or heard most frequently every day, I would include on that list the words "I love you." You may have already spoken those words today, or perhaps someone has spoken them to you. The point is that people are constantly using the words "I love you," but I doubt that most of the people using those words would define love in the way Paul does, writing by the inspiration of the Holy Spirit, in 1 Corinthians 13. And that's unfortunate because what we have in 1 Corinthians 13 is the quintessential definition of love—a kind of love that pleases God and makes us powerful tools in our Christ-centered ministries.

Thus far in this book, we've seen that, according to the Bible, when we tell someone, "I love you," we are telling that person that he or she can count on us to:

1. Be long-suffering;
2. Be kind;
3. Not be jealous or envious;
4. Not be boastful;
5. Not be arrogant or proud;
6. Not behave unbecomingly;
7. Not insist on our own way;
8. Not be irritated or annoyed;
9. Not keep a record of the wrongs committed;
10. Not rejoice in unrighteousness;
11. Rejoice in or with the truth.

And now in this chapter I want to focus our attention on Paul's twelfth characteristic of real love found at the beginning of verse 7: "Love bears all things."

## Defining Terms

The ESV and NASB translate the Greek word *stego* that Paul uses by the word "bear." The NIV translates it as "protects." Another version says "love covers." Still another says "Love patiently accepts all things." It is elsewhere translated "never gives up."

Which of these translations is right? What is Paul really saying about love? Greek dictionaries indicate that the word used here has two primary meanings, with the context determining which meaning is to be understood in any given passage.

The first interpretation is "to bear or endure; to forbear; to put up with or to support." It is used this way in 1 Thessalonians 3:5 when Paul writes, "when I could bear it no longer . . ." In the context this is the only translation that makes sense. However, for a couple of reasons I don't think that's what Paul has in mind when he uses the word in the context of 1 Corinthians 13. In verse 4 he has already mentioned the importance of being long-suffering. The last words in verse 7, "endures all things," lead me to conclude that Paul, in the first part of the verse, isn't primarily referring to enduring or putting up with all things. That's what he means in the last part of the verse—that we should endure or bear with something or someone. We'll explore what that means in a future chapter.

The verb that Paul uses here can also mean "to cover or protect." Used in its noun form in Mark 2:4, it is translated "roof." In this Mark 2 account, Jesus was in a home in Capernaum when a great crowd of people gathered to hear Him preach. Mark says that the house was so crowded that there was no longer room, even near the door. While Jesus was preaching, four men wanted to bring a paralytic person into the immediate presence of Jesus, but they were unable to do that because the crowd was so great. So they went up to the roof and dug out an opening through which they could lower their friend into the room. The "roof" is there to protect the home from the elements. It also serves to keep people from seeing inside the house. Therefore, it functions as a means of protection.

The verb form of the word used in 1 Corinthians 13:7, according to the Greek dictionary, can literally mean "to put a roof over what is displeasing in another person," "to throw a cloak of silence over what is displeasing in another person," "to pass over in silence or to keep confidential or to protect and preserve by covering." In other words, it means to cover over with silence, to keep secret, to hide or conceal the errors and faults of others.[1] I believe what Paul is saying in verse 7

1. William Arndt et al., eds., *A Greek English Lexicon of the New Testament* (Chicago: University of Chicago Press, 1957), 772; W. E. Vine, *Vine's Complete Expository Dictionary of Old and New Testament Words* (Nashville: Thomas Nelson, 1996), 53.

is that when we tell someone, "I love you," we are telling that person that we will function as an umbrella or roof that will shield and protect that person from harm or unnecessary and unhelpful exposure. That's a tall order, but real love is up to the challenge through the empowering work of the Holy Spirit.

In his comments on the passage, John MacArthur explains it this way: "*Stego* (to bear) basically means to cover or support and therefore protect. Love bears all things by protecting others from exposure, ridicule, or harm. Genuine love does not gossip or listen to gossip. Even when sin is certain, love tries to protect it with the least possible hurt and harm to the guilty person. Love never protects sin but is anxious to protect the sinner."[2]

What Paul says in verse 7 is exactly what Peter is saying in 1 Peter 4:8—"Above all, keep loving one another earnestly, since love covers a multitude of sins." In this verse Peter begins by telling us that the love we should have for one another should be stretched to the limits. Having given the general command, he goes on to tell us how fervent love will manifest itself toward others—it will manifest itself in covering the sins of other people. So Peter agrees with Paul that real love will shield and protect other people from unnecessary and unhelpful exposure.

When Peter and Paul make their statements about love protecting and covering, they may be thinking about a couple of verses from the book of Proverbs.

1. "Whoever covers an offense seeks love, but he who repeats a matter separates close friends" (17:9).
2. "Hatred stirs up strife, but love covers all offenses" (10:12).

## Let's Get Specific

In general, this is what love will do—it will cover all things. But let's get more specific and definitive about what it really means for

2. John MacArthur, *1 Corinthians* (Chicago: Moody, 1984), 352.

love to bear all things. When the Bible says that love bears or covers all things, does this mean that we should ignore or excuse all the sin patterns we see in another person's life? Does this mean that we should apply Proverbs 19:11 to every situation—that we should just overlook all transgressions or offenses in a person's life?

Of course not. I'll give you four reasons why I know Paul didn't mean that.

First, we know that when Paul said love covers all things, he didn't mean that we should always ignore a person's sins, because that would mean that Paul was telling us to do something that would violate what many passages of Scripture tell us to do:

- "Pay attention to yourselves! If your brother sins, rebuke him, and if he repents, forgive him" (Luke 17:3).
- "If your brother sins against you, go and tell him his fault, between you and him alone. If he listens to you, you have gained your brother" (Matt. 18:5).
- "Better is open rebuke than hidden love. Faithful are the wounds of a friend; profuse are the kisses of an enemy" (Prov. 27:5–6).
- "A rebuke goes deeper into a man of understanding than a hundred blows into a fool" (Prov. 17:10).
- "Whoever rebukes a man will afterward find more favor than he who flatters with his tongue" (Prov. 28:23).
- "[The pastor] must hold firm to the trustworthy word as taught, so that he may be able to give instruction in sound doctrine and also to rebuke those who contradict it" (Titus 1:9).
- "Declare these things: exhort and rebuke with all authority. Let no one disregard you" (Titus 2:15).
- "Preach the word; be ready in season and out of season; reprove, rebuke, and exhort, with complete patience and teaching" (2 Tim. 4:2).

Second, we know that when Paul said love covers or bears all things, he didn't mean that we should always ignore a person's sins, because there are passages of Scripture that tell us that real love will compel us to seek to restore people who have gone astray from the truth:

- Loving our neighbor will compel us to reprove that neighbor if he is in sin (Lev. 19:17–18).
- Loving our neighbor will involve doing what we can to rescue him from his wounded condition (Luke 10:25–37).
- Loving others will involve being proactive in seeking to help them overcome sin patterns in their lives (Gal. 6:1–2).
- Paul wrote a letter of rebuke to the Corinthians so that they might know how much he loved them (2 Cor. 2:4).
- Those whom Jesus loves He reproves and disciplines (Rev. 3:19).
- Those whom the Lord loves He disciplines and scourges (Heb. 12:6).

Third, we know that when Paul said love covers or bears all things, he didn't mean that we should always ignore a person's sins, because we are to love as Jesus loved, and there were many times when He rebuked people for their sins:

- "And Jesus rebuked him, and the demon came out of him, and the boy was healed instantly" (Matt. 17:18).
- "But Jesus rebuked him, saying, 'Be silent, and come out of him!'" (Mark 1:25).
- "But turning and seeing his disciples, he rebuked Peter and said, 'Get behind me, Satan! For you are not setting your mind on the things of God, but on the things of man'" (Mark 8:33).
- "But Jesus rebuked him, saying, 'Be silent and come out of him!' And when the demon had thrown him down in their midst, he came out of him, having done him no harm" (Luke 4:35).
- "While he was coming, the demon threw him to the ground and convulsed him. But Jesus rebuked the unclean spirit and healed the boy, and gave him back to his father" (Luke 9:42).

Finally, we know that when Paul said love covers or bears all things, he didn't mean that we should always ignore a person's sins, because there were many times when Paul himself rebuked people for their sins:

- He reproved the Galatians for distorting the gospel of Christ (Gal. 1–3).
- He rebuked Peter for his sin of hypocrisy (Gal. 2).
- He reproved Euodias and Syntyche for their lack of harmony (Phil. 4:2–3).
- He reproved the Corinthians for their lack of unity (1 Cor. 1).
- He rebuked them for not confronting the man who was having sexual relations with a relative (1. Cor. 5).
- He rebuked them for their arrogance (1 Cor. 8), and likewise with the Thessalonians and the Colossians. In fact, almost every epistle Paul wrote contains some sort of rebuke or reproof.

## The Covering or Restoring Process of Love

Therefore, in light of all these passages, when Paul says that real love covers or bears all things, he can't mean that we should ignore or excuse or overlook sinfulness. He can't mean that for all the reasons we've just mentioned. But then the question comes: if Paul doesn't mean that, what *does* he mean? We can get a grip on what it means to cover sins by turning to Galatians 6:1–2 and noting what Paul says there about how to deal in love with the faults and mistakes and even sins of other people:

> Brothers, if anyone is caught in any transgression, you who are spiritual should restore him in a spirit of gentleness. Keep watch on yourself, lest you too be tempted. Bear one another's burdens, and so fulfill the law of Christ.

One of the words in verse 1 that will help us understand what love should do when someone does something that displeases us or does something that we think is wrong is the word *transgression*. What Paul is saying is that before we take any action toward someone who displeases us, we must make sure that what we're dealing with is really a sin issue; we must make sure that what that person is doing that causes us to be concerned is really a violation of God's Word and not just something that irritates or upsets us. I believe this is more closely related to a matter where the person has really strayed behaviorally or doctrinally from the truth of God's Word.

This concept falls into line with other passages, which teach this specifically:

- "Pay attention to yourselves! If your brother sins, rebuke him, and if he repents, forgive him" (Luke 17:3).
- "If your brother sins against you, go and tell him his fault, between you and him alone. If he listens to you, you have gained your brother" (Matt. 18:15).
- "My brothers, if anyone among you wanders from the truth and someone brings him back, let him know that whoever brings back a sinner from his wandering will save his soul from death and will cover a multitude of sins" (James 5:19–20).

As we attempt to show love to someone in the form of covering his or her faults or sins, we must make sure that we're not merely concerned about what he or she is doing because of a preference issue. We are to make sure that our concern is not generated by a mere personality difference. It must not be generated by the fact that this person doesn't happen to like what we like, or do things the way we prefer. Our concern cannot relate to the fact that the person has different traditions or customs. We must make sure that our concern is not being aroused by cultural but not necessarily unbiblical differences. It must not be aroused by the fact that the person has different opinions, but not necessarily unbiblical ones, or that this person dresses or acts in a way that makes us uncomfortable, or thinks or talks in ways that don't make particular sense to us. The person's interests may run contrary to ours and leave us scratching our heads, wondering how he or she could have such curiosity about an object or subject that leaves us yawning. That should not concern us enough to rebuke the person for it.

No, Paul would say that when it comes to this matter of doing something to cover what is displeasing to us in other people, we must make sure that the issue under consideration is really a sin issue. If it's not a sin issue, then we can cover or bear what is displeasing to us by dealing with our own pride and selfishness and learning to be more accepting of other people's differences.

Another important guideline from Galatians 6:1 is related to the "covering" or "bearing" concept of 1 Corinthians 13:7 and comes to us from the word *caught*. The root word here is *lambanō*.

What does it mean to be caught? It may actually mean one of two things:

First, "to take by surprise." In John 8:3 we read of the scribes and Pharisees who brought to Jesus a woman who they said was caught in the act of adultery. In other passages we read about people who were caught in the act of stealing. By that we mean that the person was actually seen committing the act—that there is no doubt about his guilt. In current legal terminology, we would say that there were eyewitnesses to his acts.

Second, the Greek word *lambanō* may also mean "to capture, hold fast; seize, take possession of." It is used this way in Luke 19:12 where we read of a certain king who went into a distant country to acquire or take possession of a kingdom for himself. It is also found in 1 Corinthians 11:21 where Paul rebukes the people for what some of them were doing at their church suppers—grabbing or seizing their food before sharing it with the underprivileged.

This word is also used in the Greek version of the Old Testament on a number of occasions. For example, in Proverbs 7:22 it is used in reference to a young man who was enticed to commit immorality by an immoral woman: "All at once he follows her, as an ox goes to the slaughter, or as a stag is caught fast." Genesis 22 also uses it of the time Abraham obeyed God and took his son to Mount Moriah. Isaac said, "Behold, the fire and the wood, but where is the lamb for a burnt offering?" (v. 7). The answer comes in verse 13: "And Abraham lifted up his eyes and looked, and behold, behind him was a ram, caught in a thicket by his horns. And Abraham went and took the ram and offered it up as a burnt offering instead of his son."

Galatians 6:1 may be using the word in both senses. It may refer to someone who is caught by surprise in the very act of sin. He's caught red-handed, in other words. There are witnesses to his sin. However, I think Paul is talking here about someone who is really caught. It's not merely that he was caught (taken by surprise) in an act of sin. Instead this person is caught—trapped, held fast, in the grip of, stuck—in some sinful way of thinking, acting, speaking, responding, or reacting, and it has become a pattern in his life. It has become what the Bible calls in Ephesians 4:22 a manner of life.

Paul is saying that when we observe a person behaving sinfully, we must decide whether this is an anomaly (a one-time occurrence) that should be "covered" in the Proverbs 19:11 sense—let God deal with the person and bring him to confession and repentance—or whether it is a pattern of life in which the person is held fast and therefore needs the help of others to really cover that sinful pattern by changing and developing a new manner of life that is godly and holy. In this sense, the covering would consist of helping him to deal with and change the sinful pattern in a biblical manner.

That brings us to a third important word in Galatians 6:1, which is involved in the covering process. That word is *restore*. The word *restore—katartizō—*is found in Hebrews 12:12–13:

> Therefore lift your drooping hands and strengthen your weak knees, and make straight paths for your feet, so that what is lame may not be put out of joint but rather be healed [*katartizō*].

The word was often used to describe what a physician would do when someone broke a bone or had an elbow or shoulder that was knocked out of its socket. He would carefully set the broken bone or put the dislocated limb back in place.

The word is also used in Mark 1:19—James and John were sitting in their boat "mending" their nets. When Paul uses the word here in Galatians 6:1, he refers to someone who has developed a sinful manner of life, meaning that the person has developed a pattern of living and responding and thinking. If we love that person, we will do what we can to cover or bear his sins by helping him to put off the old sinful manner of life and put on a godly and righteous manner of life.

In reference to this aspect of covering, Jay Adams has said:

> Covering sins means not allowing offenses to come between brothers. It does not mean ignoring them. God allows no grudges or resentment. One must cover sins in such a way that they never bother him any more. If some sin keeps throwing the covers off, then you must confront the brother and bring the matter to a successful conclusion. God does not allow for unreconciled relationships. Nor does covering sins mean never offering help to another who is stuck in some trespass out of which he is not extricating himself.[3]

Indeed, covering sin means the very opposite. Covering means encouraging the person who has a sin pattern in his life to repent and come to Christ for forgiveness and then to change his way of life.

As we seek to understand what Paul means by covering all things, let us consider two passages of Scripture where the word *cover* is used in reference to sin. One is Psalm 32:1 where the psalmist says, "Blessed is the one whose transgression is forgiven, whose sin is covered." Here the psalmist equates forgiveness of sins with the covering of sins. Later in the psalm he tells us that this forgiveness and covering occurred when he confessed his sin, repented, and sought God's forgiveness. So to cover sins means that a person has recognized his sin, confessed his sin, repented of his sin, and sought God's forgiveness.

The second passage where the word is used in reference to sin is James 5:19–20. James talks about a person who "strays" from the truth— which may be referring to doctrinal or behavioral straying. James is referring to someone who has made a profession of faith and then turned from the truth to an erroneous way of thinking and living. He is referring to someone who is caught or held fast by this manner of life—about a man

3. Jay Adams, *The Christian Counselor's Commentary: Hebrews, James, I & II Peter, Jude* (Woodruff, SC: Timeless Texts, 1996), 282.

who is involved in a multitude of sins. For this person, living sinfully has become a fixed way of life. James indicates that what is happening here is so serious that unless the person turns from this pattern, he will experience death. Therefore, James tells us that this person needs to be turned around—restored. If we are able to do that (v. 20), we will save his soul from death and will cover a multitude of sins.

What James says here will help us understand what Paul is talking about when he says, "Love covers all things." He means the same thing James means—that if a person is straying from the Lord, either doctrinally or behaviorally, then loving that person will involve doing everything we can legitimately do to bring him back. So again, covering or bearing sin involves bringing a person to the place where he will acknowledge and confess his sin, seek God's forgiveness, and then turn from his sin to live a life of faith and obedience to Christ. This person needs to be restored—he needs to have his sin covered, and love will compel us to help in that process.

## A Right Attitude Is Crucial

Before we finish exploring what Galatians 6:1–3 has to say about restoration or the covering process, I want you to notice several other factors that Paul mentions in these verses. One is found in the statement that we are to carry out this restoration or covering process *in the spirit of gentleness or meekness*. What does it mean to restore in the spirit of gentleness? Well, Matthew 11:29 tells us that Jesus is our example when it comes to meekness. He said, "I am gentle and lowly in heart." He is our ultimate example of meekness. Meekness was manifested in His submission to the will of God; meekness was manifested in His compassion and concern for people in spite of the way they were living.

Restoring people in the spirit of gentleness means to deal with erring people the way Jesus dealt with Peter in John 21:15–17. Remember, Peter had already denied Christ three times. But in this passage we read:

When they had finished breakfast, Jesus said to Simon Peter, "Simon, son of John, do you love me more than these?" He said to him, "Yes, Lord;

you know that I love you." He said to him, "Feed my lambs." He said
to him a second time, "Simon, son of John, do you love me?" He said
to him, "Yes, Lord; you know that I love you." He said to him, "Tend
my sheep." He said to him the third time, "Simon, son of John, do you
love me?" Peter was grieved because he said to him the third time, "Do
you love me?" and he said to him, "Lord, you know everything; you
know that I love you." Jesus said to him, "Feed my sheep."

Restoring others in the spirit of gentleness means that we deal with
them in the meek way Paul describes in 2 Timothy 2:24–26:

And the Lord's servant must not be quarrelsome but kind to everyone, able to teach, patiently enduring evil, correcting his opponents
with gentleness. God may perhaps grant them repentance leading to
a knowledge of the truth, and they may escape from the snare of the
devil, after being captured by him to do his will.

Restoring others in the spirit of gentleness means the same thing
James was talking about in James 3:13–14:

Who is wise and understanding among you? By his good conduct
let him show his works in the meekness of wisdom. But if you have
bitter jealousy and selfish ambition in your hearts, do not boast and
be false to the truth.

He says that being meek is the opposite of being arrogant, jealous, and
selfishly ambitious. Meekness involves being peaceable, reasonable, willing to yield, merciful, and genuine in our relationships with people.
Restoring others in the spirit of gentleness means that we will:

- Be sensitive to the feelings of other people; be reluctant to do or
  say anything that would embarrass them. We will be like Jesus
  with Mary and Martha in John 11.
- Do what we can to make others feel at ease; gentle people don't
  enjoy making people squirm. We will be like Jesus with the sinning woman in John 8.

- Be willing to hear different ideas, even foolish ideas, without doing or saying anything that would belittle or demean someone else.
- Treat people with respect and dignity even though we disagree with them and think they are wrong.
- Avoid unnecessary and unhelpful criticism.
- Avoid the use of intimidation, coerciveness, violence, manipulation, or authoritarianism.
- Structure our speech according to Proverbs 15:1–2: "A soft answer turns away wrath, but a harsh word stirs up anger. The tongue of the wise commends knowledge, but the mouths of fools pour out folly."
- Structure our speech according to Proverbs 16:21–24: "The wise of heart is called discerning, and sweetness of speech increases persuasiveness. Good sense is a fountain of life to him who has it, but the instruction of fools is folly. The heart of the wise makes his speech judicious and adds persuasiveness to his lips."
- Structure our speech according to Ephesians 4:29: "Let no corrupting talk come out of your mouths, but only such as is good for building up, as fits the occasion, that it may give grace to those who hear."
- Follow the counsel of Proverbs 18:13: "If one gives an answer before he hears, it is his folly and shame."
- Approach others with the attitude of a servant rather than of a master or lord.
- Avoid talking to others about someone else's sins unless to do so is absolutely necessary for knowing how to help the person stuck in sin, for the protection of others who may be hurt by the person's sin, or for getting others involved in obtaining help for the person who is stuck in sin. To do otherwise would be gossip and slander and serve no constructive purpose and is therefore wrong and sinful.

John MacArthur put it this way:

There is a perverse pleasure in exposing someone's faults and failures. . . . That is what makes gossip so appealing. The Corinthians cared little for the feelings or welfare of fellow believers. It was every person for himself. Like the Pharisees, they paid little attention to others except when those others were failing or sinning. Man's depravity causes him to rejoice in the depravity of others. It is that depraved pleasure that sells magazines and newspapers that cater to exposés, true confessions, and the like. It is the same sort of pleasure that makes children tattle on brothers and sisters. Whether to feel self-righteous by exposing another's sin or to enjoy that sin vicariously, we all are tempted to take a certain kind of pleasure in the sins of others. Love has no part in that. It does not expose or exploit, gloat or condemn.[4]

In his discussion of what it means to restore someone in the spirit of meekness, Jay Adams has written:

> Meekness is difficult to define; it is more easily understood by describing its opposite. To say to a brother caught in sin, "Well, I guess this is to be expected. After all, how many times have I said . . . ," is to kick him when he is down. No, any such superior attitude is the opposite of meekness. Meekness acts more like this, "Brother, I am here, not because I consider myself better than you, but because in Galatians 6:1, God tells me to come. As a matter of fact, I may need you to help me out of some difficulty in the future."[5]

Paul says that, as we seek to cover the sins of erring people, we must constantly look to ourselves with the understanding that we are also susceptible to temptation. This is in keeping with what he says in 1 Corinthians 10:12: "Therefore let anyone who thinks that he stands take heed lest he fall."

This is the point: how can we be harsh and demanding to others when we are capable of being tempted and even yielding to temptation ourselves? Are we so lofty in our own holiness that we are somehow

4. MacArthur, *1 Corinthians*, 352.

5. Jay Adams, *The Christian Counselor's Commentary: Galatians, Ephesians, Colossians, Philemon* (Woodruff, SC: Timeless Texts, 1994), 58.

insulated from the power of sin? Have we somehow reached a level of sinless perfection? I don't think so.

Galatians 6:3 expands on this same concept when it indicates that as we seek to help erring brothers, we must approach them with the attitude that we are nothing. What Paul is doing here is attacking the spirit of overconfidence in oneself. Paul is warning against the attitude that Peter manifested in Matthew 26:31–35:

> Then Jesus said to them, "You will all fall away because of me this night. For it is written, 'I will strike the shepherd, and the sheep of the flock will be scattered.' But after I am raised up, I will go before you to Galilee." Peter answered him, "Though they all fall away because of you, I will never fall away." Jesus said to him, "Truly, I tell you, this very night, before the rooster crows, you will deny me three times." Peter said to him, "Even if I must die with you, I will not deny you!" And all the disciples said the same.

Paul is warning against the spirit of the Pharisee as described in Luke 18:9–14:

> He also told this parable to some who trusted in themselves that they were righteous, and treated others with contempt: "Two men went up into the temple to pray, one a Pharisee and the other a tax collector. The Pharisee, standing by himself, prayed thus: 'God, I thank you that I am not like other men, extortioners, unjust, adulterers, or even like this tax collector. I fast twice a week; I give tithes of all that I get.' But the tax collector, standing far off, would not even lift up his eyes to heaven, but beat his breast, saying, 'God, be merciful to me, a sinner!' I tell you, this man went down to his house justified rather than the other. For everyone who exalts himself will be humbled, but the one who humbles himself will be exalted."

Paul is warning against the kind of attitude the Laodiceans had in Revelation 3:17:

> For you say, I am rich, I have prospered, and I need nothing, not realizing that you are wretched, pitiable, poor, blind, and naked.

Paul is saying that as we seek to restore, to cover or bear another person's sins, we must do so with the attitude that, in and of ourselves, we have nothing to offer. We have no power. We are not the solution—Christ is! It's our job to point sinners away from ourselves and direct them to Him instead.

Paul is saying that as we seek to cover or bear another person's sins, we must do so with the attitude that in and of ourselves we have no wisdom. But God's Word has the answers, so we must come with an attitude of complete dependence on Him and His Word. When I train counselors, I tell them that the golden hour is not the hour the counselee spends with me. The golden hour is that hour he or she spends with the Word of God and the Holy Spirit. That's where the real work of change takes place.

In reference to the importance of humility in doing the restoring work of Galatians 6:1 or the covering work of 1 Corinthians 13:7, John MacArthur writes:

> One of the reasons many Christians do not bother to help fellow Christians is that they feel superior to sinners and wrongly consider themselves to be spiritually something when the truth is that they are really nothing. Their desire is not to help a stumbling brother, but to judge and condemn him. Conceit can coexist with outward morality, but it cannot coexist with spirituality. In fact, conceit is the ultimate sin, mentioned first in the list of things God hates in Proverbs 6:16–17. The Christian who thinks he is something when he is nothing needs help facing his own sin before he will be qualified to help anyone else out of his sin. If he refuses to see his own spiritual need, he deceives himself and is useless in serving God or in helping fellow believers.[6]

## In Conclusion: What Does It Mean to Say, "I Love You"?

So what does it mean for us to say, "I love you"? According to God's Word, it means that we are telling others that we will:

1. Be long-suffering with them;
2. Be kind to them;

6. John MacArthur, *Galatians* (Chicago: Moody, 1987), 181.

3.  Be glad when they succeed and not be envious of them;
4.  Not boast or brag about ourselves and try to impress them with our supposed importance;
5.  Not be arrogant or proud in our relationship with them;
6.  Not behave in a discourteous and rude way toward them;
7.  Not be selfish or self-seeking in our relationship with them;
8.  Not be annoyed or irritated with them;
9.  Not rejoice or get satisfaction out of unrighteousness;
10. Be mindful to rejoice in the ways that they reflect God's truth in their lives;
11. Tell them that we will do what we can to cover whatever is displeasing and perhaps even sinful in their life.

Love, says the inspired apostle Paul, covers or bears all things. And what does that mean? It means that on issues that are not sinful or harmful to the person or to others or a violation of biblical principle, we will put Proverbs 19:11 into practice. We will overlook. On issues that are merely a matter of preference rather than biblical principle, we will not insist that the person conform to our preferences.

It means that in some instances where the person may actually act or react wrongly, we will not make a big deal out of it. Unless it is a pattern in that person's life and unless it is seriously hindering that person's relationship with Christ and bringing harm to other people, we will refrain from bringing it to the attention of others. We must refrain from gossiping about the faults and failures and even sins of the other person.

Basically, before we make a judgment about the sinfulness of what we think the other person has done or is doing, we will make sure that we are in possession of the facts. We will practice Proverbs 18:13—not answer a matter (draw conclusions and respond) until we have gathered hard data. If we truly love, we will have a desire to protect the other person's reputation and want to think the best of that other person and want others to think the best of him also, unless, of course, the facts prove to the contrary.

It means that we will be actually grieved to discover that the other person has sinned or is sinning, and our grief will be motivated by our genuine concern for the other person and for the glory and honor of

God. If we are sure that what we have observed in the life of that other person is truly a sinful pattern, we will do everything we can to cover or help that person to overcome that sin by putting the principles of Galatians 6:1–3 or James 5:19–20 into practice.

Once we are sure that a person is caught in sin, we will seek to cover that person's sin by promoting restoration, by helping that person to turn from sin—to put off sinful patterns and put on righteous patterns. As we approach the person, we will come with a heart that is gentle and meek rather than harsh, condemnatory, judgmental, and pushy.

It means that as we seek to cover the sin of others, we will be humble because of the recognition that we too are sinners—we are no better than they are. We are, like them, totally dependent on Christ to promote change. We do not have the solutions to their problems; only Christ has! It is not our wisdom or intelligence that helps others to grow and change. It is only when the Holy Spirit applies the wisdom and insights found in God's Word that godly restoration and change will be accomplished.

If we are sure that what we have observed is a sin pattern in another person's life, and we have appropriately put Galatians 6:1–3 into practice, and the person has not responded, we will commit the whole affair to God. We will endeavor to do through our prayers what all our admonitions could not do because we believe that the things that are impossible with men are possible with God, and that the fervent prayer of a righteous person does accomplish much (Matt. 19:26; James 5:16). Thomas à Kempis says that in such a situation we should "beseech Him therefore, whose infinite wisdom knows how to bring good out of evil, that His will may be done, and His name glorified."[7]

That love covers sins means that if we are sure that what we have observed is a sin pattern in another person's life, we should examine ourselves to see what good God wants to bring into our lives through this person's unwillingness to recognize his sin and turn from it. Thomas à Kempis tells us what we should do if this should be the case:

> Remember that you have many failings of your own, by which the patience of other people will have its turn of being exercised.

---

7. Thomas à Kempis, *The Imitation of Christ* (New York: Doubleday, 1955), 38.

And if you do, as certainly you must see this, how unreasonable it is to expect you should make others in all particulars what you have them to be, when you cannot so much as make yourself what you are aware you ought to be . . . Supposing that all men to be without faults, some excellencies and virtues must be lost too, what could become of patience, what of forgiving and forbearance of one another for Christ's sake, if there were no provocations to try our temper? And such there could not be, if every man were perfect and did his duties.[8]

## A Final Summary and Challenge

All of that, my friends, is what I am convinced Paul meant when he spoke of love covering all things, and that is what God says it means to say, "I love you." And I close by asking two questions:

1. Is that what you mean when you tell someone, "I love you"?
2. Will you join with me in seeking to develop more of this kind of love?

I hope that you will make that commitment to improve the way you love others as Paul has directed in this passage. I am firmly convinced that if you and I will devote ourselves by God's grace and with the certain help of the Holy Spirit to loving others in this way, we will discover that our lives will be more instrumental in making an impact for Christ in this needy world.

## Review, Reflection, Application, and Discussion Questions

1. Why did I title this chapter "Love Provides a Strong Roof"?
2. Review what this chapter says it means to tell someone, "I love you."

8. Ibid.

3. What are the two primary ways in which the word *cover* or *bear* in 1 Corinthians 13:7 can be translated?

4. What are the four reasons for believing that Paul is saying that "love covers or protects"?

5. Summarize and reflect on the teaching of Galatians 6:1–2 and the connection of these verses to covering someone's sins.

6. What do these verses teach about how to cover someone's sins? What are the various ways we can cover someone's sins?

7. What are the two possible meanings of being "caught" in sin? Which of these interpretations is the correct one? Why?

8. What does to "restore" someone mean in Galatians 6:1–2?

9. What does it mean to restore someone in the spirit of gentleness?

10. When we are involved in the restoring process, what are some of the dangers we must avoid?

11. Review the various factors that this chapter says are involved in restoring someone in a spirit of gentleness, and then do the following things:

    a. Ask yourself whether you have ever been involved in covering someone's sins (restoring someone) in a biblical way. Who? When? How?

    b. Consider whether your action was related to loving that person.

    c. Use the suggestions about "restoring others in a spirit of gentleness" as an inventory and rate your own restoring efforts: "Yes, this is always true of me" (4); "This is frequently true of me" (3); "This is sometimes true of me" (2); "This is seldom true of me" (1); "This is never true of me" (0).

    d. Use this inventory to determine your restorative strengths and weaknesses.

    e. In keeping with the biblical teaching found in this chapter, consider how you need to change the way you seek to minister to people and to promote the restorative process.

12. And now my usual reminder: Please remember as you reflect on the love principle presented in this chapter that the purpose of this exposition, evaluation, and application is:

   a. not to discourage or destroy us;

   b. but to motivate us to see our constant need of the cross and how much we owe to Jesus—without Him we'd never make it, but praise God we are not without Him;

   c. and to motivate us to understand our constant daily need of grace—that our salvation never has been and never will be by the works we have done, but always by the work Christ has done and is doing for us; I want our studies in 1 Corinthians 13 to be a reminder that we need to live a cross-centered life; we need the application of the cross work of Jesus every day of our lives; remember there's not a day in our lives when we are so good that we don't need the cross, and there is never a day in our lives when we are so bad that what Christ did on the cross is not sufficient to provide forgiveness for us (Rom. 3:24; 5:20; Eph. 1:7; 1 John 1:7; 2:1–2);

   d. and to cause us to understand that we must and can, by His grace, put off from our lives the "unlove" that is displeasing to God and put on in our lives the love that is beautifully described in 1 Corinthians 13 so that we might become more and more like our Savior and more prolific in bearing fruit for Him as others see the grace of God at work in our lives, changing and transforming us (Eph. 4:22–24; 1 Tim. 4:7).

# 16

# BIBLICAL LOVERS ARE NOT GULLIBLE

### Is Godly Love So Naive?

Mariano DiGangi, who was pastor of the historic Tenth Presbyterian Church in Philadelphia, wrote a little booklet in which he said:

> Considering the crisis of our times, a man of insight cries out, "Love or Perish." Our affluent society is an afflicted society for lack of love. Just imagine how many marriages would be spared the heartbreak of separation and divorce if there were true love in the hearts of men and women! Think of what comfort and encouragement would brighten the lot of the poor, sick, lonely and sorrowing, if only there were more love in this world. Who can tell what new vitality would stir the church, and draw others into its fellowship, if there were real love among the professed followers of Christ? It is love we need—Christian love.[1]

In this booklet, Pastor DiGangi suggests that it is when Christians really manifest true love that new vitality will be brought into the church; and thus it is love that will draw others into the fellowship of the church.

1. Mariano DiGangi, *Christian Love* (Philadelphia: Time and Eternity, 1966), 5.

As we've worked our way through 1 Corinthians 12:31–13:8, we've seen that those thoughts are exactly in keeping with the truths that Paul has been communicating in this passage. In 1 Corinthians 12:31, after discussing the issue of spiritual gifts in ministry, Paul says, "I will show you a still more excellent way." The key Greek word used here is *hyperbolē*. Literally, Paul is saying that he wants to show us a hyperbolic way—not just a good way, not just a better way. The NASB translates the word in Galatians 1:13 as "beyond measure" and in 2 Corinthians 4:7 as "surpassing greatness." So when Paul uses this word in 1 Corinthians 12:31, he's telling us that he is going to show us not just a great way, but a surpassing or "beyond greatness" way, a way that is beyond measurement, a way for making your impact for Christ so great that it can't be measured!

## The "Surpassing Greatness" Way of Ministry

And what is that "beyond measure" way; what is that "surpassing greatness" way? It's what we've dealt with for fifteen chapters now! And the good news is that this exceptional gift is available to all Christians, not just to a chosen few. We don't have to be apostles and teachers to possess the kind of impacting life that is permeated and saturated with the right kind of love for others. Paul's point is that this kind of love far exceeds the mere possession of some extraordinary spiritual gifts.

Now let's discuss the next characteristic of this kind of love: "Love believes all things."

When you read that, your first thought might be, "What? I wasn't born yesterday! I'm no fool. I refuse to believe everything I hear!" That would be a natural reaction, especially in this day and age when deception is all around us. So let's talk about what Paul means by this remarkable admonition.

## What It *Doesn't* Mean to Believe All Things

First of all, let me assure you that Paul doesn't mean that we should live our lives in a gullible or naive way. It doesn't mean that if you see your child lifting money out of your pocketbook or wallet, you will believe him if he says he didn't do it! It doesn't mean that if you encounter a man staggering down the street with an empty whiskey bottle in his hand and smell alcohol on his breath, you'll believe him if he says that he wasn't drinking! It doesn't mean that if someone makes promises that are too good to be true, you'll put your utmost confidence in him because you want to show him love! It doesn't mean that if someone claims that a certain product will do amazing things, you must automatically believe him!

You'll be happy to hear that we don't check our common sense at the door when we understand we are to believe all things! And it doesn't just apply to the above, either. It can have spiritual implications. For instance, believing all things doesn't mean that if a man says he loves Christ and yet continually disobeys His commands, we must still unquestioningly believe him. It doesn't mean that if a woman says she loves God's people and yet is constantly criticizing and mocking them, we must believe her in the name of love. It doesn't mean that if someone says that he loves Christ and yet doesn't study His Word and doesn't love to hear the Word being preached, we must believe him. It doesn't mean that if someone says he is a hard worker and yet that person loafs around and uses his time unproductively, we must believe him.

We know this phrase doesn't mean these things because there are many verses that warn us against being gullible and naive:

- "The simple believes everything, but the prudent gives thought to his steps" (Prov. 14:15). The word translated "simple" could also be translated "gullible" or "naive."
- "The prudent sees danger and hides himself, but the simple go on and suffer for it" (Prov. 22:13).
- Eve was quite naive in the garden. She believed what Satan said about the pleasure she would experience if she disobeyed God (Gen. 3). Naive is the person who believes what the world says about the way to find happiness, about values, about God, about sex, about money.
- "Whoever trusts in his own mind is a fool, but he who walks in wisdom will be delivered" (Prov. 28:26). A fool uses his own

mind as his standard for living. And by implication this verse teaches that he won't be delivered in the end. What are we to trust as our standard? God's Holy Word!

- "The way of a fool is right in his own eyes, but a wise man listens to advice" (Prov. 12:15).
- "A fool takes no pleasure in understanding but only in expressing his opinion. . . . If one gives an answer before he hears, it is his folly and shame" (Prov. 18:2, 13). This fool doesn't delight in understanding, in gathering all the evidence so that he can make a wise decision. Instead, he goes around stating his own opinion. How many people have you encountered like that? What if his opinion is that it's okay to be a Christian and still be sexually promiscuous? What if he believes that indulging in pornography doesn't hurt anybody? What if his opinion is that God doesn't pay any attention to what we do or don't do? Believing a person like this would be more than foolish!
- Naive, foolish, and gullible is the young man who listens to the loose woman described in Proverbs 7:6–21.
- Naive, foolish, and gullible is the one who refuses to listen to godly admonitions to watch whom he runs around with and listens to, and instead listens to ungodly young people who entice him to indulge in sin and promise that it will be good for him (see Prov. 18:15).
- "Leave the presence of a fool, for there you do not meet words of knowledge" (Prov. 14:7). This passage tells us not to listen to fools, and to even leave their presence. We are told not to be gullible, not to listen to or believe everything we hear.

How can we know who these fools are? Who are these people we shouldn't listen to? The book of Proverbs tells us who they are and how to recognize them. Do any of these people sound familiar?

- "The wisdom of the prudent is to discern his way, but the folly of fools is deceiving" (Prov. 14:8). So a fool is someone who habitually lies.

- "One who is wise is cautious and turns away from evil, but a fool is reckless and careless" (Prov. 14:16). So a fool is someone who is habitually careless and arrogant.
- "How long, O simple ones, will you love being simple? How long will scoffers delight in their scoffing, and fools hate knowledge?" (Prov. 1:22). So a fool is someone who habitually hates the knowledge of God.
- "Because they hated knowledge and did not choose the fear of the LORD, would have none of my counsel and despised all my reproof, therefore they shall eat the fruit of their way and have their fill of their own devices" (Prov. 1:29–30). So a fool is someone who does not choose the fear of God, doesn't accept God's counsel, and habitually spurns godly reproof.
- "For the simple are killed by their turning away, and the complacency of fools destroys them" (Prov. 1:32). So fools are complacent about the things of God.
- "The way of a fool is right in his own eyes, but a wise man listens to advice" (Prov. 12:15). So a fool is someone who believes he is always right, and will not listen to godly counsel.
- "The vexation of a fool is known at once, but the prudent ignores an insult" (Prov. 12:16). So a fool is a person whose vexation is known at once. He is easily irritable.

To summarize, God describes the person who is speaking or teaching or living in a way contrary to the wisdom of God as found in His Word as a fool. More than that, a fool doesn't care to do anything about his foolishness. This is the person we must avoid. We shouldn't hang around this kind of person. Proverbs clearly warns us that if we spend too much time listening to these fools, we may lose our ability to discern the difference between what is right or wrong. We may be negatively and sinfully influenced by them. In other words, if we spend too much time with them, we are likely to become a fool just like them!

Because of all these warnings, we know that whatever Paul meant when he said that love believes all things, he didn't mean that we should be gullible or naive. We also know that this is not what he meant because there are many verses where discretion, discernment, evaluation, and caution are commended as good qualities. Let's examine a few passages in Proverbs and elsewhere that teach about being wise, in contrast to being fools.

- "The prudent gives thought to his steps" (Prov. 14:15). This is talking about a wise, intelligent person who is capable of making wise decisions and choices. The text says that this prudent or wise person doesn't just blindly and thoughtlessly follow the advice of someone else or even follow his own opinion or thoughts. Instead, he spends time evaluating the validity or accuracy of the advice he is given or even gives himself. He doesn't automatically believe something because it sounds good, even if the person says it beautifully or in an interesting fashion.
- "One who is wise is cautious and turns away from evil" (Prov. 14:16). This person doesn't quickly jump into things simply because it sounds like fun, or like an interesting idea. A wise person is fearful of doing anything that would displease God.
- "The prudent sees danger and hides himself" (Prov. 22:3). A prudent person does what Joseph did when he was tempted by the wife of Potiphar—he flees from any appearance of sin (Gen. 39). Elijah was prudent when being pursued by Jezebel. In 1 Kings 17:3 the Lord advises him to hide himself and he does. A prudent person does what every person who becomes a Christian does when he becomes aware of his sinfulness and the impending judgment of God—he flees to Christ and finds refuge in Him from the wrath and condemnation of God.
- "Test everything; hold fast what is good" (1 Thess. 5:21). A wise man will carefully examine whatever he is taught to make sure it is the truth of God.
- "But understand this, that in the last days there will come times of difficulty" (2 Tim. 3:1). Perilous times are coming! And these difficult times will come in the form of men who hold to a form of godliness, men who claim to believe the truth but really oppose the truth. These men are impostors, men

who deceive and are being deceived. We're told to "avoid such people" (v. 5). A wise man will use discernment to recognize these people and will avoid them.

- "There are some things in them [Paul's letters] that are hard to understand, which the ignorant and unstable twist to their own destruction, as they do the other Scriptures. You therefore, beloved, knowing this beforehand, take care that you are not carried away with the error of lawless people and lose your own stability" (2 Peter 3:16–17). Peter tells us to be on our guard against people who distort the Scriptures lest we be carried away by the error of unprincipled men who misuse the Word of God to deceive us and cause us to fall. A wise man will use discretion, always comparing what he hears to what the Word teaches.

- "Beloved, do not believe every spirit, but test the spirits to see whether they are from God, for many false prophets have gone out into the world" (1 John 4:1). We are told not to be gullible, believing everything that anyone teaches, but to put those who teach us and what they teach us to the test, to see whether they are from God. A wise man uses his head to examine the teaching he hears.

- "Now these Jews [the Bereans] were more noble than those in Thessalonica; they received the word with all eagerness, examining the Scriptures daily to see if these things were so" (Acts 17:11). God commends the Bereans and calls them noble for a couple of reasons: (1) they received what was truly Scripture with all readiness of mind and eagerness, and (2) they carefully examined what they were taught to make sure that it was biblical.

- "I know your works, your toil and your patient endurance, and how you cannot bear with those who are evil, but have tested those who call themselves apostles and are not, and found them to be false" (Rev. 2:2). Jesus commends the Ephesians because they put to the test those who called themselves apostles and weren't, and found them to be false. What standard did they use to test them? They tested them by God's Word.

During the fifty-plus years of my ministry, I've had many people tell me about something they have heard or something they've read or some words of advice they've been given or some drug that they have taken that has revolutionized their lives. And when that happens, I usually ask them to tell me how their lives have been revolutionized. I listen to what they have to say, and then I ask them, "On what passage or passages of Scripture are these new, revolutionary, life-changing insights based?" I want to see how they put these "revolutionary" tidbits to the test.

The issue as to whether or not we believe someone is not whether that someone claims to be telling the truth. The issue is not whether he seems to be a nice person. It's not even whether what the person says resonates with my experience. It doesn't matter how good his illustrations are or how many Bible verses he throws into the mix. The issue is not whether his teaching sounds good, or whether he actually throws in some Christian lingo. The issue is this: Is what he says in accordance with Scripture and with a proper interpretation of Scripture? There were and still are many who handle God's Word, but don't handle it properly or accurately.

For all these biblical reasons we know that whatever Paul meant by "love believes all things," he didn't mean that love is to be gullible or naive. Some people may think the way to make friends and influence people is to be a person who never asks questions, who never evaluates, who never challenges, who never disagrees with anyone, who is always a "yes" person, who goes along with whatever other people do or say. That is just not the way to do it!

## What It *Does* Mean to Believe All Things

That brings us to this question: If Paul didn't mean that love is gullible and naive, then what did he mean? I believe he meant that if we are loving people, we will not allow suspicion, cynicism, or a judgmental, critical attitude to become a dominant feature in our relationships. Love's believing all things means that if we are living a life of love, we will put the *best possible interpretation* on what another person has done or said until we have the facts that prove to the contrary. It means that if we do not have the cold hard facts that prove that what the other person has done is evil, malicious, or unbiblical, we will always opt for the most favorable possibility. This phrase is saying that we should believe all that is not palpably false. We should believe all that we can with a good conscience believe to the credit of another.

Concerning the practice of judgmentalism, Jerry Bridges writes, "Most of us can slip into the sin of judgmentalism from time to time. But there are those among us who practice it continually. These people have what I call a critical spirit. They look and find fault with everyone and everything. Regardless of the topic of conversation—whether it is a person, a church, an event, or anything—they end up speaking in a disparaging manner."[2]

Bridges calls judgmentalism (a critical spirit) a "respectable sin"— meaning, of course, that in the opinion of some people it's not something we need to take very seriously (unless, of course, we're the one against whom the judgmentalism is being directed). His term *respectable sin* is a tongue-in-cheek way of saying that it's one of those sins that we often tolerate and even excuse, especially if we are the perpetrator. I certainly agree with Bridges's observation that "there are those among us who practice it continually." It's obvious that there are some people for whom the spiritual disease (sin) of a critical spirit is more endemic. And I also believe he's right when he asserts that most of us, from time to time, are judgmental and are prone to indulge in faultfinding and negativism. But whether we consistently practice suspiciousness and judgmentalism or occasionally and selectively behave that way, whenever we behave this way (a practice usually motivated by pride), it must be regarded as a violation of the love principle described in 1 Corinthians 13:7.

In his comments on this phrase, John MacArthur writes, "Love will always opt for the most favorable possibility. If a loved one is accused of something wrong, love will consider him innocent until proven guilty. If he turns out to be guilty, love will give him credit for the best motive."[3]

2. Jerry Bridges, *Respectable Sins* (Colorado Springs: NavPress, 2007), 146.
3. John MacArthur, *1 Corinthians* (Chicago: Moody, 1984), 354.

The KJV of James 3:17 says that the truly wise person is "easy to be entreated." The Greek word (*eupeithēs*) used here means to be "easily persuaded." What James says of wisdom is comparable to what Paul says of love—love is easily persuaded to think well of another person's actions or motives unless there are cold hard facts to prove otherwise.

## Let's Get More Specific

In general, that is what it means to have a love that always trusts and believes, but now let me become more specific in terms of what it means in practice. Love's believing all things means that we won't treat people in the way that Job's so-called friends treated him in the book of Job. Job's so-called friends jumped to the conclusion that his difficulties were due to the fact that God was punishing him for some flagrant sins in his life. They refused to listen to what he had to say. They never asked him a question to gather information. Job pleaded with them to stop tormenting him and instead "keep listening to my words and let this be your comfort" (Job 21:2). But they never asked any questions to get Job's perspective. Instead, they attacked, accused, and maligned. While this was going on, they must have talked to each other about the situation. Basically, they drew conclusions, even though there was no evidence to support their conclusions.

Their conclusions clearly contradicted what the Bible says about Job. According to the Scripture, he was a mature believer who feared God and hated evil. Everything about Job validated the truth of this statement (Job 1–2). Yet his friends refused to believe anything good about Job, and in so doing, they certainly were not manifesting a love that believes all things.

What does it mean to have a love that believes all things? It means that we will avoid doing what Proverbs 16:27 says of some people: "A worthless man digs up evil, while his words are like a scorching fire" (NASB). In other words, some people go around digging up evil and then tormenting with words that are like a scorching fire. Do you know anyone like that? Are you like that? The picture here is of a person who is constantly looking for something bad in other people, and if he doesn't find it easily, he gets out a shovel and begins to dig. He is determined to discover some fault in others even if he has to manufacture it. His mouth becomes a flamethrower from which words that scorch and burn, belittle or demean, and destroy other people come belching out. Believing all things means that we won't be like this man.

What does it mean to have a love that believes all things? It means that we must avoid doing what Proverbs 17:20 says of some people: "A man of crooked heart does not discover good, and one with a dishonest tongue falls into calamity." This man finds no good in other people. This is the person who has a suspicious or judgmental attitude toward other people. It really doesn't matter what the others do! It will never be quite good enough. He always expects more than the others have done and feels they could have and should have done better.

Or this is the person who has such a suspicious attitude that if someone does something positive toward him, he thinks that the other person did it for a wrong reason. He is always suspicious of the other person's motives—believing that whatever was done was for a selfish reason. Believing all things means that we will not function in this way toward other people.

What does it mean to have a love that believes all things? It means that we must avoid doing what some of the Corinthians did with the apostle Paul, as described in 1 Corinthians 4:4–5:

> I am not aware of anything against myself, but I am not thereby acquitted. It is the Lord who judges me. Therefore do not pronounce judgment before the time, before the Lord comes, who will bring to light the things now hidden in darkness and will disclose the purposes of the heart. Then each one will receive his commendation from God.

What does it mean to have a love that believes all things? It means that we must avoid doing what some people were doing with Paul in 1 Thessalonians 2. Without a shred of solid evidence, they accused Paul of being in the ministry to please men, which could not have been further from the truth. They accused him of using flattering speech. They accused him of being greedy and seeking glory from men. What were they thinking? They accused him of being authoritarian and of being selfish, even though all the evidence proved these assessments to be ridiculously false.

What does it mean to have a love that believes all things? It means that we must guard our own attitudes when we must criticize, admonish, or rebuke someone who is doing wrong. We must make sure that our own motives are pure and keep from trying to tear that person down in order to build ourselves up. Our motive when rebuking or correcting must always be to help him and to protect others. We are to take ourselves completely out of the equation when we take issue with someone else.

This was the great error of the Pharisees. Luke 18:9 says, "He [Jesus] also told this parable to some who trusted in themselves that they were righteous, and treated others with contempt." Jesus then went on to tell them about the Pharisee and the tax collector. Matthew 23:23 also depicts their self-righteousness: "Woe to you, scribes and Pharisees, hypocrites! For you tithe mint and dill and cumin, and have neglected the weightier matters of the law: justice and mercy and faithfulness. These you ought to have done, without neglecting the others. You blind guides, straining out a gnat and swallowing a camel!" They were concerned with externals, and their desire was to criticize others—all from a wrong motive. And don't forget James 4:11–12:

> Do not speak evil against one another, brothers. The one who speaks against a brother or judges his brother, speaks evil against the law and judges the law. But if you judge the law, you are not a doer of the law but a judge. There is only one lawgiver and judge, he who is able to save and to destroy. But who are you to judge your neighbor?

What does it mean to have a love that believes all things? It means that we must be very careful about criticizing with a party spirit. In Luke 9:49–50 John came to Jesus and said, " 'Master, we saw someone casting out demons in your name, and we tried to stop him, because he does not follow with us.' But Jesus said to him, 'Do not stop him, for the one who is not against you is for you.' " Who was this man who was doing miracles? More than likely, he was one of the seventy other disciples mentioned in Luke 10:1 who were not part of the original twelve. Concerning this man, there was no evidence that he was teaching false doctrine or deceiving the people. Yet John and presumably others were condemning him. Why did they do this? The reason John gave was that they didn't know him because he wasn't of their own group.

This text should not be regarded as directions about what we should do with someone who is without any doubt preaching error and false doctrine and is misleading people. When a person is clearly teaching error, love for God, love for the truth, and love for people would compel us to oppose and expose him because the rest of the Bible commands us to expose error. "Take no part in the unfruitful works of darkness, but instead expose them" (Eph. 5:11). Luke 9 applies to what we should do when we are tempted to criticize others simply because we don't know them! It may also be applied to situations where we may know who certain people are, but we suspect that they are in error because they are not part of our group or don't attend our meetings or conferences. Without hard, solid evidence, we judge that they must be liberal or that they must be false teachers. Luke 9 warns us not to say or do this kind of thing for the reason that John gave.

What does it mean to have a love that believes all things? It means that we must be very careful about judging the motives of others. We must be careful about thinking or saying such things as, "I know why he does or says this or that." For example, we must be careful about saying or thinking, "I know he does what he does because he is materialistic. He loves money." Or "I know he does what he does because he's power-hungry! He just wants to run everything." How about this one? "She does what she does because she wants attention. She has to get her own way in everything." Or "they must have a real pride problem." Or "he doesn't do things we think are right because he is unspiritual." Brethren, we need to be careful about judging motives because we can't really know what is going on in a person's heart! Too many times we try to take over the Holy Spirit's role. The Holy Spirit can read what's going on inside others' hearts—we can't!

Scripture makes it clear that some people were constantly judging the motives of Paul and others, and they were wrong to do it! In 1 Corinthians 4:4–5 Paul says:

> I am not aware of anything against myself, but I am not thereby acquitted. It is the Lord who judges me. Therefore do not pronounce judgment before the time, before the Lord comes, who will bring to light the things now hidden in darkness and will disclose the purposes of the heart. Then each one will receive his commendation from God.

We need to remember that judging people's actions for the purpose of helping them is one thing, but judging their motives is another. Love and humility should compel us to be very careful in saying, "He is doing this because . . ." (other passages warning against acting this way include Prov. 16:2 and 1 Sam. 16:7). God is the only one who has the right and ability to definitively examine our hearts.

What does it mean to have a love that believes all things? It means that we must follow Psalm 15:2–3:

> He who walks blamelessly and does what is right
> and speaks truth in his heart;
> who does not slander with his tongue
> and does no evil to his neighbor,
> nor takes up a reproach against his friend . . .

The text says that we are not to do evil to other people. In the Bible the word *evil* is used in two ways. It is a word sometimes used to describe moral evil and sometimes situational evil. An example of using it in the first way is Job 1:1; 2:3: "There was a man in the land of Uz whose name was Job, and that man was blameless and upright, one who feared God and turned away from evil. . . . And the LORD said to Satan, 'Have you considered my servant Job, that there is none like him on earth, a blameless and upright man, who fears God and turns away from evil?'" In Ecclesiastes 12:1 we read, "Remember also your Creator in the days of your youth, before the evil days come." In this context "before the evil days" means "before you get old and have a lot of physical problems."

In particular this text is telling us about two ways that we can do both moral and situational evil to people.

We can do evil by slandering another person. Whenever we slander someone, we are doing evil. We do evil to the person *about* whom we are speaking, and we do evil to the person *to* whom we are speaking.

So then what is slander? Slander involves two things:

1. It involves saying something that may or may not be true that defames another person or damages his reputation. A person's name is one of his most valuable assets, as stated in Proverbs 22:1: "A good name is to be chosen rather than great riches, and favor is better than silver or gold."
2. It also involves saying something negative about another person that may be true, but that serves no good, constructive, godly, positive purpose.

When we spread information that is not based on rock-solid evidence, we may be guilty of lying and we certainly are engaged in slander. And beyond that, if we share negative information about someone that is true but serves no positive, uplifting purpose, it is a violation of the law of love as expressed in 1 Corinthians 13. That, my friends, is slander. And it would violate the teaching of Psalm 15:3 and also the "love believes all things" principle of 1 Corinthians 13:7.

In his commentary on Psalm 15, Charles Spurgeon included Richard Turnbull's comment on slander. Turnbull said, "The viper [snake] wounds none but such as it bites, the poisonous herbs . . . kill none but such as taste, or handle . . . and so come near them; but the poison of slanderous tongues is much more rank [dangerous] and deadly; for that hurts and slays, wounds and kills, not only near, but afar off, not only at hand, but by distance of place removed, not only at home, but abroad . . . and spares neither the living nor the dead."[4]

Charles Spurgeon also included Bishop Taylor's comment on slander: slander is a crime that "is a conjugation of evils, and is productive

4. Quoted, and modernized, from Charles Spurgeon, *The Treasury of David* (Byron Center, MI: Associated Publishers, 1970), 1:207.

of infinite mischiefs; it undermines peace, and saps the foundation of friendship; it destroys families, and rends in pieces the very heart and vitals of love; it makes an evil man a party and witness, and judge, and executioner of the innocent."[5]

Spurgeon also included Peter Baro's comments: "It is no less grievous to hurt a man with the tongue than with a sword; nay, oft times the stroke of a tongue is more grievous than the wound of a spear."[6] We can do real evil to people by slandering them. If we love them, we will not think the worst of them, nor will we want anyone else to think the worst of them. Instead, we will think the best of them unless the facts drive us to another conclusion; and if we love them, we will want others to think the best of them unless the facts drive us to think otherwise.

Psalm 15:2–3 also indicates that we can do evil by taking up a reproach:

> He who walks blamelessly and does what is right
> > and speaks truth in his heart;
> who does not slander with his tongue
> > and does no evil to his neighbor,
> > > nor takes up a reproach against his friend . . .

This text is saying that we not only do evil when we are the perpetrators of slander, but also do evil when we listen to a demeaning, slanderous report from others and then take up the slanderous report and actually pass on what we have heard to other people. Gossip works this way, especially when we embellish each evil tidbit for greater sensationalism. I wish I could say that Christians just don't do that, yet I know they do.

Peter Baro explains the meaning of not taking up a reproach:

> It seems for the most part to be enough for us if we can say, that we feign [imagine] not this or that, nor make it up from our own heads, but only tell it forth as we heard it from others, without adding

5. Ibid., 1:206.
6. Ibid., 1:205.

anything of our own brain. But as oft as we do this we fail in our own duty [duty of love], in not providing for our neighbor's credit, [and instead] we gather up, and by telling them forth, disperse them abroad . . . when as by all means possible [we should] wish and do well unto our neighbor. . . . You who travel toward eternal life must not only not devise false reports and slanders against other men, but also not so much as have them in your mouth. . . . And you must not assist or maintain them in slandering; but by all honest and lawful means, [you must] provide for the credit and estimation of your neighbor so much as lies in you.[7]

According to Psalm 15:3, it is not only wrong for us to slander another person, but also wrong for us to easily or quickly receive or believe an evil report about another person. And more than that, the text is telling us that it is certainly wrong to pass an evil report on to someone else. And all of that is certainly in keeping with what Paul is saying in 1 Corinthians 13:7. In other words, because love always trusts and is not instinctively and habitually suspicious, it will certainly resist initiating slander, receiving slander or gossip, or passing it on to others.

At this point, you may be wondering: If that's what love is, is it ever right to share negative information about someone else with other people? The answer to that question is a definite yes. In fact, there are times when not sharing negative information would be a violation of the love principle.

When would not sharing negative information about someone be a violation of the love principle? Failing to share negative information would be a violation of the love principle when not sharing would be harmful to the person who is committing sin. For example, it would be right to share negative information:

- if a person is behaving in a way that is *clearly* a violation of Scripture;
- if you have rock-solid evidence based on fact and not suspicion or rumor;

7. Ibid., 1:206.

- if the wrong he is doing is a pattern in his life and not merely an event;
- if, in accordance with Matthew 18:15 and Galatians 6:1, you have personally tried to help the person and failed. Then, Matthew 18:16 says, you are to enlist the help of others to turn him from his sinful behavior. And if you don't, you would be violating the love principle of 1 Corinthians 13 because real love is always concerned about the well-being of a person God has brought into your life who is clearly and consistently sinning against God.

Failing to share negative information about a person would also be a violation of the love principle when not sharing would be harmful to other people. There are a number of places where Paul publicly shares negative information about people. For instance, in 2 Timothy 2:17–18 he says that

> their talk will spread like gangrene. Among them are Hymenaeus and Philetus, who have swerved from the truth, saying that the resurrection has already happened. They are upsetting the faith of some.

He tells us about these men to warn us. He says that their teaching is unbiblical and will lead to ungodliness, upsetting the faith of some. So by telling others what they have done, he is attempting to spare others the same problem.

Paul did the same thing in 2 Timothy 4:14–15. This time he spoke of a man named Alexander.

> Alexander the coppersmith did me great harm; the Lord will repay him according to his deeds. Beware of him yourself, for he strongly opposed our message.

It was not unloving for Paul to tell Timothy—and us—about these men because Paul had rock-solid evidence of what these people were doing and teaching, and that it was unbiblical. He had rock-solid evidence that their teaching was dangerous to others, and so love for others compelled him to share this negative information about these men.

This means that if we discreetly share negative information about someone out of a sincere desire to protect other people from harm, we are not involved in slander. In fact, when done with this motive, the sharing may really be an act of love. In every instance, the motive for sharing is the key to whether it is an act of love or an act of malice and therefore a violation of the "love always believing" principle.

## Summary

What does it mean to have a "love believes all things" kind of life? I've tried to communicate to you just what that phrase means and what it does not mean. As we've sought to understand what Paul meant by the phrase "love always trusts" or "love believes all things," we've seen that Paul can't mean that we should automatically believe everyone and anyone. It's clear from a study of Scripture and even from the examples of Jesus and Paul that 1 Corinthians 13:7 is not encouraging us to be gullible and naive. It is not encouraging us to close our eyes to the evil that is all around us; it is not saying that we should never hold anyone accountable for wrongdoing, that we should never rebuke or expose. In fact, if we did that we would be *un*loving because "love does not rejoice at wrongdoing, but rejoices with the truth" (1 Cor. 13:6).

As we have sought to understand what Paul meant by the phrase "love always trusts" or "love believes all things," we've also noted from a positive perspective that what he means is that a person who loves in the way God wants him to love will not possess a suspicious, judgmental, or hypercritical pattern of thinking or living. In the words of Proverbs 14:15, "the prudent gives thought to his steps." He will not be careless or arrogant, but instead will be cautious and prudent. This wise man will not make snap judgments either way. He will not automatically think negatively or make judgments on the basis of innuendo, rumor, or assumptions. He will not slander or even say anything negative about or to someone else until he is sure he has the facts. And even then, he will not share it with anyone but God, unless he does so in an attempt to help the person doing the wrong or to protect someone who may be hurt or influenced by what that person is saying or doing.

This text is saying that if you are a loving person, the focus of your life, the attitude you carry through life, should basically be the attitude described in Philippians 4:8: "Finally, brothers, whatever is true, whatever is honorable, whatever is just, whatever is pure, whatever is lovely, whatever is commendable, if there is any excellence, if there is anything worthy of praise, think about these things."

As I close this chapter, I want to ask you two questions:

First, if I were to ask you who profess to be Christians, "Do you want to influence others for Christ? Do you want to be fruitful for Him?" I know that each of you, as a believer, would say yes. Romans 7:4 says, "Likewise, my brothers, you also have died to the law through the body of Christ, so that you may belong to another, to him who has been raised from the dead, in order that we may bear fruit for God." God saves us that we might bear fruit for Him. So I'm sure you would agree with me that there is nothing more exciting and desirable than knowing that you are making a mark for Christ. In comparison with this, there is nothing else that comes close. This is more desirable than being a great athlete, being a movie star, being an author of a best seller, being a successful businessman, having a big home, or having a bank account with millions of dollars. These things don't even come close to the joy of being an influence for Christ. If you are a believer, I'm sure you don't want to come to the end of your days on earth and be like that fig tree of which Jesus spoke in Matthew 21:19: "May no fruit ever come from you again!" I'm sure you would rather be like the tree described in Psalm 1:3: "He is like a tree planted by streams of water that yields its fruit in its season, and its leaf does not wither. In all that he does, he prospers." Well, if you want to be like that tree, please listen to Paul. He says in 1 Corinthians 12:31 that the way to do that surpasses greatness. The "beyond measure" way of doing this is by developing a life that is permeated and saturated by the kind of love described in 1 Corinthians 13.

Second, do you want to have a church that makes a powerful impact for Christ on our community and world? Well, if you love Christ, I'm sure you would like to see our world filled with churches that are functioning as the salt of the world and the light of the world. What is it that will cause our churches to be more powerful influences for Christ? I am convinced, on the basis of 1 Corinthians 13, that the kind of church that will make a powerful impact is a church full of people who manifest the kind of love described in this great passage.

By this time you may be convinced of the central role love plays in being an effective Christian, but you may be left with a question about how this kind of love can be developed and sustained. To this point in this book I've given some suggestions about an answer to that question. In the last two chapters I will discuss the last two characteristics of real love found in the rest of verse 7 (chap. 17) and then conclude the whole study by giving some suggestions about how to develop and sustain the kind of love described in 1 Corinthians 13 (chap. 18).

For now, I'd like to encourage you to recognize the importance that this kind of love can play in your life. I want you believers to know that you *can* have a life that is characterized by this kind of love, and I want to tell you who are not Christians yet that you cannot develop or sustain this kind of love. This is possible only for believers. What Paul has to say here is not for everyone. Of course, everyone should love this way, but not everyone can love this way. It requires the empowering work of the Holy Spirit. Without Him, we can't come close to this kind of love. So if you know you are not a Christian, and you want a life that is characterized by this kind of love, your first concern should be to recognize your need of forgiveness for your sins. Your greatest need is to be born again; your greatest need is to come to Jesus Christ, repenting and believing on Him (John 1:12–13). If you are reading this and you know that you are not a believer, please seek out a mature believer to help you come to Christ. My fervent prayer is that God will help you do that.

## Review, Reflection, Application, and Discussion Questions

1. What doesn't Paul mean when he says, "Love believes all things"?

2. What are the proofs that "love believes all things" doesn't mean that we should be gullible or naive as we interact with people?

3. Summarize and reflect on the teaching of Proverbs 14:7, 15 and 22:3.

4. According to the book of Proverbs, what are the characteristics of a person whom the Bible would classify as a fool? Study some of the verses and seek to explain what the phrases describing a fool mean. What does a foolish person do and not do?

5. What does it mean to be a prudent person?

6. From a positive perspective, what is Paul saying about a person who in "love believes all things"?

7. What can we learn about real love from the example of Job's friends?

8. What do we learn about real love from the interaction between our Lord and John in Luke 9:49–50?

9. What may we learn about what real love won't do from Psalm 15:3?

10. Explain the terms used in Psalm 15:3. What is slander? What does it mean to take up a reproach against someone?

11. What figures of speech or graphic terms do some of the men (Peter Baro, Bishop Taylor, Richard Turnbull) whom I quoted from Spurgeon's *Treasury of David* use in describing slander?

12. What are the biblical guidelines that we should keep in mind before sharing negative information about others?

13. Why is it sometimes a loving thing to share negative information with others?

14. After studying this chapter, have you identified any ways in which you are strong or weak in the practice of this characteristic of real love?

15. And now my usual reminder: Please remember as you reflect on the love principle presented in this chapter that the purpose of this exposition, evaluation, and application is:

   a. not to discourage or destroy us;

   b. but to motivate us to see our constant need of the cross and how much we owe to Jesus—without Him we'd never make it, but praise God we are not without Him;

   c. and to motivate us to understand our constant daily need of grace—that our salvation never has been and never will be by the works we have done, but always by the work Christ has done and is doing for us; I want our studies in 1 Corinthians 13 to be a reminder that we need to live a cross-centered life; we need the application of the cross work of Jesus every day of our lives; remember there's not a day in our lives when we are so good that we don't need the cross, and there is never a day in our lives when we are so bad that what Christ did on the cross is not sufficient to provide forgiveness for us (Rom. 3:24; 5:20; Eph. 1:7; 1 John 1:7; 2:1–2);

   d. and to cause us to understand that we must and can, by His grace, put off from our lives the "unlove" that is displeasing to God and put on in our lives the love that is beautifully described in 1 Corinthians 13 so that we might become more and more like our Savior and more prolific in bearing fruit for Him as others see the grace of God at work in our lives, changing and transforming us (Eph. 4:22–24; 1 Tim. 4:7).

# 17

## REAL LOVE IS HOPEFUL AND TENACIOUS

Some time ago Carol and I were asked to speak to a group of seminary students and their wives in a class on the Christian home. Carol spoke about the role the wife has in her husband's ministry, and I spoke on the importance of the pastor's marriage in his ministry. After we spoke, we had a question-and-answer time in which the students and their wives could fire questions at us. The first question we were asked was, "What were the most important things you tried to teach your children?" Carol responded, "The most important things we tried to teach our children were to love God's Word and to recognize that it is sufficient for all the issues of life." I said, "From my perspective there were two things that I considered as the most important things that I wanted to teach my children: one was to love God with all their heart, soul, and strength, and the second was to love their neighbor as they loved themselves. In comparison to these two things, everything else was relatively unimportant." Then I went on to say, "We may not have done a good job at doing these two things, but those were the two things that we were most concerned about."

If you were to ask me a similar question about what I wanted to teach the people in the congregations I pastored, I would say the same thing. If you were to ask me the same question about my ultimate goal in the biblical counseling classes I teach at Grace School of Ministry, I would say the same thing. Certainly I want to teach my students how to use God's Word in helping people, but over and beyond all of that, I want to promote in them a love for God and a love for people; not only do I want them to love to counsel people, I want them to love the people whom they counsel.

I say all of that for many reasons, one of them being what Jesus said in Matthew 22:37–39:

> You shall love the Lord your God with all your heart and with all your soul and with all your mind. This is the great and first commandment. And a second is like it: You shall love your neighbor as yourself.

Another is what Paul said in 1 Timothy 1:5 about the goal of his instruction (ministry) being to produce people who loved with a clear conscience and a sincere faith. And another reason for aiming my family and public ministry toward encouraging a real 1 Corinthians 13 kind of love in people is related to what Paul said in 1 Corinthians 12:31–13:13. As we noted in previous chapters, but important enough to summarize again, he emphasizes the importance of love with several statements:

- The love way is the "surpassing greatness" way to a fruitful ministry (12:31).
- Having a life filled with love is more important for effective ministry than linguistic ability, than unusual insights and knowledge, than mountain-moving faith, than extreme generosity, and than being so committed to a cause that you would be willing to be a martyr (13:1–3).
- "So now faith, hope, and love abide, these three; but the greatest of these is love" (13:13).
- Christians should pursue love more than any of the extraordinary gifts of the Spirit (14:1).
- The gift of prophecy and knowledge will be done away, but love will never fail (13:8–12). "Love," says Paul, "in contrast to

extraordinary spiritual gifts, abides forever." The word Paul uses
to describe what happens to prophecy and knowledge means "to
be abolished" or "to be stopped" or "to become inoperative or
unnecessary." The gift of tongues will cease. It will stop because
there won't be any need for them.

John MacArthur says that the gift of tongues is like a battery that
has a limited energy supply and a limited life span. When its limits are
reached, its activity automatically ends.[1]

- In verse 8 Paul says, "Love never fails." The Greek word *piptō*,
  which is the "fails" part of "never fails," was used to describe a
  leaf that falls to the ground, withers, and decays. The idea of
  this phrase is that at no time will love ever fail, wither, or decay.
  At no time will the importance and value of love be abolished.
  Paul is saying that (extraordinary) spiritual gifts (such as the
  gift of receiving and understanding new special revelation and
  speaking in tongues) are only for a time, but love will last for
  all eternity.
- When Paul says, "Love never fails" he is not saying that love is
  a spiritual formula that guarantees success in every endeavor.
  What he is saying is that "whenever and wherever Christians are
  successful in their living and ministry, it will always be through
  love . . . No godly work can be accomplished without love.
  Success will not always be a part of love, but love will always be
  a part of spiritual success."[2]

From all of this we can see that Paul is saying that if we want
to make a maximum impact for Christ, we must be people whose
lives are permeated and saturated with love; we must be people
whose lives just drip with it! In previous chapters we have noted
thirteen of the characteristics of this love that will enable us to
make a maximum impact for Christ in our home, churches, and

1. John MacArthur, *1 Corinthians* (Chicago: Moody, 1984), 359.
2. Ibid., 358.

world. In this chapter I intend to explain and apply the fourteenth and fifteenth characteristics of love as they are found at the end of verse 7 of chapter 13.

## Real Love Hopes All Things

The Bible makes it clear that a Christian has every reason to be filled with hope. In fact, you will find the word *hope* used thirty-one times in the New Testament. When the word *hope* is used in Scripture, it is often accompanied by adjectives that describe the nature of the hope. Sometimes it is accompanied by the word *good*, sometimes by the word *blessed*, sometimes by the word *living*, sometimes by the word *better*, sometimes by the word *fullness*.

Christianity is a religion that is filled with hope, and when the word *hope* is used, it is not referring to a "hope so" kind of thing, but to a rock-solid expectation of good. The Greek dictionary for the New Testament tells us that the word *hope*, as used in Scripture, is referring to a "favorable and confident expectation of good."[3] Reflect on the precious truths about hope found in the following verses.

- First Peter 1:3 states that we are born again to hope. The world is filled with people who have no hope or people who have a dead hope or a false hope (Eph. 2:12). But Christians have every reason to have hope because Jesus Christ was raised from the dead. Jesus Christ our Redeemer and Savior is alive, and that gives us reason to have a favorable and confident expectation of good. Because Christ has been resurrected, we can joyfully sing, "I serve a risen Savior, He's in the world today; I know that he is living whatever men may say; I see his hand of mercy; I hear his voice of cheer; And just the time I need him, he's always near. He lives, he lives, Christ Jesus lives today! He walks with me and talks with me along life's narrow way. He lives, he lives,

3. W. E. Vine, *Vine's Complete Expository Dictionary* (Nashville: Thomas Nelson, 1996), 311.

salvation to impart! You ask me how I know he lives? He lives within my heart."

- Colossians 1:27 declares, "Christ in you, the hope of glory"; 1 Timothy 1:1 reminds us that Christ is our hope. He is the basis or ground and substance of our hope.

- Titus 1:2 tells us that the God who cannot lie has given to those who believe in Christ the hope of eternal life, which is not referring just to quantity of life (longevity), but to a super quality of life.

- Second Thessalonians 2:16 informs us that God has loved us and given us eternal comfort and a good hope by grace. In other words, this text is saying that because He loves us, God comforts us in the midst of our trials by giving us a good hope, a hope that is good in terms of what it contains. A hope that is good because of what it does for us, in that it brings us comfort, encouragement, and steadfastness.

- Colossians 1:23 speaks of the hope of the gospel. The word *gospel* literally means "good news." Paul is telling us that the gospel brings to us a message of hope in that it has the power to save us and bring us near to God (Eph. 2:12; Rom. 1:16).

- In Romans 5:2 Paul says that "we rejoice in hope of the glory of God," meaning that we have a hope that we will see the glory of God in all its fullness. Now we see it in part; now we know in part; now we see His glory dimly as in a mirror; but in the future (after death or the second coming of Christ) we will see His glory face-to-face (1 Cor. 13:9–12).

- Hebrews 6:19 declares that we have a hope that is steadfast and sure, a hope that functions like an anchor, a hope that keeps us steady in the midst of the raging storms of life.

- Titus 2:13 reminds us that we have a blessed hope, even the appearing of the glory of our great God and Savior, Jesus Christ. We believe as angels said in Acts 1:9–11 that the same Jesus who was here on earth is coming back. We believe that when He comes, He will bring with Him the kingdom. When He comes, the bodies of the dead will be raised, and we will forever be with the Lord (1 Thess. 4:13–18).

- Romans 15:13 asserts that our God is the God of hope, who causes us to abound in hope by the power of the Holy Spirit.
- Romans 15:4 declares that God has given us the Scriptures to encourage us and promote perseverance and give us hope in the midst of opposition and rejection and severe trials.
- First Corinthians 13:13 informs us that we have an abiding hope, a hope that doesn't come and go, a hope that is forever certain and reliable. "So now faith, hope, and love abide."
- Hebrews 6:18 assures us that our hope is based on the character and the promises of a God who is all-loving, all-wise, all-powerful, all-righteous, and unchangeable. Our hope, says this verse, is based on the promises of God, who cannot lie. Because of His holy character, it is impossible for Him to lie; it is impossible for Him to say that He is going to do something that He will not do. This hope, which is based on the promises of a God who cannot lie, is an anchor for us. This hope is sure and steadfast. It will never disappoint us; it will never let us down.
- Proverbs 10:28 tells us that the hope of the righteous brings gladness and joy because it will be fulfilled, whereas the hope of the wicked will bring disaster because it will not be fulfilled. Our hope brings gladness because it is based on the solid foundation of the promises of a God who cannot lie. Because our hope is based on the promises of a God who cannot lie, we can know, as Proverbs 4:18 says, that our path is as a shining light that leads more and more unto the perfect day. Because of the wonderful promises of God, we can look to the future with anticipation, with joy and exuberance, because we know that the best is yet to come.

While this is a long list, it is in no way an exhaustive one. The Bible brims with hope!

The effect that these scriptural truths about hope should have on us reminds me of an older lady who was about to die. When she knew her time of departure from this world was drawing near, she asked her pastor to come and discuss her funeral service. She said,

"At my funeral service here are some of the things I would like to occur. I want these hymns to be sung [and she told him which ones]. I'd like you to preach about heaven. And when I'm put in a casket, I want you to make sure that they put several things in the casket with me. I want you to make sure that they put a Bible in the casket with my body because I want people to know that I loved the Bible. I also want you to make sure they put a spoon and a fork in the casket." When she mentioned the spoon and the fork, the pastor said, "I can understand why you would want a Bible, but why a spoon and a fork?" The woman replied, "Pastor, remember that when we have those church dinners, after we've eaten the main course, someone often tells us to keep our spoons and our forks because the best part of the meal is yet to come—meaning, of course, that we're going to have dessert. Well, Pastor, when I lie in my casket and people walk by, I want them to know that the best for me and for all Christians is yet to come."

That older lady was right. She had a hope for the future that was based on the infallible promises of her God, who could not lie. Others might make promises that they will not keep, but not so with God because, as the Bible says, "it is impossible for him to lie."

## The Relationship of Hope and Love

For all these reasons and many more, your love as a Christian is to be a hopeful love. But what does hope have to do with love? Why does Paul list hope as a characteristic of love?

- The Christian can manifest the kind of love described in 1 Corinthians 13, a love that is long-suffering and kind, a love that is not jealous, a love that will cause him to refrain from bragging and from behaving in an unbecoming way toward other people.
- The Christian can manifest this kind of love because he has a rock-solid basis for believing that nothing that ever happens to him or around him will ever put him in a hopeless situation.

- The Christian can manifest this kind of love because he has no reason for any kind of doubt about the final outcome of his life.

- The Christian can manifest this kind of love because he doesn't interpret reality by what he sees with his eyes, or by what apparently makes sense to him or to others, or by what others say about the way he should respond to trials and abuse, rejection and disappointment.

- The Christian can manifest this kind of love because he has a hope based on the promise of Romans 8:28 that God is causing all things to work together for good.

- The Christian can manifest this kind of love because he has a hope based on the truth of Matthew 19:26: no person or situation is a hopeless case.

- The Christian can manifest this kind of love because he has a hope based on the truth of Job 23:10—"He knows the way that I take; when he has tried me, I will come out as gold."

- The Christian can manifest this kind of love because he has a hope based on the truth of Jeremiah 29:11 where God says, "I know the plans that I have for you . . . plans for welfare and not for calamity to give you a future and a hope" (NASB).

- The Christian can manifest this kind of love because he has a hope based on Isaiah 41:10 where the God who cannot lie and has all power promises that He will always be with us to strengthen, help, and uphold us with His righteous right hand.

- The Christian can manifest this kind of love because he knows that he has a place and a treasure in the life to come. As 1 Peter 1:3–4 promises, "Blessed be the God and Father of our Lord Jesus Christ! According to his great mercy, he has caused us to be born again to a living hope through the resurrection of Jesus Christ from the dead, to an inheritance that is imperishable, undefiled, and unfading, kept in heaven for you."

Paul says that the kind of love that will make us a powerful influence for Christ, the kind of love that will cause us to make an impact on others, is a hopeful love. It's the kind of love that Peter describes in 1 Peter 3:8–15 where he tells us that we should not return evil for evil or insult for insult, but rather we should give a blessing. In verse 15 Peter writes that if we manifest that kind of behavior toward others, there will be people who will want to ask us about the hope that is in us. When you show that kind of love, you will be bombarded by people who recognize that you can love that way only because you have hope.

## The Last Characteristic of Real Love

In our study of God's definitive description of real love, we come to the fifteenth and last characteristic of the kind of love that will make us powerful witnesses for Christ, which, according to the last phrase in verse 7, is a love that will endure all things.

In the original, the word used here is *hypomenō*, which literally means "to bear up under pressure" or "to bear up courageously" or "to remain patient in the midst of opposition." In some contexts the word used here means to abide or to remain in a place instead of leaving it. John MacArthur says that this word was a military term used of an army holding a vital position at all costs. It was used to describe a situation in which every hardship and suffering was to be endured patiently in order to hold fast.[4]

This is the word that Paul used in Romans 12:12 when he said we are to persevere in tribulation. In other words, Paul is saying that we should not quit or run away when we experience tribulation. That thought leads us to ask the question: In what ways or areas should we persevere when experiencing tribulation? In the context of Romans 12, Paul is saying that even in the midst of tribulation, we are to:

- Continue to use the spiritual gifts that God has given us (vv. 4–8).
- Continue our devotion to one another in brotherly love (v. 9).
- Continue giving preference to one another in honor (v. 10).
- Continue being diligent (v. 11).

4. MacArthur, *1 Corinthians*, 355.

- Continue being fervent in spirit (v. 11).
- Continue rejoicing in hope (v. 12).
- Continue being devoted to prayer (v. 12).
- Continue contributing to the needs of the saints (v. 13).
- Continue practicing hospitality (v. 13).
- Continue blessing those who curse us (v. 14).
- Continue weeping with those who weep and rejoicing with those who rejoice (v. 15).
- Continue associating with poor people (v. 16).
- Continue feeding our enemies when they are hungry (vv. 18–20).
- Continue overcoming evil with good (v. 21).

The word *hypomenō* is a word that Jesus used in Matthew 10 when He sent His disciples out on a missionary journey. In verses 5–15 our Lord tells them what He wants them to do on this missionary journey. Before they go, He also informs them about the treatment they will receive. He says they will be delivered up to the courts, they will be scourged in the synagogues, they will even be brought before governors and kings because of their identification with Him. He informs them that their own families will rise up against them and cause them to be put to death; He informs them that they will be hated by people from every class for "my name's sake." He pulls no punches about the difficulties they will experience as they go out on His behalf.

Having given them their mission assignments and how-to instructions, Jesus then goes on to tell them how they should and shouldn't respond to the hardships they will experience. In verses 19–20 He says to them that in the midst of the hardships they will experience, they should not be anxious, and later He tells them three times that they should not allow themselves to be controlled by fear (vv. 26, 28, 31). Our Lord, of course, knows what happens when people are controlled by worry or fear. He knows that when people are overcome with anxiety or fear, they may become hysterical. He is aware that when people worry, they sometimes become immobile and just plain quit or give up. When people become anxious, they sometimes become obsessed with the problem they are encountering and think of nothing else. They are sometimes pulled in different directions in an attempt to find relief, running from one thing to another, becoming very unstable. Sometimes they make foolish decisions and behave in ungodly ways. They are sometimes willing to do almost anything to get rid of their problems, including doing that which only exacerbates their difficulties. They often become self-absorbed, thinking only of themselves. They sometimes run to solutions that are really non-solutions. Our Lord, of course, knows what happens when people become anxious and fearful, and so He warns them not to do so.

In verse 22 Jesus gives the disciples additional information about what they should do when they are under pressure. He tells them that they should endure, remain faithful, remain obedient, and continue to do what is right in spite of the opposition. In this verse Jesus is saying, "Don't throw in the towel. Don't allow opposition and persecution to cause you to abandon your responsibility or deviate from My directions. Don't allow persecution and hardship to cause you to turn away from Me or lead you to stop acting the way you should act and doing what I told you to do" (vv. 6–15).

In other words, He is saying that in the midst of tribulation, they are to endure. They are to remain faithful under the pressures they will certainly face.

But Jesus is very realistic, and so He not only warns them not to become anxious and fearful. He not only tells them to endure, but also tells them why they shouldn't worry and should endure. In Matthew 10 He mentions several reasons why they shouldn't allow themselves to be paralyzed by worry and fear and why they should persevere.

At this point, it would be interesting to take a detour from the main purpose for which I have referenced the Matthew passage and spend some time considering the reasons our Lord gives for not being anxious or afraid or disobedient to His directions. However, I will resist that temptation because my main purpose for referencing Matthew 10 is to demonstrate what Paul means when he speaks of the endurance of love. I want us to see from these cross-references that the original word *hypomenō*, translated "endures" in 1 Corinthians 13:7, means that if we have real love, it will continue; it will persevere in the presence of great pressure—and even danger.

To bring all that back to our study of real love in 1 Corinthians, where Paul says, "Love endures [*hypomenō*] all things," what Scripture is saying is that the kind of love that will make us a powerful witness for Christ will be tenacious. It won't quit when problems come, when things get tough, when things don't go the way we want them to go.

What Paul is saying is that the kind of love that will impact others for Christ is like the love described in Proverbs 17:17—"A friend loves at all times, and a brother is born for adversity." In the Hebrew this verse from Proverbs really begins with the words "At all times a friend loves." What this verse, along with 1 Corinthians 13:7, is saying is that a real friend loves you when you are rich and when you are poor; when you are well and when you are sick; when you are nice and when you are nasty; when you are up and when you are down; when you are happy and when you are sad; when you are young and when you are old. Proverbs 17:17, along with 1 Corinthians 13:7, is telling us that the person who loves in the 1 Corinthians 13 way loves in every circumstance. If I am discouraged, a person who has persevering love will not abandon me or condemn me, but seek to encourage me. If I am choosing a wrong path, a person who loves in the 1 Corinthians 13 way will love me enough to lovingly and gently correct me. If I actually do choose the wrong way, a person who loves in the 1 Corinthians way will love me enough to lovingly rebuke me. If I am in need of comfort, a person who has persevering love will seek to comfort. If I am in need of a different perspective from the one I already have, a person who has enduring love will seek to provide for me a new perspective.

In commenting on the statement that a true friend loves at all times, William Arnot said, "Many will court you while you have much to give. When you need to receive, the number of your friends will diminish, but their quality will be improved. Your misfortune, like the blast of wind on the thrashed corn, will drive the chaff away, but the wheat will remain where it was. How very sweet sometimes is the human friendship that remains when sore adversity has sifted it."[5]

5. William Arnot, *Studies in Proverbs* (Grand Rapids: Kregel, 1978), 504.

What Paul is saying is that the kind of love that will help you to make a powerful impact for Christ is like the love that Hosea had for his wife, who had abandoned him. Even after his wife was unfaithful, Hosea refused to quit. He pursued her until he finally won her back. His love for her was not based on or derived from her performance, but rather from God's amazing grace and love.

When I think of *hypomenō* (a persevering, enduring) love, I think of the love that Jonathan had for David. When David was in the king's favor, Jonathan was there to support him. First Samuel 18:3 says, "Jonathan loved [David] as his own soul." He loved him so much that he was willing to give David his armor and even gladly give up his right to the kingship so that David could become king. Later, when David fell out of favor with the king and the king wanted to destroy him, Jonathan did everything he could to protect and defend him to the point where the king became so upset with Jonathan that he actually tried to kill him.

When I think of *hypomenō* (a persevering, enduring) love, I also think of a young lady who lived during the time of the Civil War. In the middle of the Civil War between the North and the South, a young man who had just become engaged was drafted into the army. Because of this, the wedding was postponed. The young soldier managed to get through most of the conflict without injury, but at the Battle of the Wilderness he was severely wounded. His bride-to-be, not knowing of his condition, read and reread his letters, counting the days until he would return. Suddenly the letters stopped coming. Finally she received one, but it was written in an unfamiliar handwriting. It read, "There has been a terrible battle. It is very difficult for me to tell you this, but I have lost both my arms. I cannot write myself. So a friend is writing this letter for me. While you are as dear to me as ever, I feel I should release you from the obligation of our engagement."

The letter was never answered. Instead, the young woman took the next train and went directly to the place where her loved one was being cared for. On arrival she found a sympathetic captain, who gave her directions to the soldier's cot. Tearfully, she searched for him. The moment she saw the young man, she threw her arms around him and kissed him. "I will never give you up!" she cried. "These hands of mine will help you. I will take care of you."

This story, my friends, is an illustration of the nature of the love that Paul is describing in 1 Corinthians 13. The love he is describing is an *agapē* love that never gives up, never ends, never dies, never fails; it abides and endures forever, in contrast with all the other spiritual gifts such as prophecy and knowledge and tongues and working of miracles. They all will fail, but the value and importance of love will never fail.

When I think of *hypomenō* (a persevering, enduring) love, I think of the love that J. Robertson McQuilkin had for his wife when at age fifty-eight she developed severe Alzheimer's disease and needed constant care. His story is told in a book titled *A Promise Kept*. At the time when she developed the disease, he was the president of Columbia International University. Because she needed constant care, McQuilkin, out of love for his invalid wife, resigned from his position so that he might take care of her.

An unmarried man who read the book wrote:

> For a young single it's easy to fantasize about the joys of having a lifelong love—often at the neglect of counting the true cost of actually having one. This small but powerful book shows that cost, and how one man remained faithful to his wife despite it.
>
> Robertson, a distinguished man high in Christian academic circles, is shocked when his vivacious wife Muriel is diagnosed with Alzheimer's. Gradually, she begins to succumb to its ravages and is forced to abandon her popular radio show and speaking engagements. As the disease takes its toll on Muriel, Robertson devotes more and more time to watching over her. He leaves his work and other pursuits to care for her because without his presence, she becomes fearful and agitated. Only with him near is she happy and content. Eventually she becomes totally dependent upon him, unable to perform rudimentary tasks or even converse.
>
> But the heart of the story is that he remains with her gratefully, and with a loving attitude. He is not an angry or resentful caretaker. Of course, he is not thrilled to watch his lovely, intelligent wife slide

into helpless dementia. But he sees his caretaking as a holy task, one entrusted to him by God. Indeed, she "took care" of him for decades, so he finds it a privilege to return the favor. I would say that his attitude and actions are examples for anyone. Elisabeth Elliot once wrote that marriage is the abandonment of self. Robertson lovingly exemplifies that principle in the midst of a heart-breaking situation—all for the glory of God.[6]

In the life of Robertson McQuilkin we have a great example of *hypomenō* enduring love demonstrated in the midst of tremendous pressure and tribulation. That is what Paul is talking about when he speaks of a love that endures or perseveres.

All these illustrations are great examples of *hypomenō* (persevering, enduring) love, but the greatest example of this kind of love is the example of our God and our Savior the Lord Jesus Christ. Reflect on this great love as it is described in the following verses:

- "For God so loved the world, that he gave his only Son, that whoever believes in him should not perish but have eternal life" (John 3:16).
- "Who shall separate us from the love of Christ? Shall tribulation, or distress, or persecution, or famine, or nakedness, or danger, or sword? . . . For I am sure that neither death nor life, nor angels nor rulers, nor things present nor things to come, nor powers, nor height nor depth, nor anything else in all creation, will be able to separate us from the love of God in Christ Jesus our Lord" (Rom. 8:35, 38–39).
- "But God shows his love for us in that while we were still sinners, Christ died for us" (Rom. 5:8).
- "But God . . . because of the great love with which he loved us . . . made us alive together with Christ" (Eph. 2:4–5).
- "In this the love of God was made manifest . . . that God sent his only Son into the world, so that we might live through him. In this is love, not that we have loved God, but that he

6. From a reader's review of *A Promise Kept* on Amazon.com Web page.

loved us and sent his Son to be the propitiation for our sins"
(1 John 4:9–10).

- "[He] loves us and has freed us from our sins by his blood"
(Rev. 1:5).
- "I have been crucified with Christ. It is no longer I who live,
but Christ who lives in me. And the life I now live in the flesh I
live by faith in the Son of God, who loved me and gave himself
for me" (Gal. 2:19–20).
- Paul said that the love of Christ is so incredibly broad and deep
and high and long—so great that we can't even begin to comprehend how great it is—he says it is beyond our knowledge
or comprehension (Eph. 3:17–19). Therefore, it is also beyond
our ability to describe; the best we can do in describing it is
extremely inadequate.

Nevertheless, reflect on and be enthralled by the love of Christ as
it is described in the following quotes:

Concerning the love of Christ, Samuel Rutherford said:

To think that you could comprehend the love of Christ is as if a child
could take the globe of earth and sea in his two short arms. The love of
Christ is like a great ocean, whose depths are unfathomable. There is a
height in this love, to which no human intelligence can soar; a depth
which no created mind can penetrate. In viewing the love of Christ, there
lies a wide unbounded prospect before us. The mental vision wanders at
liberty over this illimitable range. The love of Christ is circumscribed by
no limits; it is bounded by no horizon: it is one vast expanse in which
the soul may lose itself in wonder, delight, and admiration. It is like a
great ocean, whose depths are unfathomable.[7]

Of the immensity of Christ's love, Robert Murray McCheyne wrote:

Paul says: "The love of Christ passes knowledge." It is like the blue
sky into which you may see clearly, but the real vastness of which you

---

7. www.GraceGems.org/Books2/Harsha – *Thoughts on the Love of Christ.*

cannot measure. It is like the deep, deep sea, into whose bosom you can look a little way, but its depths are unfathomable. It has a breadth without a bound, length without top, and depth without bottom. If holy Paul who was so deeply taught in divine things; who had been in the third heaven, and seen the glorified face of Jesus said this; how much more may we, poor and weak believers, look into that love, and say, It passes knowledge![8]

Reflect on and be amazed at the greatness of the love of Christ as it is reflected in the following poems (hymns):

In 1875, Samuel Francis spent some time meditating on the love of Christ. From his time of meditation he was moved to write:

O the deep, deep love of Jesus, Vast, unmeasured, boundless, free!
Rolling as a mighty ocean In its fullness over me!
Underneath me, all around me, Is the current of Thy love
Leading onward, leading homeward To Thy glorious rest above!

O the deep, deep love of Jesus, Spread His praise from shore to shore!
How He loveth, ever loveth, Changeth never, nevermore!
How He watches o'er His loved ones, Died to call them all His own;
How for them He intercedeth, Watcheth o'er them from the throne!

O the deep, deep love of Jesus, Love of every love the best!
'Tis an ocean vast of blessing, 'Tis a haven sweet of rest!
O the deep, deep love of Jesus, 'Tis a heaven of heavens to me;
And it lifts me up to glory, For it lifts me up to Thee!

In 1904 William Rees, a Welshman, spent some time reflecting on the love of God and was moved to write:

Here is love, vast as the ocean, Lovingkindness as the flood,
When the Prince of Life, our Ransom, Shed for us His precious blood.
Who His love will not remember? Who can cease to sing His praise?
He can never be forgotten, Throughout Heav'n's eternal days.

8. Ibid.

On the mount of crucifixion, Fountains opened deep and wide;
Through the floodgates of God's mercy Flowed a vast and gracious tide.
Grace and love, like mighty rivers, Poured incessant from above,
And Heav'n's peace and perfect justice Kissed a guilty world in love.

Let me all Thy love accepting, Love Thee, ever all my days;
Let me seek Thy kingdom only And my life be to Thy praise;
Thou alone shalt be my glory, Nothing in the world I see.
Thou hast cleansed and sanctified me, Thou Thyself hast set me free.

In Thy truth Thou dost direct me By Thy Spirit through Thy Word;
And Thy grace my need is meeting, As I trust in Thee, my Lord.
Of Thy fullness Thou art pouring Thy great love and power on me,
Without measure, full and boundless, Drawing out my heart to Thee.

And then in 1917 Frederick Lehman, who lived in California, spent some time meditating and was moved to write about the magnitude of Christ's love:

The love of God is greater far than tongue or pen can ever tell;
It goes beyond the highest star, and reaches to the lowest hell;
The guilty pair, bowed down with care, God gave His Son to win;
His erring child He reconciled, And pardoned from his sin.

O love of God, how rich and pure! How measureless and strong!
It shall forevermore endure, The saints' and angels' song.

When the years of time shall pass away, And earthly thrones and
    kingdoms fall,
When men, who here refuse to pray, On rocks and hills and moun-
    tains call,
God's love so sure, shall still endure, All measureless and strong;
Redeeming grace to Adam's race, The saints' and angels' song.

Could we with ink the ocean fill, And were the skies of parch-
    ment made,
Were every stalk on earth a quill, And every man a scribe by trade,

To write the love of God above, would drain the ocean dry.
Nor could the scroll contain the whole, though stretched from sky
to sky.

Certainly the greatest example of the kind of love that Paul is describing in 1 Corinthians 13 is to be found in the love that our Lord Jesus Christ has for His own people. His is a love that is incomparable and incomprehensible. In comparison to the love of Jesus Christ, the love of all other people who live now or who have ever lived is woefully lacking. In reading Paul's description of love in 1 Corinthians 13, we could very easily and properly substitute the words *Jesus Christ* for the word *love*. We could take all fifteen characteristics that Paul mentions and say with total accuracy that Jesus is all these things in perfection.

What that means is that when Paul calls upon us to put on the kind of love described in 1 Corinthians 13, he is really calling upon us to seek to be more like Jesus. In 1 Corinthians 14:1, when Paul commands us to pursue love, what he's really commanding us to do is to seek to be like Jesus.

But you say, what does it mean to be like Jesus? First Corinthians 13 tells us what it means. It means that you will be a person who manifests the characteristics of love described in 1 Corinthians 13:4–8. In terms of what we've focused on in this chapter, it means that you will be a person who has a love that is motivated by hope; it means that you will have a love that is persevering, a love that endures all things and remains faithful.

As I finish this chapter, I want to ask a question and make a couple of brief statements. First I want to put a question to each of us. The question is: Do you want to be like Jesus? If you are a Christian, I know your answer to that question is an emphatic "Yes!" If you are a Christian, I know that your answer is, "Yes, more than anything else in the world I want to be like Jesus."

And I want to also say that if you are not interested in becoming more like Jesus, you probably aren't a Christian, because in Ephesians 4:15 Paul says that we as Christians are to grow up in all aspects into

Christ. Romans 8:29–30 says that God's purpose in saving us is that we might become conformed to the image of Christ. What does it mean to become more like Jesus? At least in part, it means that you and I are to grow in being the loving person Paul describes in 1 Corinthians 13.

Moreover, I can also tell you that if you and I are becoming like Jesus, if you and I are developing and manifesting the kind of love described in 1 Corinthians 13, we will make an impact for Christ in this world because verse 8 tells us that love never fails, and 1 Corinthians 12:31 informs us that the way of love is the more excellent way of impacting others for Christ.

But now, before I bring this chapter to a conclusion, I want to issue a word of caution. What I've been saying is addressed to those of you who have already come to Christ. If you've never recognized that you are a sinner in need of God's forgiveness, if you have never bowed your knee at the foot of the cross and acknowledged your sin, if you have never bowed at the cross and thanked Jesus for dying to pay the penalty for your sin, if you have never surrendered your life to Jesus and confessed Him to be your Lord, your greatest need is *not* to try to manufacture the kind of love we've been talking about. *Your greatest need at this point is to come to Christ for salvation.* And if you are concerned about your salvation, I urge you to seek out a pastor or mature Bible-believing and -knowing Christian from a Bible-preaching and -believing church and let that person help you to learn how to become a Christian.

## Review, Reflection, Application, and Discussion Questions

1. By way of review, what are the main reasons given in this chapter for making love the main goal of our ministry in the family or in the church?

2. What does the Bible mean when it uses the word *hope*? How is the Bible's usage of the word *hope* different from the way the word is commonly used in the world?

3. What are some of the adjectives the Bible uses in connection with the word *hope*?

4. In specific terms, what do you think God is trying to tell us about our hope by using these adjectives to describe it?

5. Reflect on the verses that were used in this chapter to describe the hope that God says every believer has. What, for example, is 1 Peter 1:3 telling us about our hope? Answer that question for each of the passages.

6. What does hope have to do with love? Why does Paul mention hope as a characteristic of love?

7. What does the word *endure* mean? When the word *endure* is used, what thoughts come to your mind? When someone speaks of enduring something, what is most likely going on?

8. Reflect on what Proverbs 17:17 says about real love and what that means about how love will show itself in specific situations in relation to other people.

9. Meditate on William Arnot's comments about love found in this chapter. Explain what he is really saying. Be specific.

10. Review and reflect on the examples of "enduring love" found in this chapter and evaluate the depth and validity of your own love in comparison. What was most striking about Jonathan's love for David? What was most striking about the love of the young lady for her fiancé during the Civil War? What was most striking about the love of Robertson McQuilkin for his wife? What was and is most striking about the love of Christ for His people? (Meditate on the Scripture that describes Christ's love and on the quotes and on the hymns. Seek to identify the specific ways in which the Scripture and the quotes and the hymns describe the love of Christ.)

11. Evaluate yourself in terms of the hopefulness of your own love for other family members, for other church members, and for people outside the church. Use this rating scale: "I regularly show

1 Corinthians 13 love because I'm not living for the present but for the hope I have in Christ" (4); "I often show 1 Corinthians 13 love because I'm not living for the present but for the hope I have in Christ" (3); "I sometimes show 1 Corinthians 13 love because I'm not living for the present but for the hope I have in Christ" (2); "I seldom show 1 Corinthians 13 love because I am living for the present and don't think much about the hope a Christian has in Christ" (1); "I never show 1 Corinthians 13 love because I am living for the present and don't think much about the hope a Christian has in Christ" (0).

12. Evaluate the endurance of your own love for other family members, for other church members, and for people outside the church. Use this rating scale: "I consistently show 1 Corinthians 13 love even when I am experiencing adversity, rejection, opposition, denial, hardship" (4); "I often show 1 Corinthians 13 love even when I am experiencing adversity, rejection, opposition, denial, hardship" (3); "I sometimes show 1 Corinthians 13 love even when I am experiencing adversity, rejection, opposition, denial, hardship" (2); "I seldom show 1 Corinthians 13 love when I am experiencing adversity, rejection, opposition, denial, hardship" (1); "I never show 1 Corinthians 13 love when I am experiencing adversity, rejection, opposition, denial, hardship" (0).

13. Having read and reflected on the contents of this chapter, write out what you think you should do in response.

14. And now my usual reminder: Please remember as you reflect on the love principles presented in this chapter that the purpose of this exposition, evaluation, and application is:

a. not to discourage or destroy us;

b. but to motivate us to see our constant need of the cross and how much we owe to Jesus—without Him we'd never make it, but praise God we are not without Him;

c. and to motivate us to understand our constant daily need of grace—that our salvation never has been and never will be by the works we have done, but always by the work Christ has done and is doing for us; I want our studies in 1 Corinthians 13 to be a reminder that we need to live a cross-centered life; we need the application of the cross work of Jesus every day of our lives; remember there's not a day in our lives when we are so good that we don't need the cross, and there is never a day in our lives when we are so bad that what Christ did on the cross is not sufficient to provide forgiveness for us (Rom. 3:24; 5:20; Eph. 1:7; 1 John 1:7; 2:1–2);

d. and to cause us to understand that we must and can, by His grace, put off from our lives the "unlove" that is displeasing to God and put on in our lives the love that is beautifully described in 1 Corinthians 13 so that we might become more and more like our Savior and more prolific in bearing fruit for Him as others see the grace of God at work in our lives, changing and transforming us (Eph. 4:22–24; 1 Tim. 4:7).

# 18

## Biblically Based Guidelines for Becoming a Biblical Lover of People

S everal years ago D. A. Carson wrote an article titled "A Church That Does All the Right Things, But . . ." In this article he described the situation of the church at Ephesus as it is related in Revelation 2:4. Of this church he wrote:

> They still proclaim the truth, but no longer passionately love Him who is the truth. They still perform good deeds, but no longer out of love, brotherhood, and compassion. They preserve the truth and witness courageously, but forget that love is the great witness to truth. It is not so much that their genuine virtues have squeezed love out, but that no amount of good works, wisdom, and discernment in matters of church discipline, patient endurance in hardship, hatred of sin, or disciplined doctrine, can ever make up for lovelessness.[1]

1. D. A. Carson, "A Church That Does All the Right Things, But . . . ," *Christianity Today*, June 29, 1979, 30.

Carson's article extolled the importance of love by asserting that all our good works and all our theological correctness can never make up for lovelessness.

As we've noted again and again in this book, the inspired apostle who wrote 1 Corinthians 12:31–13:8 would have voiced a hearty "amen" to Carson's conclusion.

To this point, we've exposited and applied verses 1–3 where Paul establishes the fact that, in terms of having an effective ministry, having a life filled with the right kind of love is the most important element. In these verses, Paul established the truth that without love, everything else we have and do adds up to zero. After expositing verses 1–3, we did a careful study of the fifteen characteristics of the kind of love that will make us powerful in our witness for Christ.

After reading the previous chapters describing what real love in God's style is, some of you may be saying, "Wayne, I think I now have some understanding of what real love is. In fact, as I have read I have become more and more aware that there are some aspects of love in which I am somewhat or even greatly deficient."

In the first seventeen chapters of this book I've mentioned some things that will help us to develop, sustain, and improve our love quotient. At this point I want to devote a whole chapter to giving you a biblical answer to the question about how to develop and sustain the kind of love described in 1 Corinthians 13.

We've all heard the statement that "repetition is *the* key to learning." I'm not sure that I'm ready to say that repetition is *the* key, but I am ready to say that it certainly is one of the keys. I say that because *some* of what I write will be a review of the application portions found in several of these chapters. I emphasize the word *some* because much of what I write in this chapter will be new or a different way of saying what I have already said. I will be pulling together some suggestions from other chapters, but I will also be adding many biblically based thoughts that have not been previously included in this book. In my judgment, adding some concise and biblically based "how to" information to the "what to" information that we mainly focused on in chapters 1–17 is essential. One person said something like this: "I've always appreciated the striking beauty of 1 Corinthians 13, but I have also been devastated by the powerful message contained there. It makes me uneasy to read or hear about God's definition of love. It's beautiful, to be sure, but what a sweep. I am really glad you have carefully explained and applied this passage, but I need help in knowing how to develop and sustain this kind of love."

That was one person's request, and this chapter is intended to fulfill the desire of that man and anyone else who is serious about knowing not only what real love is, but also how to develop and sustain it on a practical level. I've called the principles I'll outline and explain "Biblically Based Guidelines for Becoming a Biblical Lover of People."

*Biblically based directive #1 is that if you want to develop and sustain this 1 Corinthians 13 kind of love, you must first be a Christian.* It is just not possible to live this kind of love without the strength and guidance of the Holy Spirit. And without faith in Christ, you don't have access to that particular resource.

It is important to recall that when Paul wrote 1 Corinthians 13, he was writing to a select group of people. First of all, as you may remember, he was writing to those who had been set apart in Christ Jesus, which was a way of saying that they were united to Christ and dedicated to Him. Second, these were people who were witnessing to others about Christ and possessed a great deal of knowledge about Him. According to verse 6, these were people who were convinced about the truth of the gospel message and had embraced the message of the cross. So when Paul tells us in 1 Corinthians 14:1 to pursue the kind of love he has just described in chapter 13, he is also writing to the same select group of people—those who are united to Christ and are now indwelt by the Holy Spirit.

It might help to recall other passages where Paul wrote concerning people who are *not* believers in Christ. For instance, in Romans 3:9 he states that before people come to Christ they are under the control of sin. They don't and can't love God in the way He should be loved, and they don't and can't love their neighbor in the way that God wants them to love their neighbor. It's as simple as that.

In another passage, Romans 8:8, he says that unbelievers are in the flesh and cannot please God. Part of pleasing God involves possessing and manifesting the kind of love described in 1 Corinthians 13.

In Titus 3:3 we read, "For we ourselves were once foolish, disobedient, led astray, slaves to various passions and pleasures, passing our days in malice and envy, hated by others and hating one another." In verses 4–8 he explains that this is truly what we were like before we were given faith in Christ, but then God saved us and delivered us from the control of sin and selfishness. When He did that, He saved us, washed us, and renewed us. He poured out His mercy on us richly so that now we can engage in good deeds. You see, it's only after He empowers us that we can live obedient lives to Him.

To say these things about people who are not Christians doesn't sound very nice or loving—but, my friends, we are not saying these things! God is! And what God says is that no one can truly love in the 1 Corinthians 13 way without being a Christian. However, that's not all the Bible says about this. It also says that when we have been born again, God gives us a new nature so that we have the potential to love in this way. And if you and I would say anything less than that, we would not only be unbiblical—we would also be unloving.

If you have not yet embraced Christ as your Savior, it doesn't have to stay that way! The exciting news is that God's Word says the beginning of a new potential for loving this way can be yours if you will come to Christ! It says you can be saved—delivered from the control of sin and selfishness. But to have this new potential, you must first come to Christ!

I'm convinced that this is the message of the apostle Paul, but it's also the message of the whole Bible. For example, when we turn to 1 Peter 1:22–23, we find Peter saying that we should and can have a genuine, fervent love of the brethren because we have been born again—because our souls have been purified. Second Peter 1:1–7 says that we who are Christians can escape the corruption that is in the world because of our selfish desires, and we can by God's power experience moral excellence. Part of that moral excellence is possessing the ability to manifest brotherly kindness and love—no, not perfectly but progressively, as we continue to walk in obedience and love.

When we turn to 1 John 4:7–19, the apostle John is saying the same thing. In verses 7–8 he says:

> Beloved, let us love one another, for love is from God, and whoever loves has been born of God and knows God. Anyone who does not love does not know God, because God is love.

These verses are saying at least two things: (1) if you really know God and are born of God, you can be a loving person; and (2) if you don't love, it's because you have not been born of God and you don't really know Him.

In a sermon John Piper preached on 1 John 4:7–19, he has some very helpful things to say:

> John's point in this passage is that in the new birth, this aspect of the divine nature becomes part of who you are. The new birth is the imparting to you of divine life, and an indispensable part of that life is love. God's nature is love, and in the new birth that nature becomes part of who you are. Look at verse 12: "No one has ever seen God; if we love one another, God abides in us and his love is perfected in us." When you are born again, God himself is imparted to you. He dwells in you and sheds abroad in your heart his love. And his aim is that this love be perfected in you. Notice the phrase "his love" in verse 12. The love that you have as a born-again person is no mere imitation of the divine love. It is an experience of the divine love and an extension of that love to others. . . .
>
> In 1 John 4:10, the apostle John says: "In this is love, not that we have loved God but that He loved us and sent His Son to be the propitiation for our sins." In this statement the apostle John is emphasizing that the nature and the origin of love does not lie in our response to God. That is not where love starts. That is not mainly what love is. Love is, and love starts with God. And if anything we feel or do can be called love, it is because we are connected with Him by the new birth. . . .
>
> John has not forgotten what he wrote in verse 7–8. "Whoever loves has been born of God and knows God. Anyone who does not

love does not know God, because God is love." So when he says, "We *ought* to love each other," he means *ought* the way fish ought to swim in water and birds ought to fly in the air and living creatures ought to breathe and peaches ought to be sweet and lemons ought to be sour and hyenas ought to laugh. And born-again people ought to love. It's who we are. This is not mere imitation. For the children of God, imitation becomes realization. We are realizing who we are when we love. God's seed is in us. God's Spirit is in us. God's nature is in us. God's love is being perfected in us. . . .

What's unique about the Christian life is that there is also the internal impulse that comes from being born again and having the very love that sent the Son into the world pulsing through our souls by the life of God within. The new birth enables us to experience the manifestation of God's love in history as an internal reality of God's Spirit within us. . . .

I want to say to you what the apostle John says to us all in verse 11: "Beloved, if God so loved us, we also ought to love one another." If we are regenerate people, we are loving people. If we are born again, the love of God is within us. "We know that we have passed out of death into life, because we love the brothers" (1 John 3:14).[2]

The point John Piper and I want to sound out, loud and clear, is that because we as Christians have been born again, we and we only now have the capacity to love in the 1 Corinthians 13 way. If you are a Christian, if you have been born again, take heart! Please don't let the truth of 1 Corinthians 13 discourage you. Let your heart be encouraged because one of the blessings that God bestows on us when we become Christians is the potential for being a genuinely loving person.

*Biblically based directive #2 for developing and sustaining a 1 Corinthians 13 love is suggested by what Paul says in 1 Corinthians 14:1. He commands us to pursue love.* The Greek word translated "pursue" is *diōkō*. Looking at two places where Scripture uses the same word will

---

2. Paraphrased from a sermon on the *Desiring God* Web site: www.desiringgod.org/ResourceLibrary/Sermons/ByScripture/46/2686_The_New_Birth_Produces_Love/.

help us to understand what Paul means when he says we should "pursue" love. We find the word *diōkō* used in Romans 9:30–31 where Paul writes, "What shall we say, then? . . . Israel who pursued [*diōkō*] a law that would lead to righteousness did not succeed in reaching that law." He's saying that the Jews diligently pursued a right standing with God! They, however, tried unsuccessfully to get it by their own works rather than by receiving it as a gift from God by faith in Christ. How strenuously did they pursue it? One example of how diligently they pursued righteousness by their own works is found in Matthew 23:23, which says that in an attempt to make themselves righteous they even tithed mint and dill and cumin.

From this example we learn something about the meaning of the word *pursue* (*diōkō*). In an attempt to win a right standing with God through their own efforts, the Israelites were largely diligent, meticulous, dedicated, and determined. For us, who have already been brought into a right relationship with God through Christ alone, by grace alone, through faith alone, pursuing love doesn't mean that we must follow their example in terms of what they did, nor for the reason they did what they did (i.e., to acquire a right standing with God).

It *does* mean that we should use the same kind of diligence and dedication to develop and sustain love as the Israelites did to attain righteousness. It *does* mean that we must constantly recognize its importance and be willing to put forth a diligent, dedicated, and determined effort to acquire the love described in 1 Corinthians 13 in our response to God's love for us.

Paul's usage of the word *diōkō* in Galatians 1:13 gives us another very meaningful illustration of what it means to pursue. "For you have heard of my [Paul's] former life in Judaism, how I persecuted the church of God violently and tried to destroy it." Before his conversion to Christ, Paul says he pursued the church beyond measure. He actually went for the *hyperbolē* (beyond measure) pursuit of Christians to destroy Christianity. In other words, he's saying that the way he persecuted the church cannot be measured or described—that it exceeded anything you can imagine.

When we turn to Acts 8:3, we have a description of what Paul meant when he said he pursued the church. Luke tells us, "But Saul was ravaging the church, and entering house after house, he dragged off men and women and committed them to prison." In Acts 9:1–2 Luke continues:

> But Saul, still breathing threats and murder against the disciples of the Lord, went to the high priest and asked him for letters to the synagogues at Damascus, so that if he found any belonging to the Way, men or women, he might bring them bound to Jerusalem.

From all these passages we can learn something about what it means to pursue love. With the same degree of intensity with which Saul once pursued the church, we should pursue love.

To pursue love means that you must want to be a loving person and you recognize love's importance to yourself and to others. It means you are determined to show love—even when it's hard to do. In order to do this, you'll have to spend some time considering just how to show love. Pursuing love means that you are willing to discipline yourself to develop and manifest love. Developing and sustaining this kind of love won't come automatically or easily. It will come as the result of a sustained, dedicated, and focused effort to follow the biblical directives delineated in this chapter. It will be produced as we discipline ourselves for the purpose of acquiring the godly characteristic of love (1 Tim. 4:7).

*Biblical directive #3 for developing and sustaining the kind of love that will make us a powerful influence for Christ is that we must abide in Christ.* Shortly before His crucifixion, our Lord met with His disciples and gave them an extended time of instruction. Part of that pre-crucifixion instruction is found in John 15 where He issues the same command two times. In verse 12 He gives this command: "This is my commandment, that you love one another as I have loved you," and then in verse 17 He repeats the same command: "These things I command you, so that you will love one another." In this passage He not only commands them to love one another, but also gives them some other instructions that will help them to actually obey this command. The same "how to" instructions are repeated in slightly different ways in several verses. They are, for example, given in verse 5 where He uses a metaphor to describe our relationship with and complete dependence on Him: "I am the vine; you are the branches."

In verses 4 and 5 Jesus enlarges on this idea that we must be in a close, continuing, and dependent relationship with Him if we are going to bear the fruit of love. "Abide in me," Jesus admonishes, "and I in you. As the branch cannot bear fruit of itself, unless it abides in the vine, neither can you, unless you abide in me. I am the vine; you are the branches. Whoever abides in me, and I in him, he it is that bears much fruit, for apart from me you can do nothing."

In these verses, Jesus teaches us that any strength or fruit-bearing potential we have comes from a close relationship with Him. His point is that it is just as impossible for us to bear the fruit of love, or any other godly characteristic, out of our own personal resources as it is for the branch of a grape plant to bear fruit without being attached closely to the vine. It is obvious to any observant person that when a branch bears fruit, it is really the vine bearing the fruit through the branch. An unattached branch bears no fruit and is good for nothing except to be cast aside and burned. A loosely attached branch (a branch that has been partially detached) will bear no fruit or else it will bear very little fruit.

The quality of the fruit a branch produces is only as good and as plentiful as the health and robustness of the vine to which it is attached. For a branch to bear fruit it must have a close, not a superficial, connection with the vine. More than that, if a branch is to bear much fruit it must be attached to a good, healthy vine. Being aware of these facts helps us to understand the practical meaning of Jesus' statement in verse 1 that He is the true vine.

The wonderful, encouraging, life-changing truth in these words is that since we are, by God's grace, united to the Lord Jesus Christ, the one in whom love is perfectly exemplified and manifested, we can also bear much fruit if we remain closely attached to Him and dependent on Him.

But what does it mean to abide in Him? The word *abide* carries with it the idea of remaining or continuing. I may visit many places, but I don't abide in these places. Abiding means that I reside in a place. Abiding means that it's the place I live. Abiding means that Jesus Christ is the center of my life. Unless this is true, I can't call what I'm doing abiding. Unless this is true, I'm just a tourist, paying a visit.

In the context of John 15, abiding in Jesus means that I'm abiding in His Word (v. 7). It means that I think about His Word, that I live in His Word. It means that His Word has taken up residency and presidency in my life. It means that I respect His Word, that I welcome His Word, that I meditate on His Word. Unless this is what is happening in my life, I can hardly say I am abiding in Christ.

Abiding in Him is equated with keeping His commandments (v. 10). If I am abiding in Him, I will want to please Him. What He wants for my life, His will, His convictions about right and wrong, about the practical issues of life, about how to live and how to function will be supremely important to me. And if this is not true of me, I'm not abiding in Christ.

Abiding in Him is equated with abiding in His love (v. 9). Abiding in Him means that I think much about His love, which, according to Paul, surpasses knowledge—it is beyond our ability to comprehend or fully understand (Eph. 3:18–19). Abiding in Him means that I am rooted and grounded in His love (Eph. 3:17). Being rooted in His love means that I am planted in His love, that I draw my strength and nutrition from His love. Being grounded means that the reality of His love produces stability and security in my life. It's the foundation on which my life is built. Abiding in His love involves continually meditating on the deep, deep love of Jesus, which as Samuel Francis said in his great hymn is "vast, unmeasured, boundless, free, rolling as a mighty ocean in its fullness over me." Abiding in His love includes enjoying and experiencing His love. It involves recognizing and appreciating the greatness and immensity of His love.

What happens as we abide in Him, as we focus on Him, as we think about Him? Deborah Howard makes this helpful comment: "When we spend a great deal of time with someone, we naturally take on some of his or her traits. Perhaps we take on certain phrases . . . or distinct characteristics. . . . In the same way when we spend more and more time with Christ through prayer and study we begin to take on His characteristics. In other words, we become more Christlike as we spend time with Him."[3]

What Deborah writes here is right in line with what Jesus intimates happens as we abide in Him. He is the personification of love, and as we spend time with Him (if we abide in Him), we will become like Him and He will bear the fruit of love in and through our lives. Fruit-bearing, on our part, according to Jesus, is connected to our abiding or remaining in Him, which means that He is the one who enables us to bear the fruit. It is as we abide in Him, as we reflect on His great love for us, that we are inspired and empowered to love in the way He loved and still loves.

*Biblical directive #4 for developing and sustaining the kind of love that will make us a powerful witness for Christ is that we must be filled with the Holy Spirit and must learn to walk in or by the Spirit.* In Ephesians 3:16 Paul prays that God might cause us to be strengthened with power by the Spirit in the inner man so that Christ may dwell in our hearts by faith and so that we might be rooted and grounded in love.

In Ephesians 5:25 Paul instructs husbands that they are to love their wives as Christ loved the church. They are to love their wives as they love themselves. He also tells wives to submit to their husbands. But before he tells them that, he issues a command in Ephesians 5:18 that they must be filled with the Spirit. Without the filling of the Spirit, husbands and wives will be unable to function in the way God wants them to function in marriage. Without the filling of the Spirit, we will not be able to love in the 1 Corinthians 13 way.

What, then, does it mean to be filled with the Spirit? It means that we are yielded completely to the Holy Spirit. It means that we are under His control. It means that we are depending on Him to enable us to do and be what God wants. It means, as Colossians 3:16 indicates, that we are letting the Word of God dwell richly in our lives. It means

3. Deborah Howard, *Where Is God in All of This?* (Phillipsburg, NJ: P&R Publishing, 2009), 46.

that our minds are filled with Scripture, which is the Spirit's book (2 Peter 1:20–21). It means, as Galatians 5:16 states, that we are walking in and by the Spirit.

John MacArthur explains what it means to walk in or by the Spirit:

> To walk by the Spirit and thereby not carry out the desires of the flesh articulates the same principle as to "put on the Lord Jesus Christ, and make no provision for the flesh in regard to its lusts" (Rom. 13:14). To walk by the Spirit is to "behave properly as in the day" whereas to carry out the desire of the flesh involves such things as "carousing, . . . drunkenness, . . . sexual promiscuity and sensuality." . . . The two behaviors are mutually exclusive, so that at all times in our Christian lives we are either walking by the Spirit or are functioning in fleshly desire, but never both at the same time.
>
> The life walked by the Spirit is the Christlike life, the saturation of the believer's thoughts with the truth, love, and glory of His Lord and the desire to be like Him in every way. It is to live in continual consciousness of His presence and will, letting "the Word of Christ richly dwell within you" (Col. 3:16). . . . Surely it is no different from being "filled with the Spirit" (Eph. 5:18), a phrase referring to the controlling power exerted by the Spirit on a willing Christian.[4]

In other words, being filled with the Spirit and walking by the Spirit are absolutely essential if we are to love in the 1 Corinthians 13 way. Both of these expressions mean that we must live in conscious dependence on the Spirit of God and walk in accordance with Him. Doing this, says Paul in Galatians 5:13–26, is a key to being delivered from living a life that is dominated and controlled by the desires of the flesh. According to Scripture, being filled with and walking by the Spirit will have tremendous practical results in our lives. Being filled with and walking by the Spirit will deliver us from a lifestyle that is characterized by outbursts of anger, jealousy, disputes, contentiousness, argumentativeness, and selfishness (see Gal. 5:15–21).

4. John MacArthur, *Galatians* (Chicago: Moody, 1987), 154.

As believers in Christ, being filled with and walking by the Spirit means that we will be enabled to live a life characterized by love and service to other people (Gal. 5:13–14). Being filled with and walking by the Spirit means that we will bear fruit of the Spirit, which according to Galatians 5:22–23 is love, joy, peace, patience, kindness, goodness, faithfulness, gentleness, and self-control. The promise of Scripture is that when we, as children of God, walk in dependence on and in submission to His control, the Holy Spirit will *cause* us to bear this fruit, with the first aspect of that fruit being biblical love.[5]

*Biblical directive #5 for developing the impactful love described in 1 Corinthians 13 is that we must constantly expose ourselves to solid biblical teaching and exhortation on the meaning of love.* "Now concerning brotherly love . . . you yourselves have been taught by God to love one another" is the statement of Paul in 1 Thessalonians 4:9. The Thessalonian Christians needed to be taught to love one another. According to this text and many others, knowing how to love one another in a biblical way doesn't come automatically or naturally. It is something that the Thessalonians, as well as we ourselves, need to be taught.

Hebrews 10:24 emphasizes the same thought. God, through the writer of this passage, tells us that when we meet with other believers, we ought to be thinking about how we can stimulate one another to love and good works. In other words, to be the loving people we ought to be, we need the thoughtful stimulation (the provocation, the admonishment, the exhortation) of other believers.

In 1 Timothy 1:5 Paul highlights the important role that teaching plays in developing and sustaining love: "the aim of our charge is love that issues from a pure heart and a good conscience and a sincere faith." These God-inspired words from Paul are also clearly telling us that God uses instruction to produce genuine love. But they are also teaching us more than that. Paul is telling us that the whole focus or goal of his teaching ministry was to produce love in the hearts of

5. For a fuller explanation of what it means to walk in or by the Spirit, see Wayne A. Mack, *God's Solutions to Life's Problems* (Tulsa: Hensley, 2002), 179–94; for more on the filling of the Spirit, see John MacArthur, *Ephesians* (Chicago: Moody, 1996), 245–69.

his hearers. What Paul is saying is that the right kinds of instruction and love—truth and love, knowledge and love—go together in the Christian life and ministry. Truth is essential, but the goal of teaching truth is not mainly cerebral (intellectual), but life-transforming. In particular, Paul is indicating that the goal he had in mind when he preached and taught was to change lives and in particular to produce genuine biblical love in his hearers. He is indicating that one of the means by which God produces 1 Corinthians 13 love is through solid preaching of His Word.

Philippians 1:9 is still another passage that emphasizes the connection between love and truth. In this text, Paul prays that the love of the Philippians might abound in real knowledge and discernment. In a message on this text Pastor Ligon Duncan said:

> Paul is concerned for the Philippians and for you and me to increase in us a true, practical, character-transforming, biblical knowledge of God. . . . [Here] the Apostle Paul puts love and knowledge side by side, and he does not see them in competition or opposition to one another. In fact, the Apostle Paul will make it clear that there can be no love without this true knowledge, and there can be no true knowledge without love. Anyone who claims to have knowledge but does not manifest love does not have the knowledge. Anyone who claims to love but who does not do it in accordance with knowledge is not loving as a Christian. For the Apostle Paul, love and knowledge go together. Love increases true knowledge of God and results from true knowledge of God, and true knowledge of God is to accompany Christian love and produce it. And so he prays that they would grow in the knowledge of God.
>
> This is so important for us. We come from a tradition of Christians that care much about truth, and rightly so. But the more we truly know the truth, the more we ought to manifest that truth in Christian love, so that our reputation ought to be those who care with deep conviction about truth and who love generously and lavishly because of that deep conviction about the truth. How countercultural would that be in our world today, where most people think that in order to love you can't believe that anything is true; if you really want to love, you've got to decide either that there is no truth, or that everything

is true, no matter how ridiculous. And here's the Apostle Paul saying, no, gospel love is manifested precisely and only where true truth is embraced about God.[6]

Summing up this guideline, Scripture indicates that to become and remain truly biblical lovers of the 1 Corinthians 13 type, we need to regularly expose ourselves to solid teaching of the Word (through preaching, through good literature, through biblically saturated music) that will convict us of our lack of love and then remind us in specifics of what real love is and also teach us how to demonstrate it in practical ways to people in our homes, churches, and world.

Our need for regularly receiving this kind of teaching is certainly indicated by the fact that God put 1 Corinthians 13 in the Bible. The fact that He uses the Hebrew words for "love" 500 times in the Old Testament and the Greek words for "love" 370 times in the New Testament certainly highlights the important role that love should play in our lives. If God refers to love that frequently in Scripture, we ought to regard that as a signal indicating how we need to avail ourselves of teaching on love. God gave us His Word as well as preachers who faithfully exposit and apply that Word so that we might be taught, reproved, corrected, and trained and thereby thoroughly equipped for every good work, including the good work of loving others in the 1 Corinthians 13 way (2 Tim. 3:16–17). In reference to this good work of being a biblical lover, there can be no substitute for regularly exposing ourselves to the faithful proclamation of God's Word.

*Biblical directive #6 for developing and sustaining the kind of love that will bear fruit for God is that you must be willing to die.* What? Perhaps you may think you didn't read that right. I can assure you, that's really what I mean.

In John 12:23 Jesus said, "The hour has come for the Son of Man to be glorified." On a couple of previous occasions (John 2:4; 7:8) Jesus said that His hour or time had not yet come. Yet in this verse we hear Him say, "The hour has come." What hour was He talking

6. From Ligon Duncan's Web site—sermon on Philippians 1:6–11.

about? It was this: the hour or time for His crucifixion; the hour when the weight of the sins of His people would be placed on Him; the hour when He who knew no sin was made sin for us that we might be made the righteousness of God in Him (2 Cor. 5:21); the hour when He would be delivered up to the cross that the penalty for our sin might be paid and that we might be forgiven; the hour when He would bear our sins in His body on the cross so that we might die to sin and live to righteousness (1 Peter 2:24); the hour when He, the just one, suffered on behalf of the unjust so that He might bring us to God (1 Peter 3:18); the hour when, according to His own words, He would be glorified (John 12:23).

In this text Jesus is saying that there is a connection between His dying and His being glorified. And that brings up the question: What was He talking about? How would dying on the cross be a means of glorifying Him?

There were many ways in which His dying would bring Him glory. But for now, I'll mention only a couple, namely, that if Jesus had not died, none of us would ever be saved; none of us would ever be people who devote our lives to Him; none of us would ever be singing His praises; none of us would ever be going out to tell others about Him. If the love of Jesus for His Father and for us had not caused Jesus to die, we would not be looking forward to spending eternity with Him where we will be singing, "Worthy is the Lamb that was slain." For Jesus to be glorified, He had to love us and die for us. For Jesus to bring forth fruit, He had to die.

And the same is true of us. Jesus begins with this truth about Himself—the hour has come for the Son of Man to be glorified, and this will happen the same way the grain of wheat falls into the ground and dies. Then He makes the truth about Himself a truth about His followers. Will we hate our lives in this world? Will we follow Him on the path to Calvary? Will we serve the Son in this way? Will we let the truth about the Son of Man become truth about us?

In John 12:24 Jesus uses an illustration from agriculture that all of us understand. He says that unless a grain of wheat dies it remains alone, but if it dies it brings forth much fruit. One grain of wheat can be the means of producing many other grains of wheat, but for that to occur it has to die.

The main point Jesus is making doesn't really have anything to do with farming. We are the grain of wheat in this verse. What Jesus is saying is that if we are going to bring forth fruit, we must be willing to die to self—we must be willing, on a daily basis, to die to our selfishness and self-centeredness. The main point has everything to do with our being like grains of wheat. A grain of wheat brings blessing to no one until it falls into the ground and dies. Until that happens, a grain of wheat remains alone. And so it is with us. Until we are willing to die to our selfishness, we remain alone in our self-absorbed, self-asserting, self-enhancing prison. But if we, like the grain of wheat, are willing to die in the figurative ways I've just mentioned, we will bear much fruit.

But you may ask, "What does dying have to do with developing and sustaining the kind of love that will make us a powerful influence for Christ?" Answer: to develop and sustain any of the characteristics of love described in 1 Corinthians 13 will require a kind of dying, and unless we are willing to die to self, we will never develop and sustain any of the precious characteristics of love that Paul mentions.

- Paul says that love is long-suffering; and the truth is that if we are going to develop that aspect of love, we will have to die to the desire for an untroubled life.
- Paul says that love is kind; and if we are going to develop this kindness aspect of love, we are going to have to die to harshness, vindictiveness, retaliation, and maliciousness.
- Love is not jealous; if we are going to develop and sustain this aspect of love, we are going to have to be willing to die to the desire for unshared affection or unrivaled attention.
- Love does not brag or boast and is not proud or arrogant; that means that we must die to the desire to call attention to our successes or think of ourselves more highly than other people.
- Love does not behave in an unbecoming fashion; that means that we must die to behaviors and conversations that may offend others.

- Love doesn't seek its own; we must die to the dominance of our own desires and preferences.
- Love is not provoked; we must die to irritability and impatience and to our desire for a life with no frustrations.
- Love does not keep a record of wrongs; that means dying to bitterness and a desire for revenge.
- Love doesn't rejoice in iniquity; we must die to taking pleasure in our own sin or the sin of others.
- Love rejoices in or with the truth; we must die to all lying, dishonesty, and deceitfulness.
- Love covers all things; that means dying to the desire to expose the sins and faults of others.
- Love believes all things; that means dying to a critical and judgmental and suspicious attitude toward others.
- Love hopes all things; we are to die to a pessimistic, negative attitude toward people and our circumstances in life.
- Love endures or perseveres; that means dying to the desire to run away from the pain of trials and difficulties that sometimes come with obedience to the Lord.[7]

## The Summation

To summarize, each of us needs to ask ourselves some important questions and remind ourselves of some important truths:

- Am I willing to pay the price to have a love that makes an impact on others?
- Am I willing to pay the price of love at home, the price of love at my work, the price of love in my neighborhood, the price of love in my church, the price of love in the body of believers? And the next question is this: Am I willing to die? If we are, then the promise of John 12:24 will surely become a reality:

7. I am indebted to John Piper for some of the thoughts about love's requiring dying, especially to his sermon on John 12:24–25 found on the Desiring God Web site.

we will bear much fruit, we will lovingly impact others, we will live forever, we will be with the Lord, and the Father will honor us.

- Make no mistake about the cost of love. Real love, impactful love is costly. It cost our Lord while He interacted with men during His life. It cost our Lord suffering and death on the cross. And it will cost us some kind of dying as well.

While you and I may not be called upon to literally die because of our love for Christ, count on it, we are called upon to be a grain of wheat that falls into the ground and dies to self. We are called on to say no to ourselves and to take up our cross daily and follow Him. And I remind you that following Him means following Him to death—death to self and our sinful self-centeredness.

The message of Jesus to those of us who call ourselves Christians is still the same as it was in the first century. It is a call for us to be willing to be a grain of wheat that falls into the ground and dies. It is the message that we are to love one another as He has loved us. It is a message that we should love one another with the 1 Corinthians 13 kind of love.

How can we develop and sustain that kind of love? My answer (which I'm convinced is a biblical answer) in summary is that we must:

1. Make sure that we have really repented of our sins and believed on the Lord Jesus Christ. We must make sure that we are really saved.
2. Pursue love. We must run after it with the same determination and effort with which Paul persecuted Christians.
3. Abide or remain in Christ—spend time with Him, thinking about Him, thinking about His great love. We must let His Word abide in us.
4. Learn to walk in the Spirit and submit to the filling or controlling of the Holy Spirit on a daily basis.
5. Make sure that we are taught about the nature and meaning of love on a regular basis by attending a church where we are challenged to love and by reading literature that will challenge us to love.

6. Engage in the daily practice of dying—dying to self and our self-centeredness.

There you have the essentials for becoming and remaining a biblical lover of the type described in 1 Corinthians 13. There you have a description of how to become a person who makes a powerful impact on others for Jesus Christ. There is a way to become that person, and that way is delineated in the six guidelines that we have discussed in this chapter. Will you put that way into practice and continue to do so? I commit myself to following these guidelines, and I pray that you will also.

## Review, Reflection, Application, and Discussion Questions

1. Reflect on the Scripture that makes it clear that 1 Corinthians 13 love can be developed and sustained only by Christians. What biblical justification is there for making such a statement?

2. Summarize in your own words the main points that John Piper makes about love in his exposition of 1 John 4:7–19.

3. What is involved in pursuing love as Paul tells us to do in 1 Corinthians 14:1? What biblical illustrations can help us to understand the specifics of pursuing love?

4. From a study of John 15, what can we learn about what it means to abide in Christ?

5. Explain what the metaphor about Christ's being the vine and our being the branches is teaching us about developing and sustaining love.

6. Explain what walking in the Spirit and being filled by the Spirit means.

7. What is the relationship between walking in the Spirit and developing and sustaining love?

8. Why do we need to make sure that we are constantly exposed to solid biblical teaching if we are going to develop and sustain 1 Corinthians 13 love? What is the biblical basis for saying that this is an important guideline?

9. What are the practical implications for carrying out this guideline?

10. What is meant by the statement that for us to develop and sustain 1 Corinthians 13 love, we must die?

11. In what ways must we die in order to bear the fruit of love?

12. Why is our death so important for being a 1 Corinthians 13 lover of people?

13. Summarize the most important challenges you have received from reading this book.

14. In what ways do you need to improve in your development and continuance of 1 Corinthians 13 love?

15. And now my usual reminder: Please remember, as you reflect on the biblical directives presented in this chapter, that the purpose of this exposition, evaluation, and application is:

    a. not to discourage or destroy us;

    b. but to motivate us to see our constant need of the cross and how much we owe to Jesus—without Him we'd never make it, but praise God we are not without Him;

    c. and to motivate us to understand our constant daily need of grace—that our salvation never has been and never will be by the works we have done, but always by the work Christ has done and is doing for us; I want our studies in 1 Corinthians 13 to be a reminder that we need to live a cross-centered life; we need the application of the cross work of Jesus every day of our lives; remember there's not a day in our lives when we are so good that we don't need the cross, and there is never a day in our lives when we are so bad that what Christ did on the

cross is not sufficient to provide forgiveness for us (Rom. 3:24; 5:20; Eph. 1:7; 1 John 1:7; 2:1–2);

d. and to cause us to understand that we must and can, by His grace, put off from our lives the "unlove" that is displeasing to God and put on in our lives the love that is beautifully described in 1 Corinthians 13 so that we might become more and more like our Savior and more prolific in bearing fruit for Him as others see the grace of God at work in our lives, changing and transforming us. This can be true of us if we will follow the directives presented in this chapter (Eph. 4:22–24; 1 Tim. 4:7).

# INDEX OF SCRIPTURE

303